SMASHING
NODE.JS

JAVASCRIPT EVERYWHERE

Guillermo Rauch

WILEY

A John Wiley and Sons, Ltd, Publication

This edition first published 2012
© 2012 Guillermo Rauch

Registered office
John Wiley & Sons Ltd, The Atrium, Southern Gate, Chichester, West Sussex, PO19 8SQ,
United Kingdom

For details of our global editorial offices, for customer services and for information about
how to apply for permission to reuse the copyright material in this book please see our
website at www.wiley.com.

A catalogue record for this book is available from the British Library.

ISBN 978-1-119-96259-5 (paperback); ISBN 978-1-119-96311-0 (emobi);
978-1-119-96309-7 (epdf); 978-1-119-96310-3 (epub)

Set in 10/12 Minion Pro
Printed in the U.S. at Command Web

PUBLISHER'S ACKNOWLEDGEMENTS

Some of the people who helped bring this book to market include the following:

Editorial and Production
VP Consumer and Technology Publishing Director: Michelle Leete
Associate Director–Book Content Management: Martin Tribe
Associate Publisher: Chris Webb
Assistant Editor: Ellie Scott
Development Editor: Brian Herrmann
Copy Editor: Chuck Hutchinson
Technical Editor: Goddy Zhao
Editorial Manager: Jodi Jensen
Senior Project Editor: Sara Shlaer
Editorial Assistant: Leslie Saxman

Marketing
Associate Marketing Director: Louise Breinholt
Senior Marketing Executive: Kate Parrett

Composition Services
Compositor: Andrea Hornberger
Proofreader: Linda Seifert
Indexer: Potomac Indexing, LLC

ABOUT THE AUTHOR

Guillermo Rauch (San Francisco, CA) is CTO and co-founder of San Francisco-based education startup LearnBoost. Rauch is the inventor of several renowned Node.JS projects, and has been a speaker at JSConf as well as Node.js workshops.

CONTENTS

FOREWORD

MOST WEB APPLICATIONS have both a client side and a server side. Implementing the server side has traditionally been complex and cumbersome. Creating a simple server required expert knowledge about multi-threading, scalability, and server deployment. An additional complication is that web client software is implemented using HTML and JavaScript whereas server code most often is implemented using more static programming languages. This split forces the programmer to use multiple programming languages and make early design decisions about where certain program logic should reside.

A few years ago, it would have been unthinkable to implement server software in JavaScript. Poor runtime performance, toy-like memory management, and lack of operating system integration all had to be fixed before JavaScript could be considered as a viable solution for servers. As part of Google Chrome, we designed the new V8 JavaScript engine to tackle the first two problems. V8 is available as an open source project with a simple API for embedding.

Ryan Dahl saw the opportunity in bringing JavaScript to the server side by embedding V8 into an OS integration layer that featured asynchronous interfaces to the underlying operating system. That was the inception of Node.JS. The benefits were obvious. Programmers could now use the same programming language on both client and server side. The dynamic nature of JavaScript made it trivial to develop and experiment with server code freeing the programmer from the traditional slow tool-heavy programming model.

Node.JS became an instant success, spawning a vibrant open source community, supporting companies, and even necessitating its own conference. I would attribute this success to a combination of simplicity, improved programming productivity, and high performance. I'm pleased V8 played a small part in this.

This book will take the reader through all steps of creating the server side of a web application on top of Node.JS including how to organize asynchronous server code and interface to databases.

Enjoy the book,

Lars Bak, Virtual Machinist

INTRODUCTION

Late in 2009, Ryan Dahl announced a technology named Node.JS (http://nodejs.org/) at a JavaScript conference in Berlin. Interestingly, and to the surprise of the attendees, this technology wasn't designed to run in the browser, the land that JavaScript had conquered and that many developers thought it would always be confined to.

This technology was about *running JavaScript in the server*. That simple phrase immediately sparked the imagination of the audience, which celebrated the announcement in standing ovation.

If done right, we could write web applications in just one language.

That was, undoubtedly, the first thought in everyone's minds. After all, to produce a rich and modern web application, one *must* be proficient with JavaScript, but server technologies are varied and require specialization. As an example, Facebook recently revealed that its codebase has four times the number of lines of JS than PHP, its back-end language of choice.

But what Ryan was interested in showing went beyond that simple yet powerful premise. Ryan showed that the "hello world" program of Node.JS creates a web server:

```
var http = require('http');
var server = http.createServer(function (req, res) {
  res.writeHead(200);
  res.end('Hello world');
});
server.listen(80);
```

It so happens this webserver is not just a toy, but a high-performance web server that happens to fare just as well (or even better) than established and tested software like Apache and Nginx in a multitude of scenarios. Node.JS was presented as a tool specifically aimed to design network applications *the right way*.

Node.JS owes its incredible speed and performance to a technique called the *event loop* and the fact that it runs on top of V8, the JavaScript interpreter and virtual machine that Google created to make their Chrome web browser run impossibly fast.

When it comes to web development, Node.JS changes the panorama. You are no longer writing scripts that are executed by a web server you install separately, such as the traditional LAMP model, which usually involves PHP and Apache.

Taking back control of the web server, as you'll see, resulted in a new category of applications being developed on top of Node.JS: real time web apps. Very fast data streaming between a server and thousands of concurrent clients is common currency in Node. This means that not only are you going to be creating more efficient programs, but you'll be part of a community that's pushing the boundaries of what we thought was achievable in the web world.

With Node, you are in charge. And with that capability comes a set of new challenges and responsibilities that this book carefully examines.

APPROACH

First and foremost, *Smashing Node.JS* is a book about JavaScript. Your knowledge of JavaScript is absolutely required, and therefore I dedicate an initial chapter to the concepts of JavaScript that, in my opinion and experience, matter most.

As you learn later, Node.JS strives to create an environment where the browser developer feels comfortable. Common expressions that are not part of the language specification but were added by browsers instead, such as `setTimeout` and `console.log`, are still available in Node.JS to this end.

After you make it past the "memory refreshing" phase, you go right into Node. Node comes with a lot of useful modules as part of its *core*, and a revolutionarily simple package manager called NPM. This book teaches you to build things leveraging only the Node core modules, and then a selection of the most useful abstractions the community has built on top of it, that you can install with NPM.

Before we jump into a module designed for solving a specific problem, I usually try to go through the hurdles of solving the same problem without them first. The best way to understand a tool is to understand why the tool exists in the first place. Therefore, before you learn about a web framework, you'll learn why it's better than using Node.JS HTTP primitives. Before you learn how to build an app with a cross-browser real time framework like Socket. IO, you'll learn the limitations of barebones HTML5 WebSockets.

This book is all about examples. Every step of the way you'll be building a small application or testing out different APIs. You can execute all the code examples in this book with the `node` command, which you can use in two different ways:

- Through the node REPL (Read-Eval-Print Loop). In the same spirit as the Firebug or Web Inspector JavaScript consoles, this approach allows you to type in some JavaScript code, press Enter, and get it executed, right from your operating system's command-line interface.
- As files that are run through the `node` command. This approach requires that you use a text editor, which you obviously already have. I personally recommend vim (http://vim. org) for this purpose, but any of them are good.

In most cases, you'll be writing the code examples step-by-step, reproducing the way it was built the first time around. I'll guide you through different challenges and refactors. When you hit important milestones, I usually include a screenshot of what you should be seeing, either in your terminal or in a browser window, depending on what you're developing.

Sometimes, no matter how much thought went into the construction of these examples, problems are inevitable. I put together a collection of resources that can aid you.

RESOURCES

Should you get stuck on any part of the book, there are a few ways you can get help.

For general Node.JS support, check out the following:

- The Node.JS mailing list (http://groups.google.com/group/nodejs)
- On the `irc.freenode.net` server, the `#nodejs` channel

For help related to specific projects, such as `socket.io` or `express`, check out the official support channels or, if none are available, general forums such as Stack Overflow (http://stackoverflow.com/questions/tagged/node.js) certainly prove helpful.

The majority of Node.JS modules are hosted on GitHub. If you're certain you've found a bug, locate their GitHub repository and contribute a test case.

Try your best to identify whether your problem is Node.JS or JavaScript related. It's usually best to keep your Node.JS help requests strictly Node related.

If you want to discuss a specific issue about this book, you can reach me at `rauchg@gmail.com`.

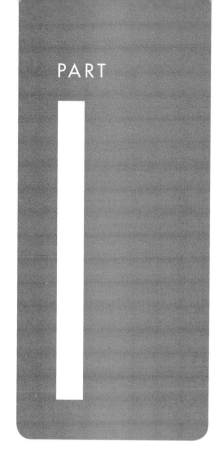

PART

I

GETTING STARTED: SETUP AND CONCEPTS

1

THE SETUP

INSTALLING NODE.JS IS a painless process. Since its conception, one of its goals has been maintaining a small number of dependencies that would make the compilation or installation of the project very seamless.

This chapter describes the installation process for Windows, OS X, and Linux systems. For the latter, you're going to ensure that you have the correct dependencies and compile it from the source.

Note: When you see lines prefixed with $ in the code snippets in the book, you should type these expressions into your OS shell.

INSTALLING ON WINDOWS

On Windows, go to http://nodejs.org and download the MSI installer. Every release of node has a corresponding MSI installer that you need to download and execute.

The filename follows the format `node-v?.?.?.msi`. Upon executing it, simply follow the instructions in the setup wizard shown in Figure 1-1.

To ensure that the installation worked, open the shell or command prompt by running `cmd.exe` and typing `$ node -version`.

Figure 1-1: The Node.JS setup wizard.

The version name of the package you just installed should display.

INSTALLING ON OS X

On the Mac, similarly to Windows, you can leverage an installer package. From the Node.JS website, download the PKG file that follows the format `node-v?.?.?.pkg`. If you want to compile it instead, ensure you have XCode installed and follow the Compilation instructions for Linux.

Run the downloaded package and follow the simple steps (see Figure 1-2).

To ensure installation was successful, open the shell or terminal by running `Terminal.app` (you can type in "Terminal" in Spotlight to locate it) and type in `$ node -version`.

The version of Node you just installed should be outputted.

Figure 1-2: The Node.JS package installer.

INSTALLING ON LINUX

Compiling Node.JS is almost just as easy as installing binaries. To compile it in most *nix systems, simply make sure a C/C++ compiler and the OpenSSL libraries are available.

Most Linux distributions come with a package manager that allows for the easy installation of these.

For example, for Amazon Linux, you use

```
> sudo yum install gcc gcc-c++ openssl-devel curl
```

On Ubuntu, the installation is slightly different; you use

```
> sudo apt-get install g++ libssl-dev apache2-utils curl
```

COMPILING

From your OS terminal, execute the following commands:

> *Note: Replace ? with the latest available version of node in the following example.*

```
$ curl -O http://nodejs.org/dist/node-v?.?.?.tar.gz
$ tar -xzvf node-v?.?.?.tar.gz
$ cd node-v?.?.?
$ ./configure
$ make
$ make test
$ make install
```

If the `make test` command aborts with errors, I recommend you stop the installation and post a log of the `./configure`, `make`, and `make test` commands to the Node.JS mailing list.

ENSURING THAT IT WORKS

Launch a terminal or equivalent, such as XTerm, and type in `$ node -version`.

The version of Node you just installed should be outputted.

THE NODE REPL

To run the Node REPL, simply type `node`.

Try running some JavaScript expressions. For example:

```
> Object.keys(global)
```

> *Note: When you see lines prefixed with > in the code snippets in the book, you should run these expressions in the REPL.*

The REPL is one of my favorite tools for quickly verifying that different Node or vanilla JavaScript APIs work as expected. While developing larger modules, it's often useful to check a certain API works exactly the way you remember it when unsure. To that end, opening a separate terminal tab and quickly evaluating some JavaScript primitives in a REPL helps immensely.

EXECUTING A FILE

Like most scripted programming languages, Node can interpret the contents of a file by appending a path to the node command.

With your favorite text editor, create a file called my-web-server.js, with the following contents:

```
var http = require('http');
var serv = http.createServer(function (req, res) {
  res.writeHead(200, { 'Content-Type': 'text/html' });
  res.end('<marquee>Smashing Node!</marquee>');
});
serv.listen(3000);
```

Run the file:

```
$ node my-web-server.js
```

Then, as shown in Figure 1-3, point your web browser to http://localhost:3000.

In this code snippet, you're leveraging the power of Node to script a fully compliant HTTP server that serves a basic HTML document. This is the traditional example used whenever Node.JS is being discussed, because it demonstrates the power of creating a web server just like Apache or IIS with only a few lines of JavaScript.

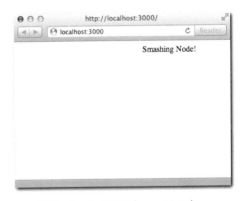

Figure 1-3: Serving a basic HTML document in Node.

NPM

The Node Package Manager (NPM) allows you to easily manage modules in projects by downloading packages, resolving dependencies, running tests, and installing command-line utilities.

Even though doing so is not essential to the core functionality of the project, you truly need to work efficiently on projects that rely on other pre-existing modules released by third parties.

NPM is a program written in Node.JS and shipped with the binary packages (the MSI Windows installer, and the PKG for the Mac). If you compiled node from the source files, you want to install NPM as follows:

```
$ curl http://npmjs.org/install.sh | sh
```

To ensure successful installation, issue the following command:

```
$ npm --version
```

The NPM version should be displayed.

INSTALLING MODULES

To illustrate the installation of a module with NPM, install the `colors` library in the directory `my-project` and then create an `index.js` file:

```
$ mkdir my-project/
$ cd my-project/
$ npm install colors
```

Verify that the project was installed by ensuring the path `node_modules/colors` was created.

Then edit `index.js` with your favorite editor:

```
$ vim index.js
```

And add the following contents:

```
require('colors');
console.log('smashing node'.rainbow);
```

The result should look like Figure 1-4.

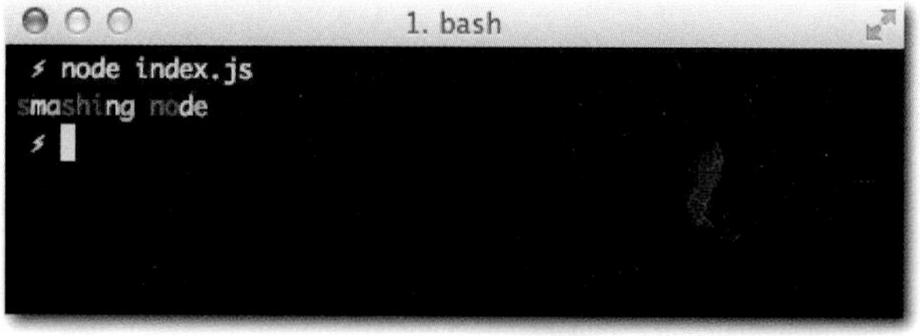

Figure 1-4: The result of installing a module

DEFINING YOUR OWN MODULE

To define your own module, you need to create a `package.json` file. Defining your own module has three fundamental benefits:

- Allows you to easily share the dependencies of your application with others, without sending along the `node_modules` directory. Because `npm install` takes care of fetching everything, distributing this directory wouldn't make sense. This is especially important in SCM systems like Git.
- Allows you to easily track the versions of the modules you depend on that you know work. For example, when you wrote a particular project, you ran `npm install colors` and that installed colors 0.5.0. A year later, due to API changes, perhaps the latest colors are no longer compatible with your project, and if you were to run `npm install` without specifying the version, your project would break.
- Makes redistribution possible. Did your project turn out fine and you want to share it with others? Because you have a `package.json`, the command `npm publish`. publishes it to the NPM registry for everyone to install.

In the directory created earlier (`my-project`), remove the `node_modules` directory and create a `package.json` file:

```
$ rm -r node_modules
$ vim package.json
```

Then add the following contents:

```
{
    "name": "my-colors-project"
  , "version": "0.0.1"
  , "dependencies": {
      "colors": "0.5.0"
    }
}
```

> Note: The contents of this file must be valid JSON. Valid JavaScript is not enough. This means that you must make sure, for example, to use double quotes for all strings, including property names.

The `package.json` file is the file that describes your project to both Node.JS and NPM. The only required fields are name and version. Normally, modules have dependencies, which is an object that references other projects by the name and version they defined in their `package.json` files.

Save the file, install the local project, and run `index.js` again:

```
$ npm install
$ node index    # notice that you don't need to include ".js"!
```

In this case, the intention is to create a module for internal use. If you wanted, NPM makes it really easy to publish a module by running:

```
$ npm publish
```

To tell Node which file to look for when someone calls `require('my-colors-project')` we can specify the `main` property in the `package.json`:

```
{
    "name": "my-colors-project"
  , "version": "0.0.1"
  , "main": "./index"
  , "dependencies": {
      "colors": "0.5.0"
    }
}
```

When you learn how to make modules export APIs, the `main` property will become a lot more important, because you will need it to define the entry point of your modules (which sometimes are comprised of multiple files).

To learn about all the possible properties for the `package.json` file, run:

```
$ npm help json
```

> *Tip: If you never intend to publish a certain project, add* `"private": "true"` *to your* `package.json`. *This prevents accidental publication.*

INSTALLING BINARY UTILITIES

Some projects distribute command-line tools that were written in Node. When that's the case, you need to install them with the `-g` flag.

For example, the web framework you're going to learn in this book called express contains an executable utility to create projects.

```
$ npm install -g express
```

Then try it out by creating a directory and running "express" inside:

```
$ mkdir my-site
$ cd mysite
$ express
```

Tip: If you want to distribute a script like this, include a flag `"bin": "./path/to/script"` *pointing to your executable script or binary when publishing.*

EXPLORING THE NPM REGISTRY

Once you get comfortable with the Node.JS module system in Chapter 4, you should be able to write programs that leverage any module in the ecosystem.

NPM has a rich registry that contains thousands of modules. Two commands are instrumental in your exploration of the registry: `search` and `view`.

If you want to search for plugins related to `realtime`, for example, you would execute the following:

```
$ npm search realtime
```

This will search all the published modules that contain MySQL in their name, tags, and description fields.

Once you find a package that interests you, you can see its `package.json` and other properties related to the NPM registry by running `npm view` followed by the module name. For example:

```
$ npm view socket.io
```

Tip: If you want to learn more about a certain NPM command, type "npm help <command>." For example, "npm help publish" will teach you more about how to publish modules.

SUMMARY

After this chapter, you should now have a working Node.JS + NPM environment.

In addition to being able to run the `node` and `npm` commands, you should now have a basic understanding of how to execute simple scripts, but also how to put together modules with dependencies.

You now know that an important keyword in Node.JS is `require`, which allows for module and API interoperability, and which will be an important subject in Chapter 4, after quickly reviewing the language basics.

You also are now aware of the NPM registry, which is the gateway to the Node.JS module ecosystem. Node.JS is an open source project, and as a result many of the programs that are written with it are also open source and available for you to reuse, a few keystrokes away.

JAVASCRIPT:

AN OVERVIEW

INTRODUCTION

JAVASCRIPT IS A prototype-based, object-oriented, loosely-typed dynamic scripting language. It has powerful features from the functional world, such as *closures* and *higher-order functions,* that are of special interest here.

JavaScript is technically an implementation of the ECMAScript language standard. It's important to know that with Node, because of v8, you'll be primarily dealing with an implementation that gets close to the standard, with the exception of a few extra features. This means that the JavaScript you're going to be dealing with has some important differences with the one that earned the language its bad reputation in the browser world.

In addition, most of the code you'll write is in compliance with the "good parts" of JavaScript that Douglas Crockford enounced in his famous book, *JavaScript: The Good Parts*.

This chapter is divided into two parts:

- **Basic JavaScript.** The fundamentals of the language. They apply everywhere: node, browser, and standards committee.
- **v8 JavaScript.** Some features used in v8 are not available in all browsers, especially Internet Explorer, because they've recently been standardized. Others are nonstandard, but you still use them because they solve fundamental problems.

In addition, the next chapter covers the language extensions and features exclusively available in Node.

BASIC JAVASCRIPT

This chapter assumes that you're somewhat familiar with JavaScript and its syntax. It goes over some fundamental concepts you must understand if you want to work with Node.js.

TYPES

You can divide JavaScript types into two groups: *primitive* and *complex*. When one of the primitive types is accessed, you work directly on its value. When a complex type is accessed, you work on a reference to the value.

- The primitive types are `number`, `boolean`, `string`, `null`, and `undefined`.
- The complex types are `array`, `function`, and `object`.

To illustrate:

```
// primitives
var a = 5;
var b = a;
b = 6;
a; // will be 5
b; // will be 6

// complex
var a = ['hello', 'world'];
var b = a;
b[0] = 'bye';
a[0]; // will be 'bye'
b[0]; // will be 'bye'
```

In the second example, b contains the *same reference* to the value as a does. Hence, when you access the first member of the array, you alter the original, so `a[0] === b[0]`.

TYPE HICCUPS

Correctly identifying the type of value a certain variable holds remains a challenge in JavaScript.

Because JavaScript has constructors for most primitives like in other languages with object-oriented features, you can create a string in these two ways:

```
var a = 'woot';
var b = new String('woot');
a + b; // 'woot woot'
```

If you use the `typeof` and `instanceof` operators on these two variables, however, things get interesting:

```
typeof a; // 'string'
typeof b; // 'object'
a instanceof String; // false
b instanceof String; // true
```

However, both are definitely strings that have the same prototypical methods:

```
a.substr == b.substr; // true
```

And they evaluate in the same way with the `==` operator but not with `===`:

```
a == b; // true
a === b; // false
```

Considering these discrepancies, I encourage you to always define your types in the literal way, avoiding `new`.

It's important to remember that certain values will be evaluate to `false` in conditional expressions: `null`, `undefined`, `''`, `0`:

```
var a = 0;
if (a) {
  // this will never execute
}
a == false; // true
a === false; // false
```

Also noteworthy is the fact that `typeof` doesn't recognize `null` as its own type:

```
typeof null == 'object'; // true, unfortunately
```

And the same goes for arrays, even if defined with `[]`, as shown here:

```
typeof [] == 'object'; // true
```

You can be thankful that v8 provides a way of identifying an array without resorting to hacks. In browsers, you typically inspect the internal `[[Class]]` value of an object: `Object.prototype.toString.call([]) == '[object Array]'`. This is an immutable property of objects that has the benefit of working across different contexts (for example, browser frames), whereas `instanceof Array` is true only for arrays initialized within that particular context.

FUNCTIONS

Functions are of utmost importance in JavaScript.

They're *first class*: they can be stored in variables as references, and then you can pass them around as if they were any other object:

```
var a = function () {}
console.log(a); // passing the function as a parameter
```

All functions in JavaScript can be named. It's important to distinguish between the function name and the variable name:

```
var a = function a () {
  'function' == typeof a; // true
};
```

THIS, FUNCTION#CALL, AND FUNCTION#APPLY

When the following function is called, the value of `this` is the global object. In the browser, that's `window`:

```
function a () {
  window == this; // true;
};

a();
```

By using the `.call` and `.apply` methods, you can change the reference of `this` to a different object when calling the function:

```
function a () {
  this.a == 'b'; // true
}

a.call({ a: 'b' });
```

The difference between `call` and `apply` is that `call` takes a list of parameters to pass to the function following, whereas `apply` takes an array:

```
function a (b, c) {
  b == 'first'; // true
  c == 'second'; // true
}

a.call({ a: 'b' }, 'first', 'second')
a.apply({ a: 'b' }, ['first', 'second']);
```

FUNCTION ARITY

An interesting property of a function is its *arity*, which refers to the number of arguments that the function was declared with. In JavaScript, this equates to the `length` property of a function:

```
var a = function (a, b, c);
a.length == 3; // true
```

Even though less common in the browser, this feature is important to us because it's leveraged by some popular Node.JS frameworks to offer different functionality depending on the number of parameters the functions you pass around take.

CLOSURES

In JavaScript, every time a function is called, a new scope is defined.

Variables defined within a scope are accessible only to that scope and inner scopes (that is, scopes defined within that scope):

```
var a = 5;

function woot () {
  a == 5; // true

  var a = 6;

  function test () {
    a == 6; // true
  }

  test();
};

woot();
```

Self-invoked functions are a mechanism by which you declare and call an anonymous function where your only goal is defining a new scope:

```
var a = 3;

(function () {
  var a = 5;
})();

a == 3 // true;
```

These functions are very useful when you want to declare *private variables* that shouldn't be exposed to another piece of code.

CLASSES

In JavaScript, there's no `class` keyword. A class is defined like a function instead:

```
function Animal () { }
```

To define a method on all the instances of `Animal` that you create, you set it on the prototype:

```
Animal.prototype.eat = function (food) {
  // eat method
}
```

It's worth mentioning that within functions in the prototype, `this` doesn't refer to the global object like regular functions, but to the class instance instead:

```
function Animal (name) {
  this.name = name;
}

Animal.prototype.getName () {
  return this.name;
};

var animal = new Animal('tobi');
a.getName() == 'tobi'; // true
```

INHERITANCE

JavaScript has *prototypical inheritance*. Traditionally, you simulate classical inheritance as follows.

You define another constructor that's going to inherit from `Animal`:

```
function Ferret () { };
```

To define the inheritance chain, you initialize an `Animal` object and assign it to the `Ferret.` prototype.

```
// you inherit
Ferret.prototype = new Animal();
```

You can then define methods and properties exclusive to your subclass:

```
// you specialize the type property for all ferrets
Ferret.prototype.type = 'domestic';
```

To override methods and call the parent, you reference the prototype:

```
Ferret.prototype.eat = function (food) {
  Animal.prototype.eat.call(this, food);
  // ferret-specific logic here
}
```

This technique is almost perfect. It's the best performing across the board (compared to the alternative functional technique) and doesn't break the instanceof operator:

```
var animal = new Animal();
animal instanceof Animal // true
animal instanceof Ferret // false

var ferret = new Ferret();
ferret instanceof Animal // true
ferret instanceof Ferret // true
```

Its major drawback is that an object is initialized when the inheritance is declared (Ferret. prototype = new Animal), which might be undesirable. A way around this problem is to include a conditional statement in the constructor:

```
function Animal (a) {
  if (false !== a) return;
  // do constructor stuff
}

Ferret.prototype = new Animal(false)
```

Another workaround is to define a new, empty constructor and override its prototype:

```
function Animal () {
  // constructor stuff
}

function f () {};
f.prototype = Animal.prototype;
Ferret.prototype = new f;
```

Fortunately, v8 has a cleaner solution for this, which is described later in this chapter.

TRY {} CATCH {}

try/catch allows you to capture an exception. The following code throws one:

```
> var a = 5;
> a()
TypeError: Property 'a' of object #<Object> is not a function
```

When a function throws an error, execution stops:

```
function () {
  throw new Error('hi');
  console.log('hi'); // this will never execute
}
```

If you use `try/catch`, you can handle the error and execution continues:

```
function () {
  var a = 5;
  try {
    a();
  } catch (e) {
    e instanceof Error; // true
  }

  console.log('you got here!');
}
```

V8 JAVASCRIPT

So far you've looked at the JavaScript features that are most relevant to dealing with the language in most environments, including ancient browsers.

With the introduction of the Chrome web browser came a new JavaScript engine, v8, which has been quickly pushing the boundaries by providing us with an extremely fast execution environment that stays up-to-date and supports the latest ECMAScript features.

Some of these features address deficiencies in the language. Others were introduced thanks to the advent of client-side frameworks like jQuery and PrototypeJS, because they provided extensions or utilities that are so frequently used it's now unimaginable to consider the JavaScript language without them.

In this section you'll learn about the most useful features that you can take advantage of from v8 to write more concise and faster code that fits right it with the style of code that the most popular Node.JS frameworks and libraries adopt.

OBJECT#KEYS

If you wanted to obtain the keys for the following object (a and c)

```
var a = { a: 'b', c: 'd' };
```

Then normally iterate as follows:

```
for (var i in a) { }
```

By iterating over the keys, you can collect them in an array. However, if you were to extend the Object.prototype as follows:

```
Object.prototype.c = 'd';
```

To avoid getting c in the list of keys you would need to run a hasOwnProperty check:

```
for (var i in a) {
  if (a.hasOwnProperty(i)) {}
}
```

To get around that complication, to get all the own keys in an object, in v8 you can safely use

```
var a = { a: 'b', c: 'd' };
Object.keys(a); // ['a', 'c']
```

ARRAY#ISARRAY

Like you saw before, the typeof operator will return "object" for arrays. Most of the time, however, you want to check that an array is actually an array.

Array.isArray returns true for arrays and false for any other value:

```
Array.isArray(new Array) // true
Array.isArray([]) // true
Array.isArray(null) // false
Array.isArray(arguments) // false
```

ARRAY METHODS

To loop over an array, you can use forEach (similar to jQuery $.each):

```
// will print 1 2 and 3
[1, 2, 3].forEach(function (v) {
  console.log(v);
});
```

To *filter elements out* of an array, you can use filter (similar to jQuery $.grep)

```
[1, 2, 3].forEach(function (v) {
  return v < 3;
}); // will return [1, 2]
```

To change the value of each item, you can use map (similar to jQuery $.map)

```
[5, 10, 15].map(function (v) {
  return v * 2;
}); // will return [10, 20, 30]
```

Also available but less commonly used are the methods `reduce`, `reduceRight`, and `lastIndexOf`.

STRING METHODS

To remove space in the beginning and ending of a string, use

```
'  hello  '.trim(); // 'hello'
```

JSON

v8 exposes `JSON.stringify` and `JSON.parse` to decode and encode JSON, respectively.

JSON is an encoding specification that closely resembles the JavaScript object literal, utilized by many web services and APIs:

```
var obj = JSON.parse('{"a":"b"}')
obj.a == 'b'; // true
```

FUNCTION#BIND

`.bind` (equivalent to jQuery's `$.proxy`) allows you to change the reference of `this`:

```
function a () {
  this.hello == 'world'; // true
};

var b = a.bind({ hello: 'world' });
b();
```

FUNCTION#NAME

In v8, the nonstandard property name of a function is supported:

```
var a = function woot () {};
a.name == 'woot'; // true
```

This property is used internally by v8 in stack traces. When an error is thrown, v8 shows a *stack trace*, which is the succession of function calls it made to reach the point where the error occurred:

```
> var woot = function () { throw new Error(); };
> woot()
Error
    at [object Context]:1:32
```

In this case, v8 is not able to assign a name to the function reference. If you name it, however, v8 will be able to include it in the stack traces as shown here:

```
> var woot = function buggy () { throw new Error(); };
> woot()
Error
    at buggy ([object Context]:1:34)
```

Because naming significantly aids in debugging, I always recommend you name your functions.

PROTO (INHERITANCE)

`__proto__` makes it easy for you to define the inheritance chain:

```
function Animal () { }
function Ferret () { }
Ferret.prototype.__proto__ = Animal.prototype;
```

This is a very useful feature that removes the need to:

- Resort to intermediate constructors, as shown in the previous section.
- Leverage OOP toolkits or utilities. You don't need to require any third-party modules to expressively declare prototypical inheritance.

ACCESSORS

You are able to define properties that call functions when they're accessed (`__defineGetter__`) or set (`__defineSetter__`).

As an example, define a property called `ago` that returns the time ago in words for a `Date` object.

Many times, especially in the software you create, you want to express time in words relative to a certain point. For example, it's easier for people to understand that something happened three seconds ago than reading the complete date.

The following example adds an `ago` getter to all the `Date` instances that will output the distance of time in words to the present. Simply accessing the property will execute the function you define, without having to explicitly call it.

```
// Based on prettyDate by John Resig (MIT license)
Date.prototype.__defineGetter__('ago', function () {
  var diff = (((new Date()).getTime() - this.getTime()) / 1000)
    , day_diff = Math.floor(diff / 86400);
```

```
    return day_diff == 0 && (
        diff < 60 && "just now" ||
        diff < 120 && "1 minute ago" ||
        diff < 3600 && Math.floor( diff / 60 ) + " minutes ago" ||
        diff < 7200 && "1 hour ago" ||
        diff < 86400 && Math.floor( diff / 3600 ) + " hours ago") ||
        day_diff == 1 && "Yesterday" ||
        day_diff < 7 && day_diff + " days ago" ||
        Math.ceil( day_diff / 7 ) + " weeks ago";
});
```

Then you simply refer to the ago property. Notice that you're not executing a function, yet it's still being executed transparently for you:

```
var a = new Date('12/12/1990'); // my birth date
a.ago // 1071 weeks ago
```

SUMMARY

Understanding this chapter is essential to getting up to speed with the quirks of the language and handicaps of most environments the language has traditionally been run in, such as old browsers.

Due to JavaScript evolving really slowly and being somewhat overlooked for years, many developers have invested significant amounts of time in developing techniques to write the most efficient and maintainable code, and have characterized what aspects of the language don't work as expected.

v8 has done a fantastic job at keeping up to date with the recent editions of ECMA, and continues to do so. The Node.JS core team of developers always ensures that when you install the latest version of Node, you always get the most recent version of v8. This opens up a new panorama for server-side development, since we can leverage APIs that are easier to understand and faster to execute.

Hopefully during this chapter you've learned some of the features that Node developers commonly use, which are those that are defining the present and future of JavaScript.

3

BLOCKING AND NON-BLOCKING IO

MUCH OF THE DISCUSSION about Node.JS is centered around its capabilities to handle a lot of *concurrency*. In simple terms, Node is a framework that offers developers a powerful way to design networking applications that will perform really well in comparison to other mainstream solutions, provided that they understand the tradeoffs and *what* makes Node programs perform well.

WITH GREAT POWER COMES GREAT RESPONSIBILITY

Node introduces a complexity to JavaScript that you're probably not really used to managing much in the browser: shared-state concurrency. As a matter of fact, this complexity is also inexistent in traditional models for making web applications like Apache and mod_php or Nginx and FastCGI.

In less technical terms, in Node you have to be careful about how your callbacks modify the variables around them (state) that are currently in memory. Thus, you need to be especially careful about how you handle errors that can potentially alter this state in unexpected ways and potentially render the entire process unusable.

To fully understand this, imagine the following function, which gets executed every time the user makes a request to the URL /books. Imagine also that the "state" is a collection of books that you'll ultimately use to return an HTML list of books.

```
var books = [
    'Metamorphosis'
  , 'Crime and punishment'
];

function serveBooks () {
  // I'm going to serve some HTML to the client
  var html = '<b>' + books.join('</b><br><b>') + '</b>';

  // I'm evil, and I'm going to change state!
  books = [];

  return html;
}
```

The equivalent PHP code is

```
$books = array(
    'Metamorphosis'
  , 'Crime and punishment'
);

function serveBooks () {
  $html = '<b>' . join($books, '</b><br><b>') . '</b>';
  $books = array();
  return $html;
}
```

Notice that in the serveBooks functions of both examples, you reset the books array.

Now imagine a user who requests /books twice in a row to the Node server and twice in a row to the PHP server. Try to predict what's going to happen:

- Node handles the first request and returns the books. The second request returns no books.
- PHP returns books in both cases.

The difference lies in the fundamental schemes. Node is a long-running process, whereas Apache spawns multiple threads (one per request), which start with a fresh state every time. In PHP, the next time the interpreter runs, the variable $books gets repopulated, whereas in Node, the function serveBooks gets called again, and the scope variable is not affected.

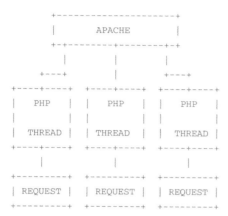

With great power comes great responsibility.

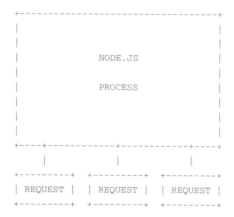

Keeping this in mind at all times is essential for writing solid Node.JS programs that don't experience problems during their executions.

An equally important aspect is understanding what is meant by blocking and non-blocking IO.

BLOCKING-NESS

Try to identify the difference between the following PHP example:

```
// PHP
print('Hello');

sleep(5);

print('World');
```

And this Node example:

```
// node
console.log('Hello');

setTimeout(function () {
  console.log('World');
}, 5000);
```

The difference is not merely syntactic (Node.JS uses a callback) because these examples epitomize the distinction between blocking and non-blocking code. In the first example, PHP `sleep()` *blocks the thread of execution*. While the program is sleeping, it's not doing anything else.

Node.JS, on the other hand, leverages the *event loop* here, so `setTimeout` is non-blocking.

This means that if you introduce a `console.log` statement immediately after the `setTimeout`, it is called immediately:

```
console.log('Hello');

setTimeout(function () {
  console.log('World');
}, 5000);

console.log('Bye');

// this script will output:
// Hello
// Bye
// World
```

What does it mean to leverage the event loop? Essentially, Node registers events and then runs an infinite loop to *poll* the kernel to know whether these events are ready to be dispatched. When they are, the associated function callbacks are fired, and it moves on. If no events are polled, Node just keeps going until new events are ready.

In contrast, in the PHP world, when `sleep` is executed, the execution is *blocked* for however long you specified, and no other instructions are executed until said time elapses, which means it's *synchronous*. `setTimeout`, instead of blocking, just registers an event for the future and lets the program continue to run, therefore being *asynchronous*.

The event loop constitutes Node's approach to *concurrency*. The same technique shown previously for timeouts is also utilized for all the IO that native modules such as `http` or `net` perform. In the same fashion that internally Node loops and triggers a notification when the timeout is complete, it uses the event loop to trigger notifications about *file descriptors*.

File descriptors are abstract handles that reference open files, sockets, pipes, and so on. Essentially, when Node gets an HTTP request from a browser, the underlying TCP connection allocates a file descriptor. If the client then sends data to the server, Node gets a notification about this and fires a callback in your JavaScript code.

A SINGLE-THREADED WORLD

It's important to note that Node uses a *single thread* of execution. It's not possible, without the help of third-party modules, to change this fact.

To illustrate what this means and how it relates to the event loop, consider the following example:

```
var start = Date.now();

setTimeout(function () {
  console.log(Date.now() - start);

  for (var i = 0; i < 1000000000; i++){}
}, 1000);

setTimeout(function () {
  console.log(Date.now() - start);
}, 2000);
```

These two timeouts print how many seconds elapsed from the moment they're set to the moment the functions are called. The output in my computer looks like Figure 3-1.

Figure 3-1: This program shows the elapsed time when each `setTimeout` is executed, which doesn't correlate to the values in the code.

What happens internally is that the event loop is *blocked* by the JavaScript code. When the first event is dispatched, the JavaScript callback is run. Because you are doing a lot of intense computation (a very long `for` loop), by the time the next iteration of the *event loop* is executed, more than two seconds have elapsed; therefore, the JavaScript timeouts don't match actual clock seconds.

This behavior is, of course, undesirable. As I explained previously, the event loop is the foundation of all IO in Node. If a timeout can be delayed, so can an incoming HTTP request or other forms of IO. That means the HTTP server would handle fewer requests per second and not perform efficiently.

For this reason, the great majority of modules available for node are *non-blocking* and perform tasks *asynchronously*.

If you have only one thread of execution, which means that as a function is running no others can be executed concurrently, how is Node.JS so good at managing a lot of network concurrency? For example, in a normal laptop, a simple HTTP server written in Node is able to handle thousands of clients per second.

For this to happen, you must first understand the concept of call stacks.

When v8 *first* calls a function, it starts what is commonly known as a call stack or execution stack.

If that function calls another function, v8 adds it to the call stack. Consider the following example:

```
function a () {
  b();
}
function b(){};
```

The call stack in this example is composed of "a" followed by "b". When "b" is reached, v8 doesn't have anything left to execute.

Return to the HTTP server example:

```
http.createServer(function () {
  a();
});
function a(){
  b();
};
function b(){};
```

In this example, whenever an HTTP client connects to Node, the event loop dispatches a notification. Eventually, the callback function is executed, and the call stack becomes "a" > "b".

Since Node is running in a *single thread*, while that call stack is being *unrolled* no other client or HTTP request can be handled.

You might be thinking, then, that Node maximum concurrency is 1! And that would be correct. Node does not offer true parallelization, because that would require the introduction of many parallel threads of execution.

The key is that you don't need to handle more than one at the same given instant, provided that the call stack executes really fast. And that's why v8 coupled with non-blocking IO are so good together: v8 is really fast at executing JavaScript, and non-blocking IO ensures the single thread of execution doesn't get hung up on external uncertainties, like reading a database or hard disk.

A real-world example of the utility of non-blocking IO is the cloud. In most cloud deployments like the Amazon cloud ("AWS"), operating systems are *virtualized* and hardware resources are shared between *tenants* (since you are essentially "renting hardware"). What this means is that if the hard drive, for example, is spinning to seek a file for another tenant, and you are trying to seek, the latency will increase. Since the IO performance for the hard drive is very unpredictable, if we blocked our thread of execution when we're reading a file, our program could behave very erratically and slowly.

A common example of IO in our applications is getting data from databases. Imagine a situation where you need to get some data from the database to respond to a request.

```
http.createServer(function (req, res) {
  database.getInformation(function (data) {
    res.writeHead(200);
    res.end(data);
  });
});
```

In this case, once a request comes in, the call stack is just composed of the database call. Since the call is non-blocking, it's up to the event loop once again to initiate a new call stack when the database IO completes. But after you tell Node "let me know when you have the database response," Node can continue to do other things. Namely, handling more HTTP clients and requests!

A topic covered throughout the book that very much has to do with the way Node is architected is *error handling,* described next.

ERROR HANDLING

First and foremost, as you saw earlier in the chapter, Node applications rely on big processes with a lot of shared state.

If an error occurs in a particular callback of a particular HTTP request, for example, the whole process is compromised:

```
var http = require('http');

http.createServer(function () {
  throw new Error('This will be uncaught')
}).listen(3000)
```

Because that exception isn't caught, the moment you try to access the web server, the process crashes, as shown in Figure 3-2.

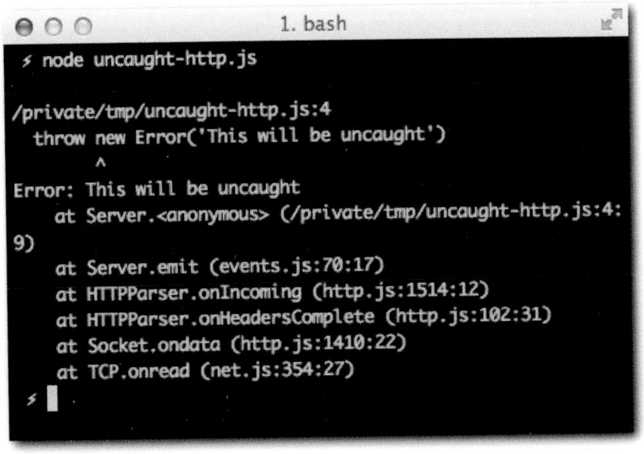

Figure 3-2: You can see the call stack from the event loop (`IOWatcher`) all the way to the callback.

Node behaves this way because the state of the process after an uncaught exception is uncertain. Things might or might not work normally afterward, and if the error is left unhandled, things might continue to fail in ways that are unexpected or can't be debugged.

This behavior changes if you add an `uncaughtException` handler. The process doesn't exit, and you are in charge of things afterward:

```
process.on('uncaughtException', function (err) {
  console.error(err);
  process.exit(1); // we exit manually
});
```

This behavior is consistent with APIs that emit `error` events. For example, consider the following example, where you make a TCP server and connect to it with the `telnet` utility:

```
var net = require('net');

net.createServer(function (connection) {
  connection.on('error', function (err) {
    // err is an Error object
  });
}).listen(400);
```

Throughout Node, many of the native modules such as `http` and `net` emit `error` events. If these events go unhandled, an uncaught exception is thrown.

Aside from the `uncaughtException` and `error` events, most of the asynchronous Node APIs take a callback where the first parameter sent is an error object or `null`:

```
var fs = require('fs');

fs.readFile('/etc/passwd', function (err, data) {
  if (err) return console.error(err);
  console.log(data);
});
```

Handling errors every step of the way in your code is essential because it allows you to write safe programs and also not lose context of where errors originate.

STACK TRACES

In JavaScript, when an error occurs, you can see the series of function calls that lead up to the error. This is called a *stack trace.* Consider the following example:

```
function c () {
  b();
};

function b () {
  a();
};

function a () {
  throw new Error('here');
};

c();
```

Run it now to obtain a stack trace like the one in Figure 3-3.

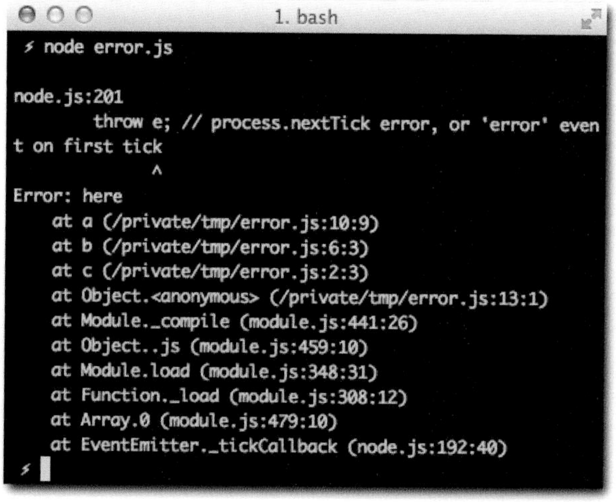

Figure 3-3: The call stack displayed by v8 for the succession of calls you defined.

In this figure, you can see the clear succession of calls that lead to the error. Now try the same thing when the event loop is involved:

```
function c () {
  b();
};

function b () {
  a();
};

function a () {
  setTimeout(function () {
    throw new Error('here');
  }, 10);
};

c();
```

When this code is executed (as in Figure 3-4), valuable information is missing from the stack trace.

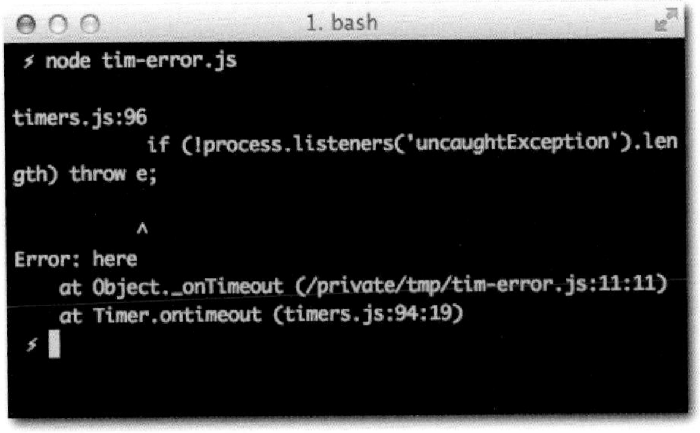

Figure 3-4: The call stack begins with the entry point of the event loop.

By the same token, catching an error of a function that's deferred so that it is called in the future is not possible. This yields an uncaught exception and the catch block doesn't execute:

```
try {
  setTimeout(function () {
    throw new Error('here');
  }, 10);
} catch (e) { }
```

This is the main reason that in Node.JS, you want to handle errors correctly every step of the way. If you are sloppy, you might find yourself with errors that are hard to track down because no contextual information is available.

It's important to mention that in future versions of Node, machinery will be in place to make errors thrown by asynchronous handlers easier to track down.

SUMMARY

You now understand how all the actors involved—the event loop, non-blocking IO, and v8—work efficiently together to give developers interfaces to write very fast networked applications.

You understand that Node offers great simplicity to the programmer by having a single thread of execution, but also that this architecture makes it unwise to perform blocking IO when you're trying to write network applications. You also understand that all the *state* is maintained in a *single memory space* for that thread, which means you need to be extra careful when writing programs.

You also clearly see that non-blocking IO and callbacks introduce new paradigms for debugging and error handling that are strikingly different from programs you write with blocking IO.

4

NODE
JAVASCRIPT

WRITING JAVASCRIPT FOR Node.JS and the browser is a remarkably different experience. Node.JS takes the basic language, and just like browsers did, adds different APIs on top of it to ensure writing code that's meant to power networked applications feels as natural as possible.

Throughout this chapter you will examine certain APIs that are not part of the language as it was conceived in its specification, but that both Node and browsers have. But more importantly, you will also go through the core Node.JS additions that are considered, as the title of this chapter implies, "Node JavaScript."

The first difference you'll look at pertains to the global object.

THE GLOBAL OBJECT

In the browser, `window` is the global object. Anything that you define in `window` becomes available to all parts of your code. For example, `setTimeout` is in reality `window.setTimeout`, and `document` is `window.document`.

Node has two similar objects that provide a cleaner separation:

- `global`: Just like `window`, any property attached to `global` becomes a variable you can access anywhere.
- `process`: Everything that pertains to the global context of execution is in the `process` object. In the browser, there's only one window, and in Node, there's only one process at any given time. As an example, in the browser, the window name is `window.name`, and in Node, the name of the process is `process.title`.

Later chapters dig deeper into the `process` object because it provides broad and interesting functionality, especially pertaining to command-line programs.

USEFUL GLOBALS

Some functions and utilities available in the browser are not part of the language specification but rather are useful things that browsers added on top, which today are generally considered to be JavaScript. These are often exposed as globals.

For example, `setTimeout` is not part of ECMAScript, but a function that browsers deemed important to implement. As a matter of fact, even if you tried, you wouldn't be able to rewrite that function in pure JavaScript.

Other APIs are in the process of being introduced to the language (and are at the proposal stage), but Node.JS adds them because they're needed for us to write our programs effectively. An example of this is a the `setImmediate` API, which in Node.JS it finds its equivalent in `process.nextTick`

This function allows you to schedule the execution of a function at the next iteration of the event loop:

```
console.log(1);
process.nextTick(function () {
  console.log(3);
});
console.log(2);
```

Imagine it as something similar to `setTimeout(fn, 1)` or "call this function in the most immediate future in an asynchronous way." You can then understand why the previous example will output the numbers in the order 1, 2, 3.

A similar example is `console`, which was originally implemented by Firebug, the Firefox plugin to aid development. As a result, Node includes a global `console` object with useful methods, such as `console.log` and `console.error`.

THE MODULE SYSTEM

JavaScript, in its pure form, is a *world of globals*. All the APIs that are normally used in the browser `setTimeout`, `document`, and so on are globally defined.

When you include third-party modules, the expectation is that they also expose a global variable (or many). For example, when you include `<script src="http://code.jquery.com/jquery-1.6.0.js">` in an HTML document, you later refer to this *module* through the global `jQuery` object:

```
<script>
  jQuery(function () {
    alert('hello world!');
  });
</script>
```

The fundamental reason for this is that in its specification, JavaScript doesn't describe an API for *module dependency and isolation*. As a result, including multiple "modules" in this way results in a pollution of the global namespace and potential naming collisions.

Node ships with a lot of useful modules that are the fundamental toolkit for building out modern applications; they include `http`, `net`, `fs`, and many more. And as you saw in Chapter 1, "The Setup," especially with the help of NPM, you can easily install hundreds more.

Instead of defining a number of globals (or evaluating a lot of code that you might not use), Node decided to introduce a simple yet extremely powerful module system, the roots of which are three globals: `require`, `module`, and `exports`.

ABSOLUTE AND RELATIVE MODULES

I use the term *absolute modules* for the ones that Node finds by internally inspecting the node_modules directory, or modules that Node ships within its core, like `fs`.

As you saw in Chapter 1, if you have a `colors` module installed, its path becomes `./node_modules/colors`.

Therefore, you can `require` that module by its *name without pointing to any directory*:

```
require('colors')
```

This particular module alters `String.prototype`, so it doesn't *export* an API. The `fs` module, however, exports a number of functions that you can leverage:

```
var fs = require('fs');
fs.readFile('/some/file', function (err, contents) {
  if (!err) console.log(contents);
});
```

Modules can also leverage the module system internally, to produce code with a clean separation of APIs and abstractions. But instead of having to declare each part of a certain module or app as a separate module with its own `package.json` file, you can leverage what I'll call *relative modules*.

Relative modules point `require` to a JavaScript file relative to the working directory. To illustrate, create two files named `module_a.js` and `module_b.js` and a third file named `main.js`, all in the same directory

module_a.js

```
console.log('this is a');
```

module_b.js

```
console.log('this is b');
```

main.js

```
require('module_a');
require('module_b');
```

Then run `main` (see Figure 4-1):

```
$ node main
```

As you can see in Figure 4-1, Node is unable to find `module_a` or `module_b`. The reason is that they weren't installed with NPM, they're not in a `node_modules` directory, and Node most certainly doesn't ship with them.

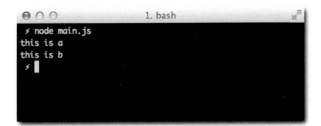

Figure 4-1: Error shown when trying to require `module_a`, which can't be found

What you need to do for this example to run is to prepend `./` to the `require` parameters:

main.js

```
require('./module_a')
require('./module_b')
```

Now run this example again (see Figure 4-2).

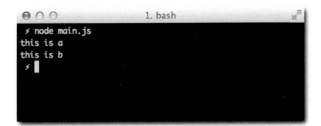

Figure 4-2: Module requirements are executed successfully

Success! The two modules execute. Next, I describe how you can make these modules expose APIs that you can assign to a variable when you call `require`.

EXPOSING APIS

For a module to expose an API that's expressed as the return value of a `require` call, two globals, `module` and `exports` ,come into play.

By default, each module exports an empty object { }. If you want to add properties to it, you can simply reference `exports`:

module_a.js

```
exports.name = 'john';
exports.data = 'this is some data';

var privateVariable = 5;

exports.getPrivate = function () {
  return privateVariable;
};
```

Now test it out (see Figure 4-3):

index.js

```
var a = require('./module_a');
console.log(a.name);
console.log(a.data);
console.log(a.getPrivate());
```

Figure 4-3: Showing the values exposed by the API of `module_a`

In this case, `exports` happens to be a reference to `module.exports`, which is an object by default. If setting individual keys in this object is not enough, you can also override `module.exports` completely. This is a common use case for modules that export constructors (see Figure 4-4):

person.js

```javascript
module.exports = Person;

function Person (name) {
  this.name = name;
};

Person.prototype.talk = function () {
  console.log('my name is', this.name);
};
```

index.js

```javascript
var Person = require('./person');
var john = new Person('john');
john.talk();
```

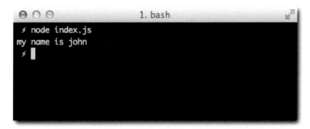

Figure 4-4: OOP-style JavaScript with Node.JS modules example

As you can see, in this `index` you no longer receive an `Object` as the return value, but a `Function`, thanks to overriding `module.exports`.

EVENTS

One of the fundamental APIs in Node.JS is the `EventEmitter`. In both Node and browser JavaScript, a lot of the code depends on events you listen on or events you emit:

```javascript
window.addEventListener('load', function () {
  alert('Window is loaded!');
});
```

The DOM APIs in the browser that deal with events are mainly `addEventListener`, `removeEventListener`, and `dispatchEvent`. They are present on a number of different objects, from a `window` to an `XMLHTTPRequest`.

The following example makes an AJAX request (in modern browsers) and listens on the stateChange to know when data is ready:

```
var ajax = new XMLHTTPRequest
ajax.addEventListener('stateChange', function () {
  if (ajax.readyState == 4 && ajax.responseText) {
    alert('we got some data: ' + ajax.responseText);
  }
});
ajax.open('GET', '/my-page');
ajax.send(null);
```

In Node, you also listen to and emit events everywhere. Node therefore exposes the Event Emitter API that defines on, emit, and removeListener methods. It's exposed as process.EventEmitter:

eventemitter/index.js

```
var EventEmitter = require('events').EventEmitter
  , a = new EventEmitter;
a.on('event', function () {
  console.log('event called');
});
a.emit('event');
```

This API a lot less verbose than the DOM equivalent, and Node uses it internally and lets you easily add it to your own classes:

```
var EventEmitter = process.EventEmitter
  , MyClass = function (){};

MyClass.prototype._proto__ = EventEmitter.prototype;
```

Therefore, all the instances of MyClass have encapsulated events support:

```
var a = new MyClass;
a.on('some event', function () {
  // do something
});
```

Events are central to Node's non-blocking design. Since Node usually doesn't "respond right away" with data (because that would imply blocking the thread while waiting on a resource), it usually *emits events* with data instead.

As an example, consider an HTTP server again. When Node fires the callback with an incoming request, all its data might not be immediately available. This is the case for example for POST requests (that is, the user submitting a form).

When the user submits a form, you normally listen on the *data* and *end* events of a request:

```
http.Server(function (req, res) {
  var buf = '';
  req.on('data', function (data) {
    buf += data;
  });
  req.on('end', function () {
    console.log('All the data is ready!');
  });
});
```

This is a common use-case in Node.JS: you "buffer" the contents of the request (data event), and then you can do something with it when you're sure all the data has been received (end event).

In order for Node to let you know that a request has hit the server as soon as possible, regardless of whether *all its data* is present or not, it needs to rely on events. Events in Node are the mechanism by which you get notified of things that haven't occurred yet, but are bound to occur.

Whether an event will be fired or not depends on the API that implements it. For example, you know that `ServerRequest` inherits from `EventEmitter`, and now you also know that it emits *data* and *end* events.

Certain APIs emit *error* events, which might or might not happen at all. There are events that only fire once (like *end*), or others that could fire more than once (like *data*). Some APIs only emit a certain event when certain conditions are met. For example, after a certain event happens some other event might be guaranteed not to be fired again. In the case for an HTTP request, you fully expect no *data* events to happen after an *end* event. Otherwise, your app would malfunction.

Similarly, sometimes for the use case of your application you only care about registering a callback for an event only once, regardless if it fires again in the future. Node provides a shortcut method for this:

```
a.once('an event', function () {
  // this function will be called only once, even if the event is triggered again
});
```

To understand what type of events are available and what their *contracts* (the "rules" the given API defines for triggering them) are, you usually refer to the API documentation of the given module. Throughout the book you'll learn the core Node module APIs and some of the most important events, but always keeping the API handy will be a very helpful habit.

BUFFERS

Another deficiency in the language that Node makes up for, besides modules, is handling of binary data.

Buffer is a global object that represents a fixed memory allocation (that is, the number of bytes that are put aside for a buffer have to be known in advance), which behaves like an array of octets, effectively letting you represent binary data in JavaScript.

A part of its functionality is the capability to convert data between encodings. For example, you can create a buffer from the base64 representation of an image and then write it down to a file as a binary PNG that can actually be used:

buffers/index.js

```
var mybuffer = new Buffer('==ii1j2i3h1i23h', 'base64'):
console.log(mybuffer);
require('fs').writeFile('logo.png', mybufffer);
```

For those not familiar with base64, it's essentially a way of writing binary data with only ASCII characters. In other words, it allows you to represent something as complex as an image in simple English characters (therefore taking up a lot more hard drive space).

Most of the Node.JS APIs that do data IO take and export data as buffers. In this example, the writeFile API from the filesystem module takes a buffer as a parameter to write out the file logo.gif.

Run it and open the file (see Figure 4-5).

```
$ node index
$ open logo.png
```

As you can see as the result of the console.log call with the Buffer object, it's a simple interface to the raw bytes that make up an image.

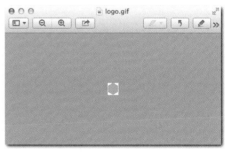

Figure 4-5: The GIF file created from the buffer base64 representation in the script showing the Node.JS logo

SUMMARY

You have now looked at the major differences between the JavaScript you write for the browser and the one you write for Node.JS.

You have a basic grasp of the APIs that Node added for patterns that are extremely common in day-to-day JavaScript but absent from the main language specification, such as timers, events, binary data, and modules.

You know the equivalent of window in Node world, and that you can leverage existing developer utilities like console.

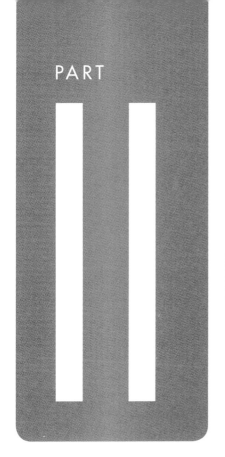

PART

II

ESSENTIAL NODE APIS

CHAPTER

CLI AND FS APIS: YOUR FIRST APPLICATION

THIS CHAPTER EXAMINES some of the most essential Node.JS APIs: those related to the handling of `stdin` and `stdout` of a process (`stdio`) and those related to the filesystem (`fs`).

As discussed in the preceding chapter, the Node approach to concurrency inherently involves the use of callbacks and events. These APIs provide

your first contact with the flow control involved in nonblocking evented I/O programming.

In addition to learning how all these APIs interact together, you create your first application: a simple command-line file explorer, whose goal is to allow the user to read and create files.

REQUIREMENTS

Start by defining what you want your program to do:

- You want the program to run on the command line. This means that the program is summoned either with the `node` command or by executing it directly, and then provides interaction with the user input and output through the terminal.
- Upon starting, the program should display the list of current directories (see Figure 5-1).

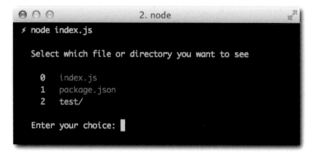

Figure 5-1: List of current directories displayed at startup.

- After you select a file, the program should output its contents.
- After you select a directory, the program should display its children.
- Then the program should quit.

Considering these cases, you can break down the project into different steps:

1. Creating our module
2. Deciding on `sync fs` versus `async fs`
3. Understanding Streams
4. Performing input and output
5. Refactoring
6. Interacting with the `fs`
7. Wrapping up

WRITING YOUR FIRST PROGRAM

You're now going to write a module based on the steps outlined above. The module is made up of a few files that you can create with any text editor.

By the end of this section you will have a fully functioning program written 100% in Node.JS.

CREATING THE MODULE

As in any other example in this book, you start by creating a directory that will contain the project. For the sake of this example, call this directory `file-explorer`.

As you learned in other chapters, it's always good practice to define a `package.json` file for your projects. This way, you can manage dependencies that are part of the NPM registry and make future publication of your modules possible.

Even though this particular example uses only APIs that are core to Node.JS (and therefore not fetched from the NPM registry), you need to create the simple `package.json`:

```
# package.json
{
    "name": "file-explorer"
  , "version": "0.0.1"
  , "description": "A command-file file explorer!"
}
```

> Note: NPM adheres to a versioning spec called **semver**. That's why instead of using "0.1" or "1" as the `version` field, you explicitly define it as "0.0.1".

To verify that your `package.json` is valid, run the command $ `npm install`.

If it works, the output should be empty. Otherwise, a JSON exception is shown (see Figure 5-2).

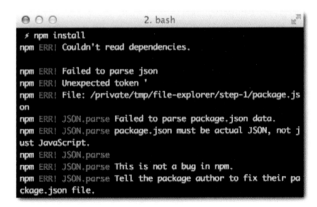

Figure 5-2: Running `npm install` with malformed JSON in `package.json`.

To continue, you are going to create a single JavaScript file to contain the entire functionality of your program: `index.js`.

SYNC OR ASYNC?

You start the file by declaring the dependencies. Because the `stdio` APIs are part of the `process` global, the only dependency you have is the `fs` module:

```
# index.js
/**
 * Module dependencies.
 */

var fs = require('fs');
```

The first thing you do upon running the program is obtain a list of files in the current directory.

One important point to keep in mind is that the `fs` API is unique in that it allows you to make both blocking and nonblocking calls. For example, if you want to get the list of present directories, you can use the following call:

```
> console.log(require('fs').readdirSync(__dirname));
```

That returns the contents immediately or throws an exception if an error exists (see Figure 5-3).

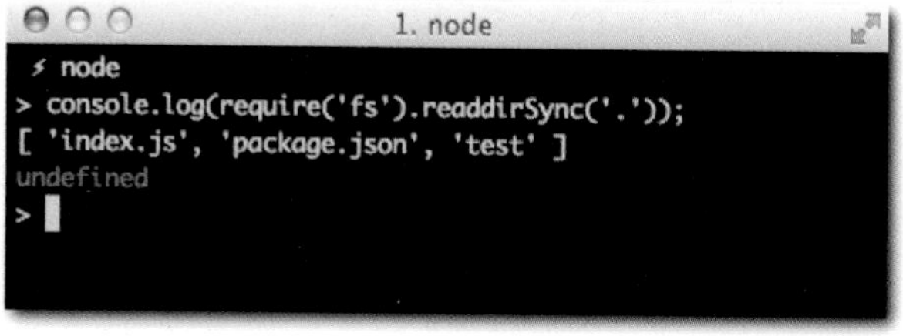

Figure 5-3: Examining the return value of `readdirSync`

The approach is obviously the asynchronous one:

```
> function async (err, files) { console.log(files); };
> require('fs').readdir('.', async);
```

This example produces the same result, shown in Figure 5-4.

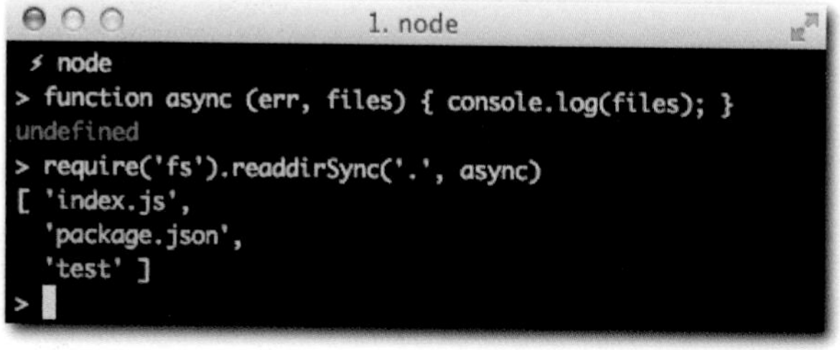

Figure 5-4: The asynchronous version of `readdir`

As discussed in Chapter 3, to create fast programs that can handle a lot of *concurrency* in only one thread, you create asynchronous evented programs.

Such are not the circumstances for this little CLI program (since only one person will be reading files at a time), but for the sake of learning the most important and challenging parts of Node.JS, you will write this in async style.

To get the list of files, you therefore use `fs.readdir`. The callback you supply provides an error object (which is `null` if no error occurs) and a `files` array:

```
# index.js
// . . .
fs.readdir(__dirname, function (err, files) {
  console.log(files);
});
```

Try executing the program! The result looks something like that in Figure 5-5.

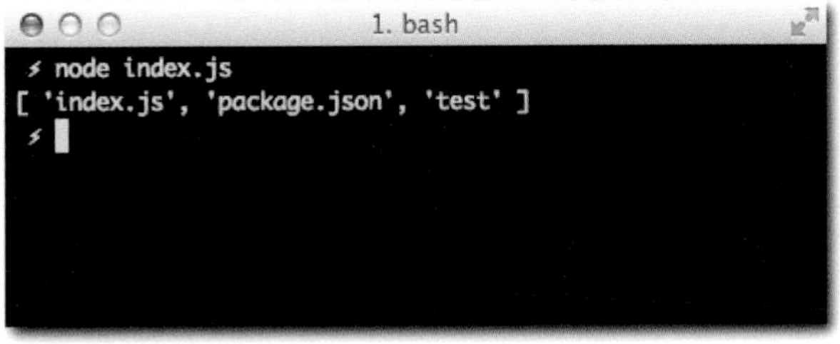

Figure 5-5: Running the example in your own node program contained in
`index.js`

Now that you understand that the `fs` module has synchronous and asynchronous methods for accessing the file system, you need to understand about streams, a fundamental concept in Node.JS.

UNDERSTANDING STREAMS

As you noticed already, `console.log` outputs to the console. In particular, `console.log` does something really specific: it *writes* to the `stdout` *stream* the string that you supply, followed by a `\n` (newline) character.

Observe the difference between the examples in Figure 5-6.

```
⊖ ○ ○                    1. bash
⚡ node example-1.js
Hello world
⚡ node example-2.js
Hello world ⚡ █
```

Figure 5-6: Writing Hello World in the first case yields a newline, but not in the second case

Now look at the source:

```
# example-1.js
console.log('Hello world');
```

and

```
# example-2.js
process.stdout.write('Hello world');
```

The process global contains three `Stream` objects that match the three Unix Standard Streams:

```
- **stdin**:  Standard input
- **stdout**: Standard output
- **stderr**: Standard error
```

These `Stream` objects are illustrated in Figure 5-7.

The first one, `stdin`, is a readable stream, whereas `stdout` and `stderr` are writeable streams.

The default state of the `stdin Stream` is paused. Normally, when a program is executed, it does something and then exits. Sometimes, however, and such is the case in this application, you need to keep the program running so that the user can enter some data.

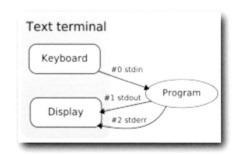

Figure 5-7: The `stdin`, `stdout`, and `stderr` objects in the context of a traditional text terminal

When you `resume` that Stream, Node watches the underlying *file descriptor* (that in Unix receives the number 0), therefore keeping the *event loop* running and not exiting your program, waiting for events to be triggered. Node.JS always exits automatically, unless it's waiting on IO.

Another property of a `Stream` is that it can have a default encoding. If you set an encoding to a stream, instead of getting a raw `Buffer`, you get an *encoded string* (utf-8, ascii, and so on) as parameters of events.

The `Stream` object is a basic building block much like an `EventEmitter` (as a matter of fact, it inherits from it). You'll be dealing with different types of Streams throughout Node, such as TCP sockets or HTTP requests. In short, *when reading or writing data progressively is involved*, streams are involved.

INPUT AND OUPUT

Now that you understand a little more about what happens when you execute your program, try to write the first part of the application, which lists files in the present directory and waits for user input:

```
# index.js
// . . .
fs.readdir(process.cwd(), function (err, files) {
  console.log('');

  if (!files.length) {
    return console.log('    \033[31m No files to show!\033[39m\n');
  }

  console.log('  Select which file or directory you want to see\n');

  function file(i) {
    var filename = files[i];

    fs.stat(__dirname + '/' + filename, function (err, stat) {
      if (stat.isDirectory()) {
        console.log('     '+i+'   \033[36m' + filename + '/\033[39m');
      } else {
        console.log('     '+i+'   \033[90m' + filename + '\033[39m');
      }

      i++;
      if (i == files.length) {
        console.log('');
        process.stdout.write('   \033[33mEnter your choice: \033[39m');
        process.stdin.resume();
      } else {
        file(i);
      }
    });
  }

  file(0);
});
```

Now look at this code line by line.

For visual separation, you output an empty line:

```
console.log('')
```

You write that no files are present to be listed if the files array is empty. The \033[31m and 033[39m that surround the text give it a red color. The last character in the example is the newline \n again, simply for visual separation.

```
if (!files.length) {
  return console.log('    \033[31m No files to show!\033[39m\n');
}
```

The next line is self-explanatory:

```
console.log('   Select which file or directory you want to see\n');
```

You define a function that is going to be executed for each member of the array. This is the first pattern of asynchronous flow control used throughout this book: **serial execution**. At the end of the chapter, you look at it in detail.

```
function file (i) {
  // . . .
}
```

You access the first filename and then obtain the Stat on it. fs.stat gives a variety of *metadata* about the file or directory:

```
var filename = files[i];

fs.stat(__dirname + '/' + filename, function (err, stat) {
  // . . .
});
```

The callback gives you, again, an error object (if any) and a Stat object. The Stat object method of interest in this case is isDirectory:

```
if (stat.isDirectory()) {
  console.log('      '+i+'    \033[36m' + filename + '/\033[39m');
} else {
  console.log('      '+i+'    \033[90m' + filename + '\033[39m');
}
```

If the path is a directory, you want to print it in a different color from files.

Next is the central piece of flow control. You increment the counter by one, and you immediately check whether you have any files left for processing:

```
i++;
if (i == files.length) {
  console.log('');
  process.stdout.write('    \033[33mEnter your choice: \033[39m');
  process.stdin.resume();
  process.stdin.setEncoding('utf8');
} else {
  file(i);
}
```

If you don't have any files left, you prompt the user for an option. Notice that you use `process.stdout.write` instead of `console.log`; you don't want a newline so that the user can type right after the prompt (see Figure 5-8):

```
console.log('');
process.stdout.write('    \033[33mEnter your choice: \033[39m');
```

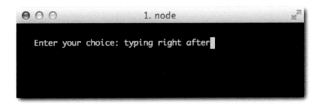

Figure 5-8: Your program so far, prompting you for `stdin` input.

This line, as discussed earlier, allows you to request input from the user:

```
process.stdin.resume();
```

This line sets the Stream encoding to utf8 so that you can seamlessly support special characters:

```
process.stdin.setEncoding('utf8');
```

On the other hand, if there's still a file to process, the function calls itself again:

```
file(i);
```

The process thus continues *serially* until all the files are processed and user input is requested. This is the first important pattern you study in this chapter.

REFACTORING

You start refactoring by adding some useful shortcuts because you're going to use `stdin` and `stdout` quite a bit:

```
# index.js
// . . .
var fs = require('fs')
  , stdin = process.stdin
  , stdout = process.stdout
```

Because you're writing code that's asynchronous, you run the risk that as the functionality grows (especially that which regards to flow control), too much nesting of functions makes the program hard to read.

To counter this, you can define functions in succession that represent each step of the async process.

First, separate the function to read the stdin:

```
# index.js
// called for each file walked in the directory
function file(i) {
  var filename = files[i];

  fs.stat(__dirname + '/' + filename, function (err, stat) {
    if (stat.isDirectory()) {
      console.log('    '+i+'   \033[36m' + filename + '/\033[39m');
    } else {
      console.log('    '+i+'   \033[90m' + filename + '\033[39m');
    }

    if (++i == files.length) {
      read();
    } else {
      file(i);
    }
  });
}

// read user input when files are shown
function read () {
  console.log('');
  stdout.write('   \033[33mEnter your choice: \033[39m');

  stdin.resume();
  stdin.setEncoding('utf8');
}
```

Notice that you're also leveraging new stdin and stdout references.

The next logical step after reading input is evaluating it. The user is asked to provide an option of which file to read. To that end, after you set the encoding for stdin, you start listening on the data event:

```
function read () {
  // . . .
  stdin.on('data', option);
}


// called with the option supplied by the user
function option (data) {
  if (!files[Number(data)]) {
    stdout.write('   \033[31mEnter your choice: \033[39m');
  } else {
    stdin.pause();
  }
}
```

Here, you check that the user input matches an existing index in the `files` array. Remember that the `files` array is part of the callback you're enclosed in (`fs.readdir`). Notice you convert the utf-8 string `data` to a `Number` for the check.

If the check is successful, you make sure to pause the stream again (back to its default state) so that after the program performs the `fs` operations described in the next step, it quits (see Figure 5-9).

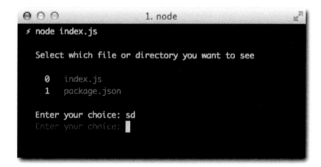

Figure 5-9: An example of a wrong choice being entered

Now that you've made progress in the user interaction aspects by presenting the user with the list of files, you can move on to actually read and display them.

INTERACTING WITH THE FS

When you know you can locate the file, it's time to read it!

```
function option (data) {
  var filename = files[Number(data)];
  if (!filename) {
    stdout.write('   \033[31mEnter your choice: \033[39m');
  } else {
    stdin.pause();
    fs.readFile(__dirname + '/' + filename, 'utf8', function (err, data) {
```

```
    console.log('');
    console.log('\033[90m' + data.replace(/(.*)/g, '    $1') + '\033[39m');
  });
  }
}
```

Notice that once again, you can specify the encoding in advance so that the event gives you a ready-for-use string:

```
fs.readFile(__dirname + '/' + filename, 'utf8', function (err, data) {
```

You then output the content `data`, adding some indentation with a regular expression (see Figure 5-10):

```
data.replace(/(.*)/g, '    $1')
```

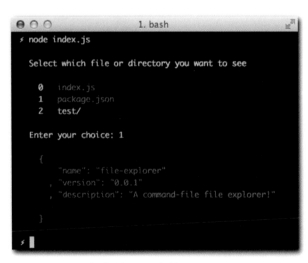

Figure 5-10: An example of reading a simple file

But what if a directory is chosen? In that case, you're supposed to output its children instead.

To avoid performing an `fs.stat` again, go back to the `file` function and save references to the `Stat` objects:

```
// . . .
var stats = [];

function file(i) {
  var filename = files[i];

  fs.stat(__dirname + '/' + filename, function (err, stat) {
    stats[i] = stat;
    // . . .
```

Now you can easily check from the `option` function. For reference, this is where you were previously executing `fs.readFile`:

```
if (stats[Number(data)].isDirectory()) {
  fs.readdir(__dirname + '/' + filename, function (err, files) {
    console.log('');
    console.log('   (' + files.length + ' files)');
    files.forEach(function (file) {
      console.log('      -   ' + file);
    });
    console.log('');
  });
} else {
  fs.readFile(__dirname + '/' + filename, 'utf8', function (err, data) {
    console.log('');
    console.log('\033[90m' + data.replace(/(.*)/g, '      $1') + '\033[39m');
  });
}
```

If you run the program now you should be able to select a directory and be presented with a list of choices of files to read (see Figure 5-11).

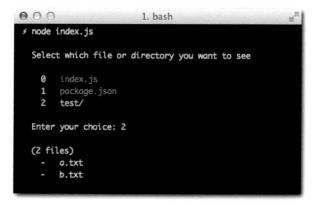

Figure 5-11: An example of reading the `test/` folder.

And you're done! Congratulations on writing your first Node CLI program.

EXPLORING THE CLI

Now that you have completed your first command-line program, it's useful to learn additional APIs that are helpful when writing similar applications that run from the terminal.

ARGV

The `process.argv` contains all the argument values with which the node program that is being run was summoned:

```
# example.js
console.log(process.argv);
```

In Figure 5-12, notice that the first element is always `node`, and the second is the path of the file being evaluated. Subsequent elements are the arguments supplied with the command.

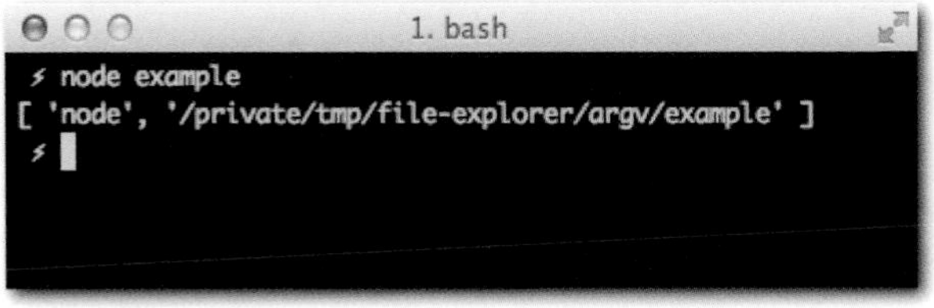

Figure 5-12: An example of the contents of `process.argv`

To obtain these elements, you can slice off the first two elements from the array (see Figure 5-13):

```
# example-2.js
console.log(process.argv.slice(2));
```

Figure 5-13: An example of the stripped-down `argv` that displays only the supplied options to the example program

Next up, you need to understand how to access the difference between the directory a program *resides at* and the one the program is *run at*.

WORKING DIRECTORY

In the sample app, you use `__dirname` to access the directory where the file that you're executing is in the filesystem.

Sometimes, however, it's preferable to look for the *current working directory* at the time the application is run. With the current implementation, if you're in your home directory and want to run this app, the result is the same as if you run it in any other directory because the location where `index.js` lives doesn't change, and therefore `__dirname` stays the same.

If you want to obtain the current working directory, you can call `process.cwd`:

```
> process.cwd()
/Users/guillermo
```

Node also provides the flexibility for changing it via `process.chdir`:

```
> process.cwd()
/Users/guillermo
> process.chdir('/')
> process.cwd()
/
```

Another aspect of the context a program is run in is the presence of environmental variables. You will learn how to access them next.

ENVIRONMENTAL VARIABLES

Node allows you to easily access variables that are part of your shell environment via the handy object `process.env`.

For example, a common environmental variable is NODE_ENV (see Figure 5-14), which is used conventionally to signal a node program whether you're in a development or production environment.

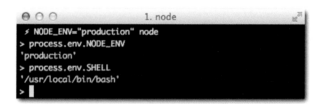

Figure 5-14: The environmental variable NODE_ENV

Controlling when to quit a program from within it is often times necessary.

EXITING

To quit your application, you can call `process.exit` and optionally supply an exit code. For example, if you want to exit with an error, it's good practice to quit with the code 1:

```
console.error('An error occurred');
process.exit(1);
```

This allows healthy interoperability between your node CLI programs and other tools in the operating system.

Another point of interoperability is the process *signals*.

SIGNALS

One of the ways processes communicate with the operating system is through signals. When you want to *signal* the process to terminate immediately, for example, you send the SIGKILL signal.

Signals in Node programs are emitted as events on the `process` object:

```
process.on('SIGKILL', function () {
  // signal received
});
```

Read on to understand how you brought colors to the example program in this chapter with escape codes.

ANSI ESCAPE CODES

To control formatting, colors, and other output preferences in a text terminal, you use *ANSI escape sequences or codes*. These special characters are recognized by the terminal emulator in a standard way.

When you include the characters that surround your text, those characters are obviously not output. These characters are called *nonprinting*.

Consider, for example, the following sequence:

```
console.log('\033[90m' + data.replace(/(.*)/g, '    $1') + '\033[39m');
```

- `\033` begins the escape sequence.
- `[` indicates color setting.
- `90` is the foreground color to bright gray.
- `m` wraps up the setting.

You might notice that on the other end you use `39`, which resets back to the default terminal color so that you partially colorize text.

You can find a complete table of ANSI escape codes at http://en.wikipedia.org/wiki/ansi_escape_code.

EXPLORING THE FS MODULE

The `fs` module allows you to read and write data through a Stream API. Unlike the `readFile` and `writeFile` methods, the allocation of memory doesn't happen all at once.

Consider the example of a large comma-separated file with millions of rows. Reading the entire file to parse it would mean a large allocation of memory all at once. A much better approach would be to read chunks at a time, look for line endings (`"\n"`) and parse progressively.

Node `Streams` are a perfect fit for this, as you'll read about next.

STREAMS

The method `fs.createReadStream` allows you to create a readable `Stream` object for a particular file.

To understand the power of streams, consider the difference between the following two examples:

```
fs.readFile('my-file.txt', function (err, contents){
  // do something with file
});
```

In this case, the callback function that you supply fires after the entire file is read, placed in RAM, and ready to use.

In the following example, chunks of varying sizes are read, and each time a callback is fired:

```
var stream = fs.createReadStream('my-file.txt');
stream.on('data', function(chunk){
  // do something with part of the file
});
stream.on('end', function(chunk){
  // reached the end
});
```

Why is this capability important? Imagine you have a large video you need to upload to a web service. You don't really need to read the *entire* video to start uploading it, so using `Stream` immediately translates into a speed advantage.

This is also the case for logging, especially with a writable stream. If you use a web app to log visitors to your website, it might not be so efficient to tell the operating system to open and close the file (and therefore seek it in your disk each time) because you'll be writing to the file a lot.

Therefore, that's a good use case for a `fs.WriteStream`. Open the file once and then call `.write` for each log entry.

Another great fit for Node's non-blocking design is watching.

WATCH

Node allows you to *watch* files and directories for changes. Watching means that upon a file (or files contained within, in the case for watching a directory) changing in the file system, you get an event in the form of a callback.

This functionality is widely used within the Node ecosystem. For example, some people prefer to write CSS stylesheets in a language that compiles down to CSS. It's often really handy to perform the compilation upon the source file being modified.

Consider the following example. First, you look for all the CSS files in the working directory and then you watch them for changes. When a change is detected, the filename is output to the console:

```
var stream = fs.createReadStream('my-file.txt');
var fs = require('fs');
// get all files in working directory
var files = fs.readdirSync(process.cwd());
files.forEach(function (file) {
  // watch the file if it ends in ".css"
  if (/\.css/.test(file)) {
    fs.watchFile(process.cwd() + '/' + file, function () {
      console.log(' - ' + file + ' changed!');
    });
  }
});
```

In addition to `fs.watchFile`, you can also leverage `fs.watch` to watch *entire directories* seamlessly.

SUMMARY

During this chapter you learned the fundamentals of writing a program in Node.JS, specifically a command-line program that interacts with the filesystem.

Despite the first example program being a good fit for the synchronous `fs` APIs, you leveraged the asynchronous ones to understand some of the intricacies of writing code that contains a lot of callbacks. Regardless, we succeeded in making the program's code expressive and completely functional.

One of the most important APIs you learned about is the `Stream`, which will appear frequently throughout the book. Almost everywhere where I/O is present, `Streams` are as well.

You also now have tools and pointers to play around and create sophisticated and useful terminal programs that leverage the filesystem, interact with other programs or get input from the user.

You will leverage these APIs (specially those pertaining to process) a lot as a Node.JS developer, even when writing web applications or more complex problems. Make sure you remember them well!

CHAPTER

6

TCP

TRANSMISSION CONTROL PROTOCOL (TCP) is a connection-oriented protocol that provides reliable and ordered delivery of data from one computer to another.

In other words, TCP is the transport protocol you use whenever you want to ensure that all the bytes you send from one point reach the other completely and in the correct order.

For these and other reasons, most protocols that you use now, such as HTTP, are built on top of TCP. When you send the HTML for a page, you want it to get to the other end in the exact form that you sent it, and if that is not possible, an error should be triggered. If even one character (byte) of the stream were to be misplaced, a browser might not be able to render the page.

Node.JS is a framework designed with the development of networked applications in mind. Today, applications in a network communicate over the transport known as TCP/IP. Therefore it's crucial that we have an understanding about how TCP/IP basically works, and how Node.JS expresses it with its amazingly simple APIs.

First, you are going to learn the characteristics of the protocol. For example, what guarantees you have when you send a message from one computer to another using TCP. If you send two messages in a row, will they get to the other end in the order you wrote them? Understanding the protocol is essential to understanding any software that leverages it. Most of the times you connect and talk to a database like MySQL, you're doing so over a TCP socket, for example.

The Node HTTP server is built on top of the Node TCP server. To us programmers, this translates into the Node `http.Server` inheriting from the `net.Server` (`net` is the TCP module).

In addition to web browsers and servers (HTTP), applications you rely on daily leverage TCP, like email clients (SMTP/IMAP/POP), chat programs (IRC/XMPP), remote shells (SSH), and a lot more.

Knowing as much as possible about TCP and familiarizing yourself with the Node.JS APIs for it will therefore help you create or understand network programs with a variety of uses and applications.

WHAT ARE THE CHARACTERISTICS OF TCP?

In order to *use* TCP, you don't really need to understand how it works internally, or what decisions were made about how the protocol works.

But that understanding can be a big help when analyzing problems with higher-level protocols and servers, such as web servers or databases.

The first thing to understand about TCP is that it's connection-oriented.

CONNECTION-ORIENTED COMMUNICATION AND SAME-ORDER DELIVERY

When you work with TCP, you can think of the communication between a client and server as a *connection* or *data stream*. This is a useful abstraction for the development of services and applications because the Internet Protocol (IP) on which TCP sits is connectionless.

IP is based on the transmission of *datagrams*. These datagrams are packets of data that are sent and received independently and whose order of arrival is arbitrary.

How does TCP ensure that these independent datagrams are part of an ordered stream?

If using IP means having potentially irregular arrival times of data packets, and these packets do not belong to any *data stream* or *connection*, how is it possible that if you open two TCP/IP connections to a server, the packets you send don't get mixed up?

The answer to these two questions is what explains the existence of TCP. When you send data in the context of a TCP connection, the IP datagrams that are sent out contain information that identifies the connection they belong to and the order in the data stream.

Imagine splitting up a message into four parts. If a server gets parts 1 and 4, and both belong to connection A, it knows to wait for parts 2 and 3 to arrive in other datagrams.

When you write a server that implements TCP, like you're going to do with Node, you simply don't worry about this underlying complexity. You always think of connections, and when you *write* to a socket, you know that the other end will receive it in that order, or if a network error occurs, the connection will be considered erroneous and aborted.

BYTE ORIENTATION

TCP doesn't know about characters, or character encodings, and rightfully so. As you saw in Chapter 4, different text encoding can result in a different number of bytes being transmitted.

TCP therefore allows you to transmit data that could be a succession of ASCII characters (1 byte each) or Unicode that could take up to 4 bytes each.

By not enforcing a particular message format, TCP offers great flexibility.

RELIABILITY

Because TCP is based on a fundamentally unreliable service, it must implement a series of mechanisms to achieve reliability based on *acknowledgments* and *timeouts*.

When a data packet is sent, the sender expects an acknowledgment (a tiny response indicating that the packet was received). If, after a certain window of time, the acknowledgment is not received, the sender retries to send the packet.

This behavior effectively deals with unpredictable conditions such as network errors and network congestions.

FLOW CONTROL

What happens when two computers communicate and one has a significantly faster connection speed than the other?

TCP also ensures a balance in the flow of packets between the two ends by means of flow control.

CONGESTION CONTROL

TCP has built-in mechanisms to ensure that rates of packet delay and loss within a network don't drastically increase to ensure a good quality of service (QoS).

Similarly to flow control, which prevents the sender from overwhelming the receiver, TCP tries to avoid congestive collapse by regulating the rate at which packets are sent, for example.

Now that you have some basic understanding of how TCP theoretically works, it's time to get practical. In order to test or play around with TCP servers, you can leverage the Telnet utility.

TELNET

Telnet is an old network protocol intended to provide a bidirectional virtual terminal. It was mostly used before SSH existed as a means of controlling remote computers, such as remote server administration. It's (no surprise!) a layer on top of the TCP protocol.

Even though it's almost completely fallen into disuse since the 2000s, almost all modern operating systems today ship with a `telnet` client (also illustrated in Figure 6-1):

```
$ telnet
```

The port over which most Telnet communications occur is 23. If you try to connect to a server over this port (`telnet host.com 23` or simply `telnet host.com`), the program attempts to *speak* the Telnet protocol over TCP.

Figure 6-1: Running the telnet utility.

But the `telnet` client program has a capability of far more interest in this case. If, by looking at the data sent, it sees that the server is speaking a protocol other than Telnet, instead of closing the connection or displaying an error, it puts the client in a *protocol-less RAW TCP mode*.

So, what happens when you try to `telnet` to a web server? To find out, check out the following example.

First, start by writing a hello world Node.JS web server and making it listen on port 3000:

```
# web-server.js
require('http').createServer(function (req, res) {
  res.writeHead(200, { 'Content-Type': 'text/html' });
  res.end('<h1>Hello world</h1>');
}).listen(3000);
```

You run it with `node server.js`. To make sure it works, you can use the quintessential HTTP client, the browser, as shown in Figure 6-2.

Figure 6-2: The browser establishes a TCP connection to localhost over port 3000, and then "talks" the HTTP protocol.

Now implement the client. To do so, establish a connection with `telnet` (see also Figure 6-3):

```
$ telnet localhost 3000
```

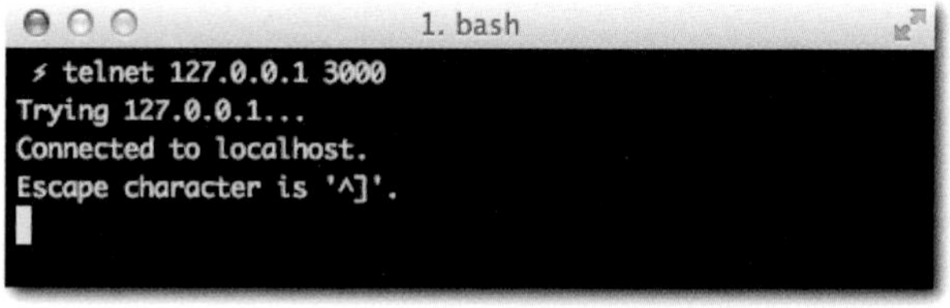

Figure 6-3: `telnet` enables you to establish a TCP connection manually using the terminal.

Based on the result in Figure 6-3, it definitely looks as though this example worked, but nothing that remotely resembles "Hello World" is coming up. The reason is that you must first create an HTTP request by *writing* to the TCP connection, which is also called *socket*. Type GET / HTTP/1.1 and press Enter twice.

The response, illustrated in Figure 6-4, should come up!

Figure 6-4: An IRC client (`Textual.app`) in action on the Mac. `Textual.app` implements the IRC protocol over TCP sockets.

In sum:

- You successfully established a TCP connection.
- You created an HTTP request.
- You received an HTTP response.
- You tested a few of the features that make TCP. The data arrived just like you wrote it in Node.JS: you first wrote the `Content-Type` header and then the response body, and everything arrived in perfect order.

A TCP CHAT PROGRAM

As you saw earlier, the main goal of TCP is enabling reliable communication between machines across networks.

The "Hello World" program of TCP chosen for this chapter is a chat application because it's one of the simplest ways to illustrate the usefulness of TCP.

Next, you're going to create a basic TCP server that anyone can connect to without implementing any sophisticated protocols or commands:

- When the server is connected, it greets you and asks for your name. It tells you how many other clients are connected.
- Upon typing in your name followed by Enter, you're considered connected.
- When connected, you can receive and send messages to other connected clients by typing and pressing Enter.

What does it mean to press Enter? Essentially, everything you write on Telnet is immediately sent to the server. Pressing Enter inserts the character \n. In the Node server, you look for this \n to know when a message has arrived completely. It's the *delimiter*.

In other words, pressing Enter is no different from writing a letter a.

CREATING THE MODULE

As usual, you start by creating the directory where your project is going to live and a `package.json` file:

```
# package.json
{
    "name": "tcp-chat"
  , "description": "Our first TCP server"
  , "version": "0.0.1"
}
```

You can test it by running `npm install`. An empty line should be printed because the project has no dependencies.

UNDERSTANDING THE NET.SERVER API

Next, create an `index.js` file to contain the server:

```
/**
 * Module dependencies.
 */

var net = require('net')
```

```
/**
 * Create server.
 */

var server = net.createServer(function (conn) {
  // handle connection
  console.log('\033[90m   new connection!\033[39m');
});

/**
 * Listen.
 */

server.listen(3000, function () {
  console.log('\033[96m   server listening on *:3000\033[39m');
});
```

Notice that you specify a callback function to `createServer`. This function gets executed *every time a new connection to the server is established.*

To test this callback, run the code to spawn your TCP to the server. When `listen` executes, it binds the server to the port 3000 and subsequently prints a message to the terminal.

```
$ node index.js
```

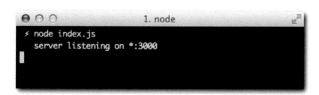

Figure 6-5: Your server will bind to the port 3000 and then display a success message.

Now, attempt a connection with `telnet`:

```
$ telnet 127.0.0.1 3000
```

In Figure 6-6, you can see the command and the "new connection!" output side by side.

As you can see, this example very much resembles the HTTP hello world. This should come as no surprise considering that HTTP is a layer on top of TCP. In this case, however, you're creating your own protocol.

The `createServer` callback passes an object that's an instance of a common occurrence in Node: a `Stream`. In this case, it passes a `net.Stream`, which is usually both readable and writable.

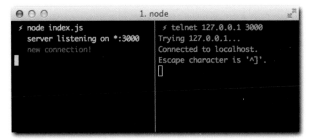

Figure 6-6: On the left, you can see the status of the server process. On the right, the client, that upon connecting makes the server print "new connection!"

Finally, another method of importance is `listen`, which allows you to *bind the server to a port*. Because this method is asynchronous, it also receives a callback.

RECEIVING CONNECTIONS

As defined in the earlier project description, as soon as a connection is established, you want to *write back* to the client with a Hello and the number of active connections.

You start by adding a counter outside the callback:

```
/**
 * Keep track of connections.
 */

var count = 0;
```

You change the connection callback to increment this counter and print the greeting:

```
var server = net.createServer(function (conn) {
  conn.write(
      '\n > welcome to \033[92mnode-chat\033[39m!'
    + '\n > ' + count + ' other people are connected at this time.'
    + '\n > please write your name and press enter: '
  );
  count++;
});
```

As you can see here, you still use shell escape codes to print out colors.

Test it now by restarting the server:

```
$ node index
```

Then connect again (see also Figure 6-7):

```
$ telnet 127.0.0.1 3000
```

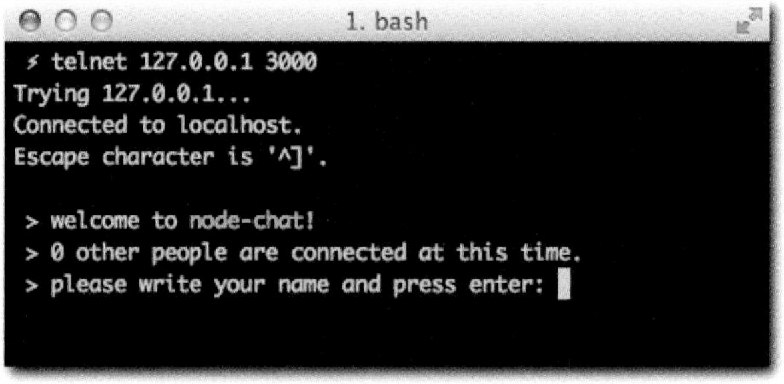

Figure 6-7: The client now receives some data upon connecting.

If you connect again, as shown in Figure 6-8, you can see the counter go up!

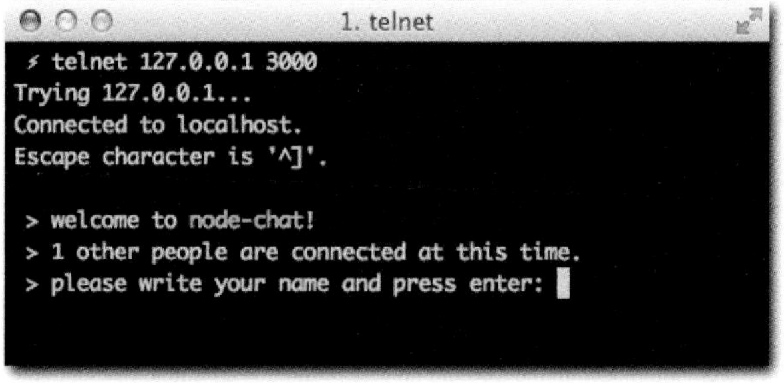

Figure 6-8: The connections counter in action

When the client emits the `close` event, you substract a unit from the counter variable:

```
conn.on('close', function () {
  count--;
});
```

The `close` event is fired by Node.JS when the underlying socket is closed. Node.JS has two events related to the connection finalization: `end` and `close`. The former is received when the client explicitly closes the TCP connection. For example, when you close telnet properly, it will send a packet called "FIN" that signals the end of the connection.

If a connection error occurs (which triggers the `error` event), `end` won't fire, since the "FIN" packet wasn't received. `close`, however, will fire under both circumstances, so it's better to use that one instead for this example.

You can end a telnet connection properly by pressing alt+[key on the Mac, and Ctrl+] on Windows.

THE DATA EVENT

Now that you have printed out some data, you also need to consider the data that comes in.

The first piece of data to handle is the nickname; you therefore can start listening on the incoming data event. Like many other APIs in Node, the `net.Stream` is also an `EventEmitter`.

To test this, print out the incoming data to the server console:

```
var server = net.createServer(function (conn) {
  conn.write(
      '\n > welcome to \033[92mnode-chat\033[39m!'
    + '\n > ' + count + ' other people are connected at this time.'
    + '\n > please write your name and press enter: '
  );
  count++;

  conn.on('data', function (data) {
    console.log(data);
  });
  conn.on('close', function () {
    count--;
  });
});
```

You then launch the server and connect a client. Try writing some data, as in Figure 6-9. On the left, as you write data, the server is passing it by `console.log`.

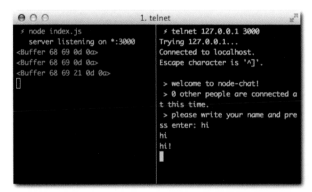

Figure 6-9: You can see the representation of the `Buffer` objects on the left for the data sent on the right.

As you can see, what you get as data is a `Buffer`. Remember I said TCP is byte oriented? Here, you can see Node complying with TCP!

At this point, you have a couple of different options. You could call `.toString('utf8')` on the `Buffer` object to get a utf8-encoded representation.

However, because at no point are you going to need data in an encoding other than utf8, you can use handy `net.Stream#setEncoding` to have Node do that for you:

```
# index.js
. . .
conn.setEncoding('utf8');
```

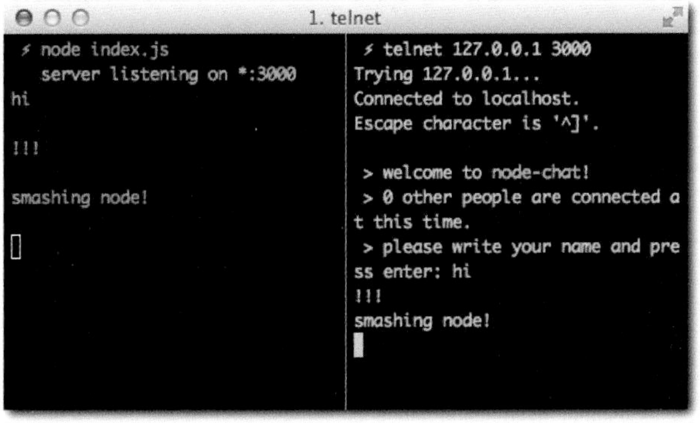

Figure 6-10: On the left, the chat messages are now output as utf8-encoded strings.

Now that you successfully passed messages back and forth between one client and the server, you can bring in the tracking of other clients to chat with.

STATE AND KEEPING TRACK OF CONNECTIONS

The counter defined earlier is part of what is normally called `state`. Node is said to deal with *shared-state concurrency* because in the example, two concurrent users alter the same state variables.

To be able to send a message and broadcast it to all other connections, you need to extend this state to keep track of who's connected.

A client is considered connected and capable of receiving messages when a nickname has been typed in.

The first thing you do is keep track of all the users who have set a nickname. To do so, you introduce a new state variable, `users`:

```
var count = 0
  , users = {}
```

Next, introduce the variable `nickname` in the scope of each connection:

```
conn.setEncoding('utf8');

// the nickname for the current connection
var nickname;

conn.on('data', function (data) {
```

When you get data, you make sure to clear the \r\n (equivalent to pressing Enter):

```
// remove the "enter" character
data = data.replace('\r\n', '');
```

If the user doesn't have a nickname, you validate it. If the nickname is not being used, you relay it to everyone that you connected (see Figure 6-11):

```
// the first piece of data you expect is the nickname
if (!nickname) {
  if (users[data]) {
    conn.write('\033[93m> nickname already in use. try again:\033[39m ');
    return;
  } else {
    nickname = data;
    users[nickname] = conn;

    for (var i in users) {
      users[i].write('\033[90m > ' + nickname + ' joined the room\033[39m\n');
    }
  }
}
```

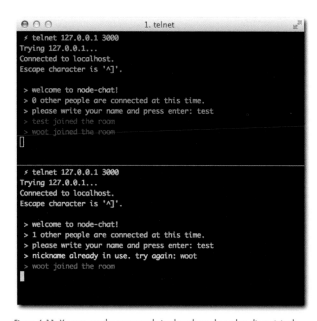

Figure 6-11: You can see the messages being broadcasted as other clients join the chat server.

However, if the user has been set, you consider that the incoming data is a message to relay to everyone else:

```
else {
  // otherwise you consider it a chat message
  for (var i in users) {
    if (i != nickname) {
      users[i].write('\033[96m > ' + nickname + ':\033[39m ' + data + '\n');
    }
  }
}
```

You check that you don't send the message to yourself by using the `i != nickname` check.

You can see in Figure 6-12 the new behavior by connecting two clients, writing in one and watching the other.

Figure 6-12: Clients get messages typed by other clients prefixed with their nicknames.

After succeeding in exchanging chat messages, you can make the final touches.

WRAP UP

When someone disconnects, you clear up the `users` array:

```
conn.on('close', function () {
  count--;
  delete users[nickname];
});
```

It's also a good idea to send a message to the rest of the users about your departure. Because you need to broadcast to all the users yet again, you can probably abstract that out as a utility:

```
// . . .
function broadcast (msg, exceptMyself) {
  for (var i in users) {
    if (!exceptMyself || i != nickname) {
      users[i].write(msg);
    }
  }
}

conn.on('data', function (data) {
  // . . .
```

The following function is self-explanatory. You can replace the other instances of broadcasting with the new reusable utility:

```
broadcast('\033[90m > ' + nickname + ' joined the room\033[39m\n');
// . . .
broadcast('\033[96m > ' + nickname + ':\033[39m ' + data + '\n', true);
```

Now you can add it to the close handler (see Figure 6-13):

```
conn.on('close', function () {
  // . . .
  broadcast('\033[90m > ' + nickname + ' left the room\033[39m\n');
});
```

Figure 6-13: After killing the first client to make it forcefully "close" the connection, you can see the departure message relayed by the server on the other clients' screens.

You're done!

After having implemented a TCP server successfully, you should learn how to implement TCP clients in Node.JS.

The client APIs will bear a lot of resemblance to other clients, such as the HTTP clients you use to query web services like Twitter, so it's crucial that you understand them fully.

AN IRC CLIENT PROGRAM

IRC, which stands for Internet Relay Chat, is yet another protocol based on TCP that's in common use. It's normally used through desktop apps, similar to the one shown in Figure 6-14, that act as clients to IRC servers.

Figure 6-14: An IRC client (Linkinus) in action on the Mac. Linkinus implements the IRC protocol over TCP sockets.

Because you successfully created a TCP server in the previous part, you're now going to create a TCP client.

Creating a client involves implementing the IRC protocol. This means that you need to make sure that incoming and outgoing data adhere to the set of commands that IRC servers "speak."

For example, to set a nickname, you send the following string:

```
NICK mynick
```

IRC is a very straightforward and simple protocol. You can achieve a lot and experience interoperability with existing applications and servers (like the one shown in Figure 6-14) with just a few simple commands.

Read on to learn how to write a very basic client in Node.JS that connects to a server, joins a room and relays a message.

CREATING THE MODULE

As usual, start by creating the directory where your project is going to live and a `package.json` file:

```
{
    "name": "irc-client"
  , "description": "Our first TCP client"
  , "version": "0.0.1"
}
```

Test it by running npm install. An empty line should be printed because the project has no dependencies.

UNDERSTANDING THE NET#STREAM API

In the same way that you use createServer, the net API offers a method called connect with an API, as follows:

```
net.connect(port[[, host], callback]])
```

If a function is supplied, it's equivalent to listening on the connect event of the resulting object.

```
var client = net.connect(3000, 'localhost');
client.on('connect', function () {});
```

is therefore equivalent to

```
net.connect(300, 'localhost', function () {});
```

In addition, similar to the API you saw previously, you can listen on data and close events.

IMPLEMENTING PART OF THE IRC PROTOCOL

You first initialize the client. Then attempt to log on to the #node.js channel on irc.freenode.net:

```
var client = net.connect(6667, 'irc.freenode.net')
```

You set the encoding to utf-8:

```
client.setEncoding('utf-8')
```

When you're connected, you send your desired nickname. In addition, you write the USER command, which is required by servers. You send data like this:

```
NICK mynick
USER mynick 0 * :realname
JOIN #node.js
```

You therefore write

```
client.on('connect, function () {
  client.write('NICK mynick\r\n');
  client.write('USER mynick 0 * :realname\r\n');
  client.write('JOIN #node.js\r\n')
});
```

Notice that after each command you need to include the delimiter \r\n. This is the equivalent to using Telnet and pressing Enter in our previous example. \r\n is also the delimiter used by the HTTP protocol to separate header lines.

TESTING WITH A REAL-WORLD IRC SERVER

Fire up an IRC client (such as mIRC on Windows, xChat on Linux, or Colloquy/Linkinus on Mac) and point it to

```
irc.freenode.net
#node.js
```

Then start the client and watch for mynick to connect:

```
![](http://f.cl.ly/items/1b3g3i1w120Z2U082I3G/Image%202011.11.07%202:31:35%20AM.png)
```

SUMMARY

This chapter described a simple implementation of a net Client. You saw it successfully interoperate with a TCP server that's not your own.

As an exercise, listen on data events and attempt to parse the incoming data so that you can print out the messages that other users send to the #node.js channel. You can then combine it with the existing code to produce an IRC bot that responds to commands automatically. For example, if someone says "date" (which you can detect in the data events), you can output the result of new Date().

Moving forward, you'll learn about HTTP, the protocol of the web that Node.JS is largely famous for. You now have a very solid understanding of the building blocks, and learning the HTTP APIs as a "layer" on top of TCP gives you true in-depth knowledge of the Node.JS core functioning.

CHAPTER

7

HTTP

HYPERTEXT TRANSFER PROTOCOL, or HTTP, is the protocol that powers the web, and, as discussed in Chapter 6, it sits on top of the TCP stack,

Throughout this chapter you'll learn how to leverage the Node.JS Server and Client APIs. Both are really easy to use to get started, but you'll also learn some of the shortcomings that come up when building actual websites and web applications with them. For that, in the coming chapters I will introduce you to abstractions that sit on the HTTP server to introduce reusable components.

Keep in mind that since you're programming both the server and the website as part of the same code, every time you make changes with your text editor to code that's running, you need to restart the Node process that powers it to have the changes reflect. At the end of this chapter I'll teach you how to leverage a tool to make this process straightforward.

To get started, let's review the anatomy of the HTTP protocol.

THE STRUCTURE OF HTTP

The protocol is structured around the concept of *requests* and *responses*, materialized in Node. JS as objects of the `http.ServerRequest` and `http.ServerResponse` constructors, respectively.

When a user first browses to a website, the user agent (the browser) creates a request that gets sent to the web server over TCP, and a response is emitted.

What do requests and responses look like? To find out, first create a Hello World Node HTTP server that listens on `http://localhost:3000`:

```
require('http').createServer(function (req, res) {
  res.writeHead(200);
  res.end('Hello World');

}).listen(3000);
```

Next, establish a telnet connection and write your own request:

```
GET / HTTP/1.1
```

After typing `GET / HTTP/1.1`, press Enter twice.

The response, illustrated in Figure 7-1, comes in right afterward!

Figure 7-1: The response produced by our HTTP server.

The response text looks like this:

```
HTTP/1.1 200 OK
Connection: keep-alive
Transfer-Encoding: chunked
```

```
b
Hello World
0
```

The first relevant section of this response is the *headers*, which you'll read about next.

HEADERS

As you can see, HTTP is a protocol in the same fashion as IRC. Its purpose is to enable the exchange of documents. It utilizes *headers* that precede both requests and responses to describe different aspects of the communication and the content.

As an example, think of the different types of content that web pages deliver: text, HTML, XML, JSON, PNG and JPEG images, and a large number of other possibilities.

The *type* of content that's sent is annotated by the famous `Content-Type` header.

Look at how this applies in practice. Bring back hello world, but this time add some HTML in there:

```
require('http').createServer(function (req, res) {
  res.writeHead(200);
  res.end('Hello <b>World</b>');

}).listen(3000);
```

Notice that the word World is surrounded by bold tags. You can check it out with the rudimentary TCP client again (see Figure 7-2).

Figure 7-2: The `Hello <b>World</b>` response

The response is just what you might expect:

```
GET / HTTP/1.1

HTTP/1.1 200 OK
Connection: keep-alive
Transfer-Encoding: chunked

12
Hello <b>World</b>
0
```

Now, however, see what happens when you look at it with a browser (see Figure 7-3).

Figure 7-3: The browser shows the response as plain text.

That doesn't look like rich text, but why?

As it occurs, the HTTP client (the browser) doesn't know what type of content you're sending because you didn't include that as part of your communication. The browser therefore considers what you're seeing as content type `text/plain`, or normal plain text, and doesn't try to render it as HTML.

If you adjust the code to include the appropriate *header*, you fix the problem (see Figure 7-4):

```
require('http').createServer(function (req, res) {
  res.writeHead(200, { 'Content-Type': 'text/html' });
  res.end('Hello <b>World</b>');

}).listen(3000);
```

Figure 7-4: The response, this time with the additional header.

The response text is as follows:

```
HTTP/1.1 200 OK

Content-Type: text/html
Connection: keep-alive
Transfer-Encoding: chunked

12
Hello <b>World</b>
0
```

Notice the header is included as part of the response text. The same response is parsed out by the browser (see Figure 7-5), which now renders the HTML correctly.

Figure 7-5: The browser now shows the word World in bold rich text.

Notice that despite having specified a header with the `writeHead` API call, Node still includes two other headers: `Transfer-Encoding` and `Connection`.

The default value for the `Transfer-Encoding` header is `chunked`. The main reason for this is that due to Node asynchronous nature, it's not rare for a response to be created progressively.

Consider the following example:

```
require('http').createServer(function (req, res) {
  res.writeHead(200);
  res.write('Hello');

  setTimeout(function () {

    res.end('World');

  }, 500);

}).listen(3000);
```

Notice that you can send data as part of multiple `write` calls, before you call `end`. In the spirit of trying to respond as fast as possible to clients, by the time the first `write` is called, Node can already send all the response headers and the first chunk of data (`Hello`).

Later on, when the `setTimeout` callback is fired, another chunk can be written. Since this time around you use `end` instead of `write`, Node finishes the response and no further writes are allowed.

Another instance where writing in chunks is very efficient is when the file system is involved. It's not uncommon for web servers to serve files like images that are somewhere in the hard drive. Since Node can write a response in chunks, and also allows us to read a file in chunks, you can leverage the `ReadStream` filesystem APIs for this purpose.

The following example reads the image `image.png` and serves it with the right `Content-Type` header:

```
require('http').createServer(function (req, res) {
  res.writeHead(200, { 'Content-Type': 'image/png');
  var stream = require('fs').createReadStream('image.png');
  stream.on('data', function (data) {
    res.write(data);
  });
  stream.on('end', function () {
    res.end();
  });
}).listen(3000);
```

By writing the image as a series of chunks, you ensure:

- Efficient memory allocation. If you read the image completely for each request prior to writing it (by leveraging `fs.readFile`), you'd probably end up using more memory over time when handlings lots of requests.
- You write data as soon as it becomes available to you.

In addition, notice that what you're doing is *piping* one `Stream` (an FS one) onto another (an `http.ServerResponse` object). As I've mentioned before, streams are a very important abstraction in Node.JS. Piping streams is a very common action, so Node.JS offers a method to make the above example very succinct:

```
require('http').createServer(function (req, res) {
  res.writeHead(200, { 'Content-Type': 'image/png');
  require('fs').createReadStream('image.png').pipe(res);
}).listen(3000);
```

Now that you understand why Node defaults to a *chunked* transfer encoding, let's talk about connections.

CONNECTIONS

If you compare your TCP server implementation and your HTTP server implementation side by side, you might notice they're similar. In both cases, you call `createServer`, and in both cases, you get a callback when a client connects.

A fundamental difference, however, is the type of object you get in that callback. In the case of the `net` server, you get a *connection*, and in the case of an HTTP server, you get *request* and *response* objects.

The reason for this is two-fold. First, the HTTP server is a *higher-level* API that gives you tools to handle the specific set of functionality and behaviors inherent to the HTTP protocol.

For example, look at the `headers` property of the request object (the `req` parameter in the example) when a common web browser accesses the server (see Figure 7-6). For this experiment, use `console.log` on the `req.headers` property:

```
require('http').createServer(function (req, res) {
  console.log(req.headers);
  res.writeHead(200, { 'Content-Type': 'text/html' });
  res.end('Hello <b>World</b>');

}).listen(3000);
```

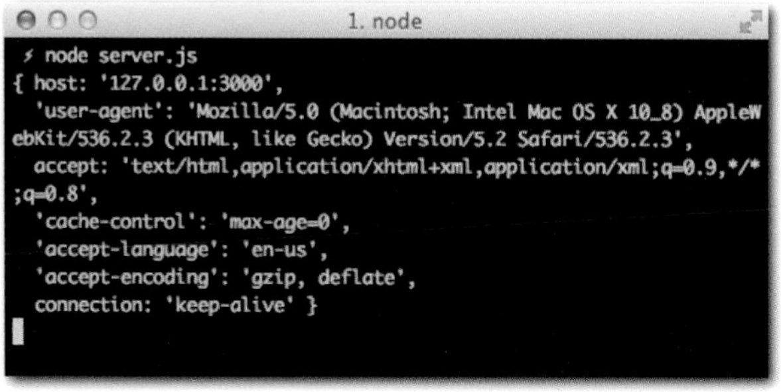

Figure 7-6: The `ServerRequest headers` property as output by `console.log`.

Notice that Node does a lot of the heavy work for you. It takes the incoming message by the browser, analyzes it (parses it), and constructs a JavaScript object that you can conveniently use from your scripts. It even makes the headers *lowercase* so that you don't have to remember if it was `Content-type` or `Content-Type` or `Content-TYPE`.

The second, even more important reason is that browsers don't use just *a single connection* when they access websites. Modern browsers can open up to eight different connections to a same host and send requests over all of them in an effort to make websites load faster.

Node wants to make it easy for you to worry just about requests and not connections. Therefore, even though you can still access the TCP connection through the property `req.connection`, you are mostly going to get involved with the request and response abstractions here.

By default, Node tells browsers to keep the connection alive and send more requests through it. This is expressed by the `keep-alive` value of the `Connection` header you saw previously. Normally this is the desired behavior in the interest of performance (since browsers don't need to waste time tearing down and restarting new TCP connections), but you can also override this header by passing a different value to the `writeHead` call, such as `Close`.

For your next project, you utilize the Node HTTP APIs to perform a real-world task: process a form that the user submits.

A SIMPLE WEB SERVER

Throughout this project you'll leverage some of the key concepts outlined above, like the `Content-Type` header.

You'll also learn how web browsers exchange encoded data as part of form submissions, and how to *parse* them into JavaScript data structures.

CREATING THE MODULE

As usual, you start by creating the directory where your project is going to live and a `package.json` file:

```
{

    "name": "http-form"

  , "description": "An HTTP server that processes forms"

  , "version": "0.0.1"

}
```

You test it by running `npm install`. An empty line should be printed because the project has no dependencies.

PRINTING OUT THE FORM

Just as in the `Hello <b>World</b>` example, you are going to print out some HTML. In this case, you want to represent a form. Place the following contents in your server.js file

```
require('http').createServer(function (req, res) {
  res.writeHead(200, { 'Content-Type': 'text/html' });
  res.end([
      '<form method="POST" action="/url">'
    , '<h1>My form</h1>'
    ,   '<fieldset>'
    ,   '<label>Personal information</label>'
    ,   '<p>What is your name?</p>'
    ,   '<input type="text" name="name">'
    ,   '<p><button>Submit</button></p>'
    , '</form>'
  ].join('')); }).listen(3000);
```

Notice that for the sake of syntax clarity, I structured the response text as an array that gets combined into a string with the `join` method. Otherwise, the example is equivalent to Hello World.

Notice that the `<form>` contains an endpoint URL `/url` and a method `POST`. Also notice that the input the user types has a name of `name`.

Now you can run the server:

```
$ node server.js
```

Next, point the browser, as shown in Figure 7-7, to see the rendered form for the HTML you output:

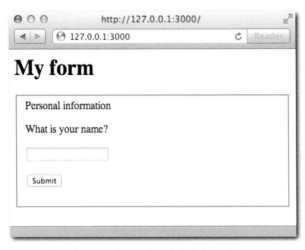

Figure 7-7: The rendered page for your form should look like this.

You can try pressing Enter. The browser then elaborates a new request (one that contains the data), but because all the code does right now is print out that HTML, the result after pressing Enter should be the same (see Figure 7-8). Type in a name and click Submit.

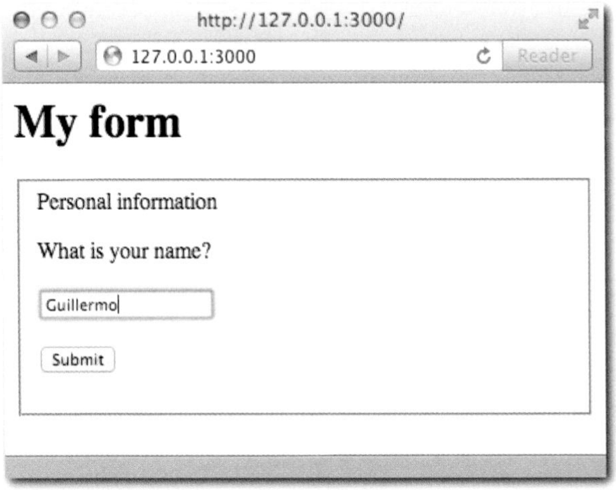

Figure 7-8: An example of the form submission.

As a result of the submission, the URL changes, but the response is constant, as shown in Figure 7-9.

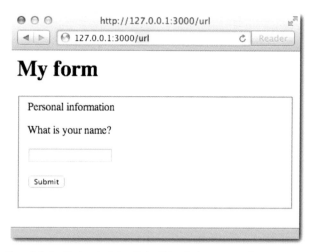

Figure 7-9: Despite the submission, Node will handle the request in the same way, therefore sending the same HTML again.

In order to have Node treat the submission request differently and produce an appropriate response, you need to learn about inspecting the request method and URL.

METHODS AND URLS

Obviously, when the user presses Enter, you want to display something different. You want to *process* the form.

To that end, inspect the url property of the request object. The code for server.js should now look like this:

```
require('http').createServer(function (req, res) {
  if ('/' == req.url) {
    res.writeHead(200, { 'Content-Type': 'text/html' });
    res.end([
        '<form method="POST" action="/url">'
      , '<h1>My form</h1>'
      , '<fieldset>'
      , '<label>Personal information</label>'
      , '<p>What is your name?</p>'
      , '<input type="text" name="name">'
      , '<p><button>Submit</button></p>'
      , '</form>'
    ].join(''));
  } else if ('/url' == req.url) {
    res.writeHead(200, { 'Content-Type': 'text/html' });
    res.end('You sent a  <em>' + req.method + '</em> request');
  }
}).listen(3000);
```

If you go to the / URL, as shown in Figure 7-10, nothing changes.

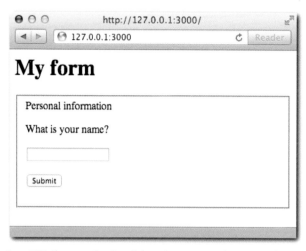

Figure 7-10: The request handler still shows the same HTML when we go to the URL.

If you type in /url, you see something like Figure 7-11. The supplied URL matches the req. url in the else if clause, and the appropriate response is produced.

Figure 7-11: What you see when you go to /url as a result of req.url changing.

However, when you enter your name through the form, you see a message like that in Figure 7-12. The reason for this is that browsers will send the form data in the HTTP method specified in the action attribute of the <form> tag. The req.method value will be POST in this case, thus producing what you see in Figure 7-12.

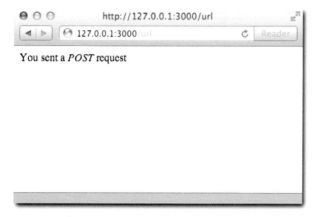

Figure 7-12: In this case `req.method` is `POST`.

As you can see, you're dealing with two different variables of the request: the URL and the method.

Node.JS puts in the `url` property everything that follows the hostname. If you navigate to `http://myhost.com/url?this+is+a+long+url`, the contents of `url` are `/url?this+is+a+long+url`.

The reigning protocol of the web, `HTTP/1.1` (as you may remember from the `telnet` example in Chapter 6), establishes different methods for a request:

- `GET` (the default)
- `POST`
- `PUT`
- `DELETE`
- `PATCH` (the newest)

The idea behind this is that an HTTP client picks a method to alter a resource on a server, which is located by its URL, with certain data as the body of the request.

DATA

When you sent HTML, you had to define a `Content-Type` along with the body of your response.

Symmetrically to a response, a request can also contain a `Content-Type` and body of data.

To process forms effectively, you absolutely need these two pieces of information. Just like the browser doesn't know if the `Hello World` is going to be HTML or plain text unless you explicitly indicate so, how do you know if the user is sending her name in JSON, XML, or plain text? The code for `server.js` should look like this now:

```
require('http').createServer(function (req, res) {
  if ('/' == req.url) {
    res.writeHead(200, { 'Content-Type': 'text/html' });
    res.end([
        '<form method="POST" action="/url">'
      , '<h1>My form</h1>'
      , '<fieldset>'
      , '<label>Personal information</label>'
      , '<p>What is your name?</p>'
      , '<input type="text" name="name">'
      , '<p><button>Submit</button></p>'
      , '</form>'
    ].join(''));
  } else if ('/url' == req.url && 'POST' == req.method) {
    var body = '';
    req.on('data', function (chunk) {
      body += chunk;
    });
    req.on('end', function () {
      res.writeHead(200, { 'Content-Type': 'text/html' });
      res.end('<p>Content-Type: ' + req.headers['content-type'] + '</p>'
        + '<p>Data:</p><pre>' + body + '</pre>');
    });
  }
}).listen(3000);
```

What is going on here? You are listening to the `data` and `end` events. You create a `body` string that gets populated with different chunks, and then you consider that you have all the data *only after* the `end` events fires and not before.

The reason for this is that Node.JS allows you to process the data as it *comes* to the server. Because data can come in different TCP packets, it's entirely possible that in real-world usage, you get a piece of the data first and sometime later you get the remainder.

Submit the form again and take a look at the response in Figure 7-13.

Figure 7-13: In this example you output the `Content-Type` and request data back to the page.

For example, when you search on Google, the URL can look like that in Figure 7-14.

Figure 7-14: The highlighted part in the URL when a search is performed is `q=<search term>`.

Notice the fragment for the search in the URL gets *encoded* in the same way the form contents do. That's why the `Content-Type` in this case is called urlencoded.

This particular fragment of URLs is also known as the *query string*.

Node.JS provides a module called `querystring` that makes it easy to *parse* those strings into data you can easily access in the same way it does with headers. Create a file `qs-example.js` with the following contents and run it (see Figure 7-15).

```
console.log(require('querystring').parse('name=Guillermo')); console.
  log(require('querystring').parse('q=guillermo+rauch'));
```

Figure 7-15: The output for the `parse` function calls.

As you can see, the `querystring` module is capable of taking a string and producing an Object data-structure from it. This parsing process is homologous to Node taking the headers from the HTTP request data and producing the `headers` object you can easily access.

You'll leverage the query string module to easily access the form field that's submitted with the form.

PUTTING THE PIECES TOGETHER

You're now ready to parse the incoming body data and display it to the user. `server.js` should now have the following contents. Notice that in the end request event we now run the body through the `querystring parse` module, you get the name key from the produced `Object` and output it back to the user. Keep in mind that name matches the `name` attribute of the `<input>` tag defined in the HTML you first output. The `server.js` code now looks as follows:

```
var qs = require('querystring');
require('http').createServer(function (req, res) {
    if ('/' == req.url) {
      res.writeHead(200, { 'Content-Type': 'text/html' });
      res.end([
          '<form method="POST" action="/url">'
        , '<h1>My form</h1>'
        , '<fieldset>'
        , '<label>Personal information</label>'
        , '<p>What is your name?</p>'
        , '<input type="text" name="name">'
        , '<p><button>Submit</button></p>'
        , '</form>'
      ].join(''));
    } else if ('/url' == req.url && 'POST' == req.method) {
      var body = '';
      req.on('data', function (chunk) {
        body += chunk;
      });
      req.on('end', function () {
        res.writeHead(200, { 'Content-Type': 'text/html' });
        res.end('<p>Your name is <b>' + qs.parse(body).name + '</b></p>');
      });
    }
}).listen(3000);
```

You point the browser and voila! (See Figure 7-16.)

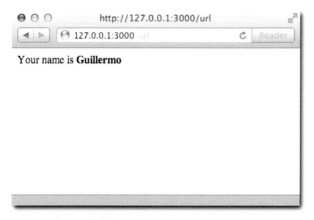

Figure 7-16: The name field that you see

BULLET-PROOFING

A problem still exists in the preceding example: what happens if no URL is matched by your conditional statements?

If you try going to the URL /test, you see that the server never responds, and the user agent (browser) just hangs.

To solve this problem, you can send back the status code 404 (Not Found) if the server doesn't know how to treat the request. Notice that in server.js you add an else clause that calls writeHead with the 404 status code:

```
var qs = require('querystring');
require('http').createServer(function (req, res) {
  if ('/' == req.url) {
    res.writeHead(200, { 'Content-Type': 'text/html' });
    res.end([
        '<form method="POST" action="/url">'
      ,   '<h1>My form</h1>'
      ,   '<fieldset>'
      ,   '<label>Personal information</label>'
      ,   '<p>What is your name?</p>'
      ,   '<input type="text" name="name">'
      ,   '<p><button>Submit</button></p>'
      , '</form>'
    ].join(''));
  } else if ('/url' == req.url && 'POST' == req.method) {
    var body = '';
    req.on('data', function (chunk) {
      body += chunk;
    });
```

```
    req.on('end', function () {
      res.writeHead(200, { 'Content-Type': 'text/html' });
      res.end('<p>Your name is <b>' + qs.parse(body).name + '</b></p>');
    });
  } else {
    res.writeHead(404);
    res.end('Not Found');
  }
}).listen(3000);
```

You can now consider your first HTTP web server complete! The code is not as clean as it could be, but you'll learn the right way to write more complex HTTP servers in the coming chapters.

Moving on, you'll learn the counterpart of the Server API: the HTTP Client.

A TWITTER WEB CLIENT

The importance of learning how to make requests to other web servers from Node.JS cannot be overstated.

HTTP has become a protocol not just for exchanging markup that's meant to be rendered and presented to the user (thanks to HTML), but also a fundamental way of transmitting data between servers in different networks. JSON is quickly becoming the de-facto standard data format for this, which puts Node.JS in a very good position to establish its server-side dominance, as the notation was born out of the JavaScript object literal syntax.

For this example, you'll learn how to query the Twitter API, get some JSON, which you'll decode into a data structure that you can loop over and produce a human-readable terminal output form.

CREATING THE MODULE

As usual, you start by creating the directory where your project is going to live and a `package.json` file:

```
{
    "name": "tweet-client"
  , "description": "An HTTP tweets client"
  , "version": "0.0.1"
}
```

MAKING A SIMPLE HTTP REQUEST

Analogous to the TCP client you created, and not by coincidence, you instantiate a `Client` object with a static method on the `http` module called `request`.

To get familiar with it, bring back the typical HTTP server:

```
require('http').createServer(function (req, res) {
  res.writeHead(200);
  res.end('Hello World');
}).listen(3000);
```

Then write a client that gets the response and prints it out in colors to the console:

```
require('http').request({
    host: '127.0.0.1'
  , port: 3000
  , url: '/'
  , method: 'GET'
}, function (res) {
  var body = '';
  res.setEncoding('utf8');
  res.on('data', function (chunk) {
    body += chunk;
  });
  res.on('end', function () {
    console.log('\n  We got: \033[96m' + body + '\033[39m\n');
  });
}).end();
```

The first thing you do is call the request method. This initializes a new `http.Client Request` object.

Notice that you collect the body in chunks in the same way you did for the requests sent from the web browser in the server section of this chapter. The remote server you're connecting to might respond in different data chunks that you need to put together to get a complete response. It might happen that all the data comes in one data event, but you can't really know.

Therefore, you listen on the end event to, in this case, log the body to the console.

In addition, you also set the default encoding on the response object to `utf8` with `setEncoding`, because all you want to print to the console is text. As an example, if you try to download a PNG image with the client, trying to print it as a `utf8` string would not be ideal.

Now run the server and then the client (see Figure 7-17):

```
$ node client
```

Figure 7-17: The response from our Hello World server is displayed after the client successfully requests it.

Next, you'll learn how to also send data along with your request.

SENDING A BODY OF DATA

Notice that after you call `request` in the preceding example, you *also* have to call `end`.

The reason for this is that after you create a request, you can continue to interact with the `request` object prior to sending it to the server.

And an example of that is if you want to *send* data to the server, as you see in the next example.

Remember the form you created in the browser? Reproduce that here, but this time for the client, use Node, and for the `<form>`, use `stdin`, incorporating the knowledge you learned in Chapter 5.

The server processes the form:

```
var qs = require('querystring');
require('http').createServer(function (req, res) {
  var body = '';
  req.on('data', function (chunk) {
    body += chunk;
  });
  req.on('end', function () {
    res.writeHead(200);
    res.end('Done');
    console.log('\n  got name \033[90m' + qs.parse(body).name + '\033[39m\n');
  });
}).listen(3000);
```

The client does the opposite. By using the `stringify` method of the `querystring` module, you can turn an object into a urlencoded body of data:

```
var http = require('http')
  , qs = require('querystring')

function send (theName) {
  http.request({
    host: '127.0.0.1'     , port: 3000
    , url: '/'
    , method: 'POST'
  }, function (res) {
      res.setEncoding('utf8');
      res.on('end', function () {
        console.log('\n  \033[90m  request complete!\033[39m');
process.stdout.write('\n  your name: ');
      });
  }).end(qs.stringify({ name: theName }));
}
```

```
process.stdout.write('\n  your name: ');
process.stdin.resume(); process.stdin.setEncoding('utf-8');
process.stdin.on('data', function (name) {
  send(name.replace('\n', ''));


});
```

Notice that data is passed to the `end` method, in the same way you do when you create a response in the server.

In this case, don't worry about the chunks of data that you can get from the server. You simply know that when `end` is called, you can print the text request complete and ask the user again for data.

Figure 7-18 shows the action side by side. On the left, the server is showing the name that's submitted with the form on the left through `stdin`.

Figure 7-18: When prompted on the right for name, I typed one in and pressed enter, which is correctly processed by the server on the left.

Now that you learned how to send data along with a request, you have seen almost the full extent of the request API. Let's continue with our main goal!

GETTING TWEETS

Now you're ready for some *real* real-world HTTP! Create a command called `tweets` that takes a search argument and displays the latest tweets about that given topic.

If you look at the documentation for the public search API for Twitter, you can see that URLs look like this: `http://search.twitter.com/search.json?q=blue+angels`.

And the result looks like this (notice I cut it short at the end)

```
{
    "completed_in":0.031,
    "max_id":122078461840982016,
    "max_id_str":"122078461840982016",
    "next_page":"?page=2&max_id=122078461840982016&q=blue%20angels&rpp=5",
    "page":1,
    "query":"blue+angels",
    "refresh_url":"?since_id=122078461840982016&q=blue%20angels",
    "results":[    {
// ...
```

Once again, the usual suspects: the search term is urlencoded (q=blue+angels), and the result is JSON. The tweets are in the `results` array in the object that forms the response.

Because you're producing a command that takes an argument, like you saw in Chapter 5, you want to access `argv`. With the `querystring` module, you produce the URL and then obtain the response data. The `method` to access the resource is obviously GET and the port 80, both of which are defaults you can skip (for the sake of clarity in this first HTTP client example, I still included the GET option).

```
var qs = require('querystring')
  , http = require('http')

var search = process.argv.slice(2).join(' ').trim()

if (!search.length) {
  return console.log('\n  Usage: node tweets <search term>\n');
}
console.log('\n  searching for: \033[96m' + search + '\033[39m\n');
http.request({
    host: 'search.twitter.com'
  , path: '/search.json?' + qs.stringify({ q: search })
}, function (res) {
  var body = '';
  res.setEncoding('utf8');
  res.on('data', function (chunk) {
    body += chunk;
  });
  res.on('end', function () {
    var obj = JSON.parse(body);
    obj.results.forEach(function (tweet) {
      console.log('  \033[90m' + tweet.text + '\033[39m');
      console.log('  \033[94m' + tweet.from_user + '\033[39m');
      console.log('--');
    });
  });
}).end()
```

When you execute it, it will validate the `processs.argv` array to know if you have a search term (see Figure 7-19), and output help text otherwise.

Figure 7-19: The command being run without a search term.

When you supply arguments, the search is executed, as shown in Figure 7-20. Twitter responds with JSON, which is looped over after being parsed in the end event handler, and output back to the user.

Figure 7-20: In this case I searched for Justin Bieber, and some interesting tweets come back.

So far you've been using the `http.request` pretty extensively. You've mostly made GET requests, which one could say are the most common. Web services usually expose more GET endpoints than POST or PUT. Sending data (a request body) along with a request is also fairly uncommon.

Node.JS tries to make the most common use case for requests easy by exposing `request.get`. The Twitter API call (with `http.request`) could be rewritten like this:

```
http.get({
    host: 'search.twitter.com'
  , path: '/search.json?' + qs.stringify({ q: search })
}, function (res) {
  var body = '';
  res.setEncoding('utf8');
  res.on('data', function (chunk) {
    body += chunk;
  });
```

```
    res.on('end', function () {
      var obj = JSON.parse(body);
      obj.results.forEach(function (tweet) {
        console.log('   \033[90m' + tweet.text + '\033[39m');
        console.log('   \033[94m' + tweet.from_user + '\033[39m');
        console.log('--');
      });
    });
})
```

The only real difference is that you don't need to call end, and you make it slightly more explicit that you're getting data. The API accepts a method parameter, which defaults to GET, so this method provides little extra usefulness.

With this improvement, we're still repeating ourselves a lot. Next up, I'll introduce you to a tool called superagent, an API that sits on top of the HTTP Client API to make these work-flows easier.

A SUPERAGENT TO THE RESCUE

More often than not, the HTTP clients you create will follow a common pattern: you want to get all the response data, execute a parser based on the Content-Type of the response, and do something with it.

When sending data to the server, the situation is similar. You'll want to make a POST request, and encode an object as JSON.

A module called superagent solves this by extending the response object with useful additions, some of which I'll show you next.

The examples in this section use superagent version 0.3.0. Create a new directory and install superagent locally inside:

```
$ npm install superagent@0.3.0
```

To get the JSON data for a request, provided the server responds with the right Content-Type that indicates the response contains JSON, superagent will automatically buffer and parse it and place it as res.body. Create a file called tweet.js with the following contents:

```
var request = require('superagent');
request.get('http://twitter.com/search.json')
  .send({ q: 'justin bieber' })
  .end(function (res) { console.log(res.body); });
```

If you run the file, you'll see the Object that results from decoding the JSON response. You can still access the raw response text b accessing res.text.

Notice that you also didn't need to encode the query string manually, since superagent knows that if you try to `send` data with a GET request, that means encoding it as part of the URL as a query string.

To set a header for the request, you can do so by calling `set`. In the following example I set the `Date` header with the request:

```
var request = require('superagent');
request.get('http://twitter.com/search.json')
  .send({ q: 'justin bieber' })
  .set('Date, new Date)
  .end(function (res) { console.log(res.body); });
```

Both `send` and `set` can be called multiple times, which makes it a *progressive* API: you can build out the object progressively, and then call `end` when you're done.

The simplicity of this API does not stop at GET requests. Similarly, superagent exposes `put`, `post`, `head`, and `del` methods.

The following example POSTs a JSON-encoded object:

```
var request = require('superagent');
request.post('http://example.com/')
  .send({ json: 'encoded' })
  .end();
```

JSON is the default encoding. If you want to change it, simply adjust the `Content-Type` of the request by calling `set`.

RELOADING HTTP SERVERS WITH UP

By now, you probably already noticed that it can get somewhat annoying to continuously reload a Node process manually in order for a web browser to reflect the changes you make to your servers code with your text editor.

The most naive way to tackle this problem is to simply reload the process every time a code change is detected. This can work well for development, but when you deploy your web servers to production, you probably want to make sure requests that are in-flight (in other words, requests that are in progress at the time you want to reload your code) are not killed along with the old process.

I developed a tool called `up` to tackle this problem in a very safe and reliable way. For development, simply install the `up` executable with NPM:

```
$ npm install -g up
```

Then, you need to ensure that you structure your code in such a way that you *export* the Node HTTP Server you want to reload, instead of calling `listen`. This is because `up` will call `listen` for you, and it needs to be able to access the Server instance. For example, create a new directory and place a file `server.js` with the following contents:

```
module.exports = require('http').createServer(function (req, res) {
  res.writeHead(200, { 'Content-Type': 'text/html' });
  res.end('Hello <b>World</b>');
});
```

Now `cd` to that directory, run the server by summoning `up` and passing the `--watch` and `--port` options:

```
$ up -watch -port 80 server.js
```

`--watch` will leverage the appropriate Node APIs to detect changes to any file in the working directory. Try pointing your browser to this server, then editing `server.js` and changing the `Hello <b>World</b>` text. As soon as you save the file, refresh your browser, and your changes are reflected immediately!

SUMMARY

You learned a lot about writing HTTP with Node. You started out by understanding the basics of HTTP from the perspective of a protocol that sits on top of TCP.

You took a careful look at the default response Node.JS produces in a Hello World example. You can recognize the default headers, and you understand why they're there.

You learned the importance of headers in HTTP requests and how to change the default one in server responses. You also have a fundamental understanding of the encoding formats that are normally used to exchange data with browsers, and what tools Node offers to parse incoming data and work with it.

After writing a working web server, you also took a look at the client APIs, which are very useful for web services interoperability in the modern web. After observing the most common use cases, you successfully queried the Twitter API, but it soon became evident that the same code was written over and over again. For that reason you were also introduced to a new API that sits on top of the core Node.JS one to make things easier. The module that's the focus of the next chapter, Connect, does the same thing for web servers, but there's a lot more to learn.

Finally, I introduced `up`, a command-line utility (also available as a JavaScript API) to make the servers you write from now on easier to test as you iterate on the code and make changes to it. Remember: in order to leverage it moving forward, make sure your modules *export* the `http.Server` instance returned by `createServer`.

WEB DEVELOPMENT

CONNECT

NODE.JS PROVIDES basic APIs for common network applications. So far, you have looked at the basic APIs for TCP servers and an API for HTTP that builds on top of it.

Most real-world applications, however, perform a series of common tasks that you probably don't want to re-implement on top of primitive APIs over and over again.

Connect is a toolkit that sits on top of the HTTP server to provide a new way of organizing code that interfaces with request and responses, around units called *middleware*.

To illustrate the benefits of code reuse through middleware, assume this sample structure for a website:

```
$ ls website/
index.html  images/
```

Under the images directory, you have four images:

```
$ ls website/images/
1.jpg  2.jpg  3.jpg  4.jpg
```

The index.html simply displays the four images, and you want to access the website through http://localhost as in other examples (see Figure 8-1):

```
<h1>My website</h1>

<img src="/images/1.jpg">
<img src="/images/2.jpg">
<img src="/images/3.jpg">
<img src="/images/4.jpg">
```

Figure 8-1: A simple static website demonstrating Connect's capabilities

To show the simplicity Connect offers for the world of HTTP applications, this chapter shows how to write this simple website with the native `http` API and later with the `connect` API.

A SIMPLE WEBSITE WITH HTTP

As usual, you start by requiring the `http` module for the server and the `fs` module for reading files:

```
/**
 * Module dependencies.
 */

var http = require('http')
  , fs = require('fs')
```

Then you initialize the server and handle the request-response cycles:

```
/**
 * Create the server.
 */

var server = http.createServer(function (req, res) {
  // ...
});
```

And finally you listen:

```
/**
 * Listen.
 */

server.listen(3000);
```

Now back to the `createServer` callback. You need to check that the URL matches a file in the directory, and if so, read the file and serve it. In the future, you might want to add more images, so you need to make sure it's dynamic enough to support this capability.

The first step is to check that the method is GET and the URL starts with `/images` and finishes with `.jpg`. If the url is `'/'`, you serve `index.html` (with the shortcut function `serve` you write later). Otherwise, you send the status `404 Not Found`, as follows:

```
if ('GET' == req.method && '/images' == req.url.substr(0, 7)
  && '.jpg' == req.url.substr(-4)) {
  // …
} else if ('GET' == req.method && '/' == req.url) {
  serve(__dirname + '/index.html', 'text/html');
} else {
  res.writeHead(404);
  res.end('Not found');
}
```

Then you use `fs.stat` to check that the file exists. You use the Node global constant `__dirname` to reference the directory where the server lives. After the first "if", you'd place the next statement.

```
fs.stat(__dirname + req.url, function (err, stat) {

});
```

You do not use the synchronous version of `fs.stat` (`fs.statSync`). If you did, you would block other requests from being processed while the files are being sought in the disk, which is undesirable for a server to handle high concurrency. For reference, we discussed this in Chapter 3.

If an error occurs, you abort the process and send the HTTP status code 404 to signal that you can't find the requested image. You also should do this if the `stat` succeeds but the supplied path is not a file, as shown here. The following snippet goes in the `fs.stat` callback.

```
if (err || !stat.isFile()) {
  res.writeHead(404);
  res.end('Not Found');
  return;
}
```

Otherwise, you serve the image. The following line follows the `if`:

```
serve(__dirname + req.url, 'application/jpg');
```

Finally, you write the `serve` function afterwards, which, as you might have guessed, takes the path of the file to serve and includes the `'Content-Type'` header which is necessary, as you saw, for the browser to know what type of resource you're sending:

```
function serve (path, type) {
  res.writeHead(200, { 'Content-Type': type });
  fs.createReadStream(path).pipe(res);
}
```

Remember the subsection about Streams in Chapter 6? An HTTP Response is a write-only Stream. And you can create a Stream from a file that's read-only. And you can `pipe` the filesystem stream to the HTTP Response! The preceding short snippet of code is roughly equivalent to this:

```
fs.createReadStream(path)
  .on('data, function (data) {
    res.write(data);
  })
  .on('end', function () {
    res.end();
  })
```

It's also the most effective and recommended method for serving static files.

Putting all the pieces together, you get

```
/**
 * Module dependencies.
 */

var http = require('http')
  , fs = require('fs')

/**
 * Create the server.
 */

var server = http.createServer(function (req, res) {
  if ('GET' == req.method && '/images' == req.url.substr(0, 7)
    && '.jpg' == req.url.substr(-4)) {
    fs.stat(__dirname + req.url, function (err, stat) {
      if (err || !stat.isFile()) {
        res.writeHead(404);
        res.end('Not Found');
```

```
      return;
    }
    serve(__dirname + req.url, 'application/jpg');
  });
} else if ('GET' == req.method && '/' == req.url) {
  serve(__dirname + '/index.html', 'text/html');
} else {
  res.writeHead(404);
  res.end('Not found');
}

function serve (path, type) {
  res.writeHead(200, { 'Content-Type': type });
  fs.createReadStream(path).pipe(res);
}
});

/**
 * Listen.
 */

server.listen(3000);
```

Now you're done! The next step is to run the following:

```
$ node server
```

Then point your browser to `http://127.0.0.1:3000`, and you should see your website!

A SIMPLE WEBSITE WITH CONNECT

This website example highlights a few common tasks frequently involved in creating a website:

- Serving static files
- Handling errors and bad or missing URLs
- Handling different types of requests

Connect, as a layer on top of the `http` API, provides some facilities to make these repeatable processes easier to implement so that you can focus on the real purpose of your application. It lets you stick to the **DRY** pattern: **D**on't **R**epeat **Y**ourself.

The example can be simplified tremendously thanks to Connect. You first create `package.json` with the dependency "connect" in a new directory.

```
{
    "name": "my-website"
  , "version": "0.0.1"
```

```
   , "dependencies": {
        "connect": "1.8.7"
   }
}
```

Then you install it:

```
$ npm install
```

Next, you `require` it:

```
/**
 * Module dependencies.
 */

var connect = require('connect')
```

You create the `http.Server` through Connect:

```
/**
 * Create server.
 */

var server = connect.createServer();
```

You `use()` the `static` middleware. You explore the concept of middleware in the next section and go in greater depth in the coming chapters. For now, it's important to understand that middleware is a simple JavaScript function. In this case, we configure the static middleware by passing some parameters to `connect.static`, which returns a function.

```
/**
 * Handle static files.
 */

server.use(connect.static(__dirname + '/website'));
```

You place `index.html` and the `images` directory under `/website` to ensure you don't serve undesired files.

Then you `listen()`:

```
/**
 * Listen.
 */

server.listen(3000);
```

Now you're done! Connect can even handle 404s for you, so also try going to `/made-up-url`.

MIDDLEWARE

To understand middleware better, go back to the node HTTP example. Remove the logic and focus for a minute on what you're trying to do:

```
if ('GET' == req.method && '/images' == req.url.substr(0, 7)) {
  // serve image
} else if ('GET' == req.method && '/' == req.url) {
  // serve index
} else {
  // display 404
}
```

As you can see, the application tries to do *only one* of three things every time a request comes. If you also want to log requests, for example, you would add this piece of code to the top:

```
console.error(' %s %s ', req.method, req.url);
```

Now imagine a larger application that can do *many* different things, depending on the different variables at play for each request:

- Log requests and how long they take
- Serve static files
- Perform authorization

These tasks can make handling code in a single event handler (the callback that you pass to `createServer`) a very convoluted process.

Simply put, middleware is made up of functions that handle the `req` and `res` objects but also receive a `next` function that allows you to do *flow control*.

If you want to write the same application using the middleware pattern, it would look like this:

```
server.use(function (req, res, next) {
  // you always log
  console.error(' %s %s ', req.method, req.url);
  next();
});

server.use(function (req, res, next) {
  if ('GET' == req.method && '/images' == req.url.substr(0, 7)) {
    // serve image
  } else {
```

```
      // let other middleware handle it
      next();
    }
  });

  server.use(function (req, res, next) {
    if ('GET' == req.method && '/' == req.url) {
      // serve index
    } else {
      // let other middleware handle it
      next();
    }
  });

  server.use(function (req, res, next) {
    // last middleware, if you got here you don't know what to do with this
    res.writeHead(404);
    res.end('Not found');
  });
```

You not only benefit from the expressive power (the ability to break down the app into smaller units), but also benefit from the reusability. As you will see, Connect already ships middleware that performs common tasks. To do request logging, you can simply use the following:

```
app.use(connect.logger('dev'))
```

And that handles logging!

The next section explains how to write middleware that alerts you when a certain request is taking a long time to respond.

WRITING REUSABLE MIDDLEWARE

Middleware that notifies you when a request is taking too long can be useful under many circumstances. For example, imagine you have a page that makes a series of requests to a database. Under your tests, everything responds within 100 milliseconds (ms), but you want to make sure you log whenever processing is taking longer than that.

You start by creating middleware in a separate module (file) called `request-time.js`.

The purpose of this module is to expose a function that returns a function. This is a very common pattern for middleware that allows for configurability. When you summoned `connect.logger` in the previous example, you passed a parameter to it, and that returns the function that eventually handles the requests.

The module for now takes a single option, the number of milliseconds after which you want to log the request as problematic:

```
/**
 * Request time middleware.
 *
 * Options:
 *   - 'time' ('Number'): number of ms after which you log (100)
 *
 * @param {Object} options
 * @api public
 */

module.exports = function (opts) {
  // …
};
```

First, you default the time to 100:

```
var time = opts.time || 100;
```

Then you return the function that will become the middleware:

```
return function (req, res, next) {
```

In the middleware itself, you should first create a timer that fires within the time specified:

```
var timer = setTimeout(function () {
  console.log(
      '\033[90m%s %s\033[39m \033[91mis taking too long!\033[39m'
    , req.method
    , req.url
  );
}, time);
```

Now you have to make sure to *clear* (that is, stop or cancel) the timer if the response finishes within 100ms. Another common pattern in middleware is to override functions (also known as *monkey-patch*) so that when other middleware calls them, you can perform a certain action.

In this case, when the response end()s, you want to clear the timer:

```
var end = res.end;
res.end = function (chunk, encoding) {
  res.end = end;
  res.end(chunk, encoding);
  clearTimeout(timer);
};
```

You first keep a reference around to the original function (var end = res.end). Then, within the overridden function, you restore the original, call it, and then clear the timer.

Finally, you should always let other middleware look at the request, so you call `next`. Otherwise, your app wouldn't do anything!

```
next();
```

The complete middleware code looks like this:

```
/**
 * Request time middleware.
 *
 * Options:
 *   - 'time' ('Number'): number of ms after which we log (100)
 *
 * @param {Object} options
 * @api public
 */
module.exports = function (opts) {
  var time = opts.time || 100;
  return function (req, res, next) {
    var timer = setTimeout(function () {
      console.log(
          '\033[90m%s %s\033[39m \033[91mis taking too long!\033[39m'
        , req.method
        , req.url
      );
    }, time);

    var end = res.end;
    res.end = function (chunk, encoding) {
      res.end = end;
      res.end(chunk, encoding);
      clearTimeout(timer);
    };
    next();
  };
};
```

To test this example, create a quick Connect app that has two different routes: one that gets resolved quickly and one that takes a second:

You start with the dependencies:

```
# sample.js
/**
 * Module dependencies.
 */

var connect = require('connect')
  , time = require('./request-time')
```

Next, create the server:

```
/**
 * Create server.
 */

var server = connect.createServer();
```

You log requests:

```
/**
 * Log requests.
 */

server.use(connect.logger('dev'));
```

Then you implement the middleware:

```
/**
 * Implement time middleware.
 */

server.use(time({ time: 500 }));
```

You implement the fast handler:

```
/**
 * Fast response.
 */

server.use(function (req, res, next) {
  if ('/a' == req.url) {
    res.writeHead(200);
    res.end('Fast!');
  } else {
    next();
  }
});
```

Then you implement the simulated slow route:

```
/**
 * Slow response.
 */

server.use(function (req, res, next) {
  if ('/b' == req.url) {
    setTimeout(function () {
      res.writeHead(200);
```

```
      res.end('Slow!');
    }, 1000);
  } else {
    next();
  }
});
```

As usual, you make the server listen:

```
/**
 * Listen.
 */

server.listen(3000);
```

You run the server:

```
$ node server
```

And then, as shown in Figure 8-2, visit `http://localhost:3000/a` with the browser (the fast route).

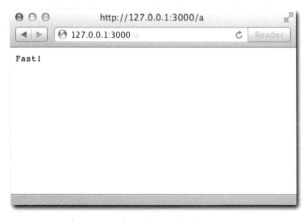

Figure 8-2: A simple route (/a) being shown to the browser.

If you look at the console shown in Figure 8-3, you can see the `logger` middleware in action.

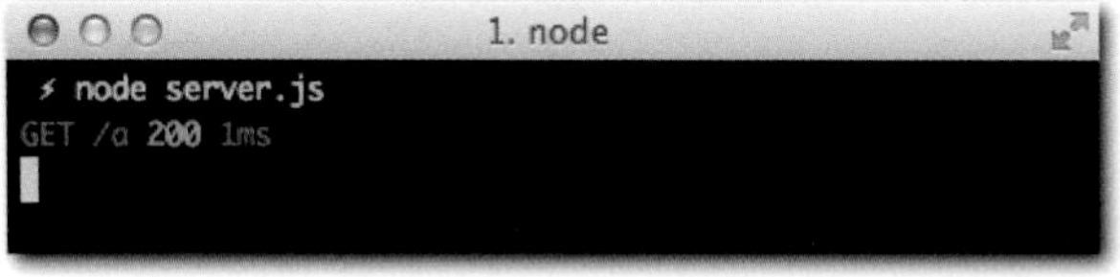

Figure 8-3: The logs shown in the console after accessing route /a

Figure 8-4 shows the slow route (`/b`).

http://127.0.0.1:3000/b
127.0.0.1:3000/b
Reader
Slow!

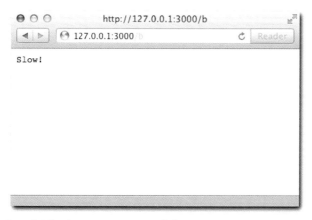

Figure 8-4: The slow route `/b` response in the browser

Figure 8-5 depicts the console and shows the middleware in action!

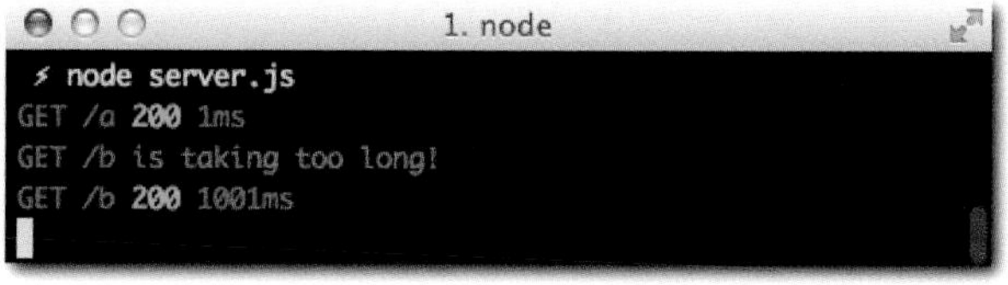

1. node
node server.js
GET /a 200 1ms
GET /b is taking too long!
GET /b 200 1001ms

Figure 8-5: The logs after accessing route `/b` reveal the warning produced by your first middleware

Next up, you'll go through some of the built-in middleware that Connect ships with due to the high level of reusability they have in common web applications.

STATIC MIDDLEWARE

`Static` middleware is probably among the most common type of middleware you will use during the development of web applications with Node.

Mounting

Connect allows middleware to be *mounted* to specific URLs. For middleware like `static`, this can be really useful because it allows you to map an arbitrary URL to any directory in your filesystem.

For example, assume you want to serve a directory called `/images` when the URL `/my-images` is requested. You can do it with mounting:

```
server.use('/my-images', connect.static('/path/to/images'));
```

maxAge

The `static` middleware takes an option called `maxAge` that specifies how long a certain resource can be cached in the client's user agent. This capability is useful when you know a certain asset is not going to change, and you don't want the user's browser to re-request it.

For example, it's common practice for web applications to *bundle up* all the client-side JavaScript into a file that represents a revision number. You can add the `maxAge` option to ensure those get cached forever:

```
server.use('/js', connect.static('/path/to/bundles', { maxAge: 10000000000000 });
```

hidden

The other option `static` takes is `hidden`. If this option is set to `true`, Connect serves files that begin with a dot (`.`) and are considered *hidden* in Unix filesystems:

```
server.use(connect.static('/path/to/resources', { hidden: true });
```

QUERY

Sometimes in your applications you have optional data associated with a URL that you send as part of the query string.

For example, consider the `url /blog-posts?page=5`. If you point your browser to that URL, then Node populates `req.url` with a string:

```
server.use(function (req) {
  // req.url == "/blog-posts?page=5"
});
```

Most likely, though, you actually want to access the value contained in that querystring.

If you implement the `query` middleware, you get a `req.query` object automatically with those values:

```
server.use(connect.query);
server.use(function (req, res) {
  // req.query.page == "5"
});
```

Again, parsing the query string is a common task for applications that Connect greatly simplifies. Just as in the `static` example where you stopped including the `require` call for the `fs` module, you no longer need to worry about using the `querystring` module.

This middleware is included automatically for you in Express, the web framework subject of the next chapter. Another very useful middleware is logger, which is described next.

LOGGER

The `logger` middleware is a useful diagnostics tool for your web application. It prints out information about incoming requests and outgoing responses to the terminal.

There are different built-in logging formats you can use

- `default`
- `dev`
- `short`
- `tiny`

For example, in order to leverage the `dev` logger format you would initialize the logger middleware as follows:

```
server.use(connect.logger('dev'));
```

Consider the following example, a typical "Hello World" HTTP server with the logger middleware in use:

```
var connect = require('connect');
connect.createServer(
    connect.logger('dev')
  , function (req, res) {
      res.writeHead(200);
      res.end('Hello world');
    }
).listen(3000);
```

Notice that I passed a series of middleware functions as parameters to the `createServer` helper function. This is equivalent to initializing a Connect server and calling `use` twice.

When you go to `http://127.0.0.1:3000` in your browser, you'll notice two lines get output:

```
GET / 200 0ms
GET /favicon.ico 200 2ms
```

The browser is requesting `/favicon.ico` and `/`, and the connect logger is displaying the method for the request, in addition to the response status code, and how long the process took.

`dev` is a concise and short logging format, giving you insight into behavior and performance while you're testing out your web apps.

The `logger` middleware allows custom strings that represent the format of your output.

Say you want to log only the method and the IP:

```
server.use(connect.logger(':method :remote-addr'));
```

You can also log headers by using the dynamic tokens `req` and `res`. To log the `content-length` and the `content-type` of the response along with how long it took to produce, you use the following:

```
server.use(connect.logger('type is :res[content-type], length is '
  + ':res[content-length] and it took :response-time ms.'));
```

Note: Remember that, in Node, request/response headers are always lowercase.

If you apply it to the original website that requests four images, you can see some interesting output, as shown in Figure 8-6. (Make sure you request on a fresh cache and clear your browser data prior to running the example.)

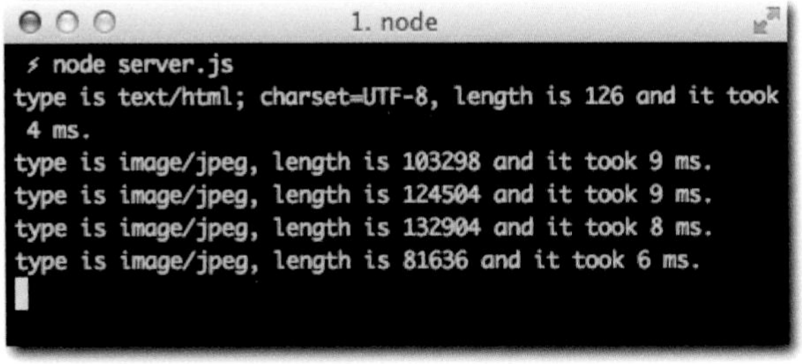

Figure 8-6: Your custom logger in action

Following is the complete list of tokens you can use:

- `:req[header]` (for example, `:req[Accept]`)
- `:res[header]` (for example, `:res[Content-Length]`)
- `:http-version`
- `:response-time`
- `:remote-addr`
- `:date`
- `:method`
- `:url`
- `:referrer`
- `:user-agent`
- `:status`

You can also define custom tokens. Say you want a shortcut called `:type` that refers to the `Content-Type` of the request; in that case, you use the following:

```
connect.logger.token('type', function (req, res) {
  return req.headers['content-type'];
});
```

The next middleware to consider is body parser, which automates another task you've been manually writing for http servers so far.

BODY PARSER

In one of the examples in the `http` module, you used the `qs` module to parse the body of a POST request.

Connect can also help here! You can leverage `bodyParser` as follows:

```
server.use(connect.bodyParser());
```

Then you can get the POST data in the `req.body`:

```
server.use(function (req, res) {
  // req.body.myinput
});
```

If you send JSON from the client in a POST request, `req.body` also is populated accordingly because `bodyParser` looks at the `Content-Type` of the request.

Handling uploads

Another function of the `bodyParser` is leveraging a module called `formidable` that allows you to access the files that the user uploaded.

For this example, you can use a shortcut way of calling `createServer` and pass all the middleware you need to it:

```
  var server = connect(
      connect.bodyParser()
    , connect.static('static')
  );
```

In the folder `static/`, you create `index.html` with a simple form to handle a file upload:

```
<form action="/" method="POST" enctype="multipart/form-data">
  <input type="file" />
  <button>Send file!</button>
</form>
```

Then you can add simple middleware to see what `req.body.file` looks like:

```
function (req, res, next) {
  if ('POST' == req.method) {
    console.log(req.body.file);
  } else {
    next();
  }
}
```

You're ready to test it! To do so, upload the file `Hello.txt`, as shown in Figure 8-7.

Figure 8-7: Uploading a sample text file from the browser

Then look at the server output, as shown in Figure 8-8.

As you can see, you get an object that describes the upload with some useful properties. Now print the upload back to the user:

```
if ('POST' == req.method && req.body.file) {
  fs.readFile(req.body.file.path, 'utf8', function (err, data) {
    if (err) {
      res.writeHead(500);
      res.end('Error!');
      return;
    }

    res.writeHead(200, { 'Content-Type': 'text/html' });
    res.end([
        '<h3>File: ' + req.body.file.name + '</h3>'
      , '<h4>Type: ' + req.body.file.type + '</h4>'
      , '<h4>Contents:</h4><pre>' + data + '</pre>'
    ].join(''));
```

```
    });
  } else {
    next();
  }
```

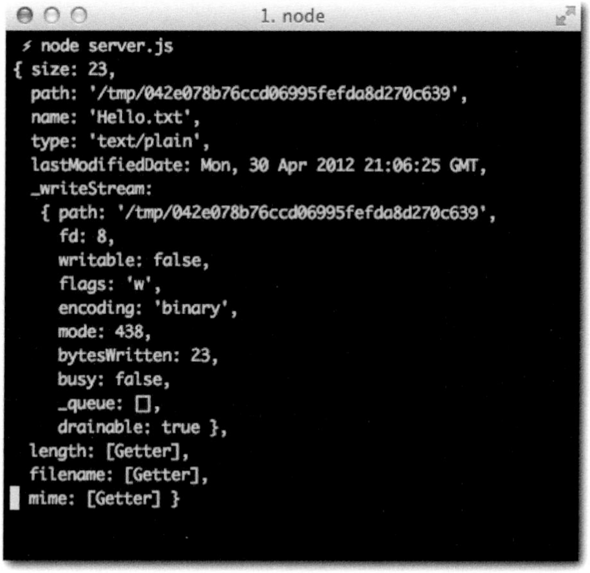

Figure 8-8: The uploaded file object representation in `req.body` shown through the console

Uploading the file again reveals its contents (see Figure 8-9).

Figure 8-9: The contents of sample file `Hello.txt` shown through the browser after the successful upload

Multiple files

If you want to handle multiple uploads, all you need to do is add `[]` to the name attribute of your input:

```
<input type="file" name="files[]" />
<input type="file" name="files[]" />
```

Then `req.body.files` contains an array of objects like the one you saw in the `Hello.txt` example before.

COOKIES

In a similar fashion to `query`, Connect can aid in the process of parsing and exposing cookies.

When a browser sends cookies, it does so through the `Cookie` header. Its format is somewhat similar to the query string of a URL. Look at a sample request that includes this header:

```
GET /secret HTTP/1.1
Host: www.mywebsite.org
Cookie: secret1=value; secret2=value2
Accept: */*
```

To access those values (`secret1` and `secret2`) without having to parse manually or use regular expressions, you can turn to the `cookieParser` middleware:

```
server.use(connect.cookieParser())
```

And, as you could expect, you can access the values through a `req.cookies` object:

```
server.use(function (req, res, next) {
  // req.cookies.secret1 = "value"
  // req.cookies.secret2 = "value2"
})
```

SESSION

In most web applications, the concept of a "user session" that spawns over multiple requests is necessary. Every time you need to "log in" to a website, you're probably leveraging some form of session system that relies on setting a cookie on the browser that is sent with subsequent requests.

Connect makes it really easy to do this. For this example, you create a simple login system. You're going to store the credentials in a `users.json` file that looks like this:

```
{
    "tobi": {
        "password": "ferret"
      , "name": "Tobi Holowaychuk"
    }
}
```

The first thing you do is `require` Connect and the users file:

```
/**
 * Module dependencies
 */

var connect = require('connect')
  , users = require('./users')
```

Notice that you can `require` JSON files! When you only need to export data, you don't need to include `module.exports`, and you can export it as JSON directly.

Next, you include the `logger`, `bodyParser` and `session` middleware. Because sessions depend on sending a cookie to the user, the `session` middleware needs to be *preceded* by the `cookieParser` middleware:

```
var server = connect(
    connect.logger('dev')
  , connect.bodyParser()
  , connect.cookieParser()
  , connect.session({ secret: 'my app secret' })
```

For security reasons, you have to supply a `secret` option when you initialize the `session` middleware.

The first middleware checks whether the user is logged in; otherwise, you let other middleware handle this task:

```
, function (req, res, next) {
    if ('/' == req.url && req.session.logged_in) {
      res.writeHead(200, { 'Content-Type': 'text/html' });
      res.end(
          'Welcome back, <b>' + req.session.name + '</b>. '
        + '<a href="/logout">Logout</a>'
      );
    } else {
      next();
    }
  }
```

The second one displays a form for logging in:

```
, function (req, res, next) {
    if ('/' == req.url && 'GET' == req.method) {
      res.writeHead(200, { 'Content-Type': 'text/html' });
      res.end([
          '<form action="/login" method="POST">'
        ,   '<fieldset>'
        ,     '<legend>Please log in</legend>'
        ,     '<p>User: <input type="text" name="user"></p>'
        ,     '<p>Password: <input type="password" name="password"></p>'
        ,     '<button>Submit</button>'
        ,   '</fieldset>'
        , '</form>'
      ].join(''));
    } else {
      next();
    }
  }
```

The next one actually checks that the credentials exist and logs in the user as a result:

```
, function (req, res, next) {
    if ('/login' == req.url && 'POST' == req.method) {
      res.writeHead(200);
      if (!users[req.body.user] || req.body.password != users[req.body.user].
 password) {
        res.end('Bad username/password');
      } else {
        req.session.logged_in = true;
        req.session.name = users[req.body.user].name;
        res.end('Authenticated!');
      }
    } else {
      next();
    }
  }
```

Notice that you modify an object called `req.session`. This object is saved whenever the response is sent, and you don't have to save it manually. You store the `name` and mark `logged_in` as `true`.

Finally, you handle the logout action in a similar fashion:

```
, function (req, res, next) {
    if ('/logout' == req.url) {
      req.session.logged_in = false;
      res.writeHead(200);
      res.end('Logged out!');
    } else {
      next();
    }
  }
```

The complete code should look like this:

```
/**
 * Module dependencies
 */

var connect = require('connect')
  , users = require('./users')

/**
 * Create server
 */

var server = connect(
    connect.logger('dev')
  , connect.bodyParser()
  , connect.cookieParser()
  , connect.session({ secret: 'my app secret' })
  , function (req, res, next) {
      if ('/' == req.url && req.session.logged_in) {
        res.writeHead(200, { 'Content-Type': 'text/html' });
        res.end(
            'Welcome back, <b>' + req.session.name + '</b>. '
          + '<a href="/logout">Logout</a>'
        );
      } else {
        next();
      }
    }
  , function (req, res, next) {
      if ('/' == req.url && 'GET' == req.method) {
        res.writeHead(200, { 'Content-Type': 'text/html' });
        res.end([
            '<form action="/login" method="POST">'
          ,   '<fieldset>'
          ,     '<legend>Please log in</legend>'
          ,     '<p>User: <input type="text" name="user"></p>'
          ,     '<p>Password: <input type="password" name="password"></p>'
          ,     '<button>Submit</button>'
          ,   '</fieldset>'
          , '</form>'
        ].join(''));
      } else {
        next();
      }
    }
  , function (req, res, next) {
      if ('/login' == req.url && 'POST' == req.method) {
        res.writeHead(200);
        if (!users[req.body.user] || req.body.password != users[req.body.user].
password) {
```

```
            res.end('Bad username/password');
          } else {
            req.session.logged_in = true;
            req.session.name = users[req.body.user].name;
            res.end('Authenticated!');
          }
        } else {
          next();
        }
      }
    , function (req, res, next) {
        if ('/logout' == req.url) {
          req.session.logged_in = false;
          res.writeHead(200);
          res.end('Logged out!');
        } else {
          next();
        }
      }
);

/**
 * Listen.
 */

server.listen(3000);
```

Now try out this simple login system. First, as shown in Figures 8-10 and 8-11, make sure basic security works.

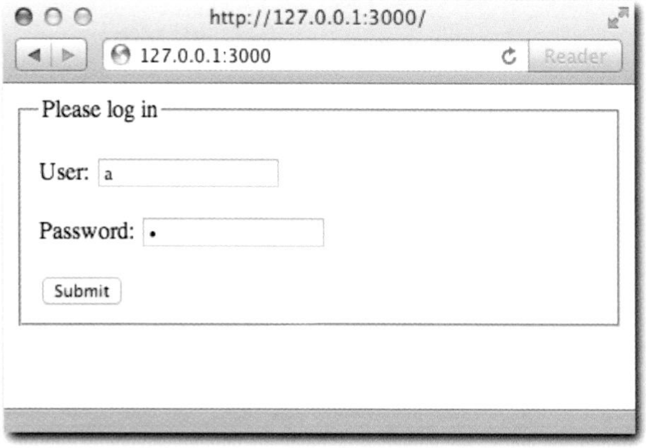

Figure 8-10: Trying out a login with bad credentials

Figure 8-11: The bad credentials result in unsuccessful login as expected

Now , as depicted in Figure 8-12, try logging in with one of the users in `users.json`.

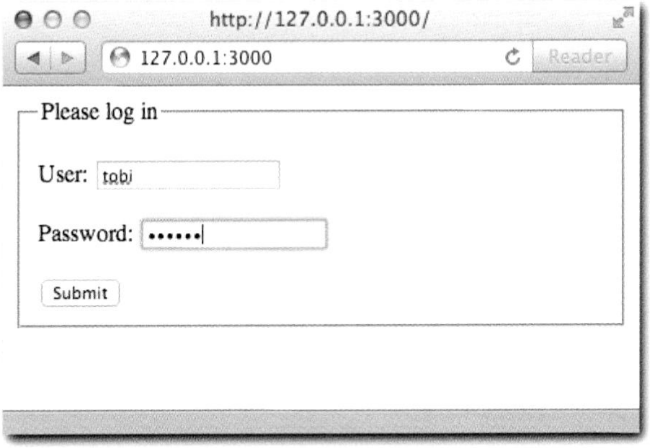

Figure 8-12: Login attempt with a valid user

Figure 8-13 illustrates a successful login.

Figure 8-13: Success page after login

In Figure 8-14, you've returned to the main page after a successful login.

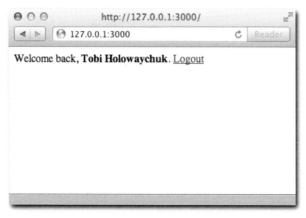

Figure 8-14: The result of going back to the main page once logged in

In order to have sessions work in a production-ready manner, you should learn how to persist them with Redis.

REDIS SESSIONS

Try the following: while logged in, restart your node server and then refresh your browser. Notice that the session is now gone!

The reason is that the default *store* for the `session` middleware is Memory. This means that the session data is stored in memory, and when the process dies, the sessions die with it.

This result is not a bad thing while you're developing applications, but it certainly can be detrimental for production applications. In those scenarios, you should swap the store with one that can persist reloading your node application, such as Redis (more on Redis in Chapter 12).

Redis is a small, fast database that a module called `connect-redis` leverages to store session data so that it lives *outside* the Node process.

You can set it up like this (you must have Redis installed):

```
var connect = require('connect')
  , RedisStore = require('connect-redis')(connect);
```

Then you include it by passing the `store` option to the `session` middleware:

```
server.use(connect.session({ store: new RedisStore, secret: 'my secret' }))
```

Now you're done! Sessions outlive your Node processes.

METHODOVERRIDE

Older browsers are incapable of creating requests (like Ajax) of certain methods such as PUT, DELETE, or PATCH. A common way to address this shortcoming for these specific user agents is to send a GET or POST request and to append a _method variable to the query string of the URL with the real intended method.

For example, if you want to PUT a resource from IE, you could send a request like this:

```
POST /url?_method=PUT HTTP/1.1
```

For your middleware to think that that request is actually a PUT request, you can include the methodOverride middleware:

```
server.use(connect.methodOverride())
```

Remember that middleware gets executed sequentially, so make sure it's placed before you include other middleware that handles requests.

BASICAUTH

For certain projects, sometimes you just need a basic authentication layer (see Figure 8-15) that's controlled by the user agent.

Figure 8-15: A login dialog shown by the browser (basic authentication)

Connect makes it really easy to add this layer through the `basicAuth` middleware.

As an example, create a toy authentication system that relies on the administration authorizing users through the command line.

You first receive user input:

```
process.stdin.resume();
process.stdin.setEncoding('ascii');
```

Then you add the `basicAuth` middleware:

```
connect.basicAuth(function (user, pass, fn) {
  process.stdout.write('Allow user \033[96m' + user + '\033[39m '
    + 'with pass \033[90m' + pass + '\033[39m ? [y/n]: ');
  process.stdin.once('data', function (data) {
    if (data[0] == 'y') {
      fn(null, { username: user });
    }
    else fn(new Error('Unauthorized'));
  });
})
```

Notice that you use the `once` method on the stdin `EventEmitter` because you only care about receiving data from the command line *once per request*.

The middleware is simple to use. It supplies the `user` and `pass` as parameters, and it supplies a callback to be invoked upon successful or failed authorization.

If the authorization succeeds, you pass `null` as the first argument (or an `Error` if it doesn't succeed) and the user object to populate `req.remoteUser` with.

You then declare the next middleware, which gets executed only if the authentication succeeds:

```
, function (req, res) { res.writeHead(200); res.end('Welcome to the protected area,
  ' + req.remoteUser.username); }
```

Then you submit your credentials (see Figure 8-16).

Figure 8-16: Filling the login dialog with sample credentials

Finally, as shown in Figure 8-17, you (in)securely authorize from the command line!

Figure 8-17: The server console reveals the authentication request which is responded to

Figure 8-18 shows the web site after a user has been authenticated via the command line.

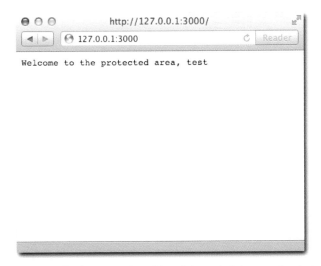

Figure 8-18: After the user is authorized through the terminal, the request is authorized

SUMMARY

In this chapter you learned the benefits of leveraging middleware as building blocks for code organization and reusability around requests and responses in HTTP servers. In this case, Connect is the module that supplies the infrastructure to do this in a very expressive way.

You compared having a single request handler in contrast with separating logic into smaller units connected by the `next` middleware function parameter.

You also looked at the middleware that Connect bundles that solves a variety of common needs for the development of websites and web applications. You now understand how to write your own middleware, and how to make them reusable through the Node.JS module system.

EXPRESS

WHEREAS CONNECT PROVIDES the foundation for the common set of *basic* tasks that are normally performed on top of the HTTP module, Express provides convenient APIs on top of Connect to build entire websites and web applications.

Throughout the examples in Chapter 8, you might have noticed most of the tasks performed in the interaction between a web browser and web server are organized around methods and URLs. The combination of these two is what is sometimes referred to as *routes*, a concept that sets the foundation for an Express app.

Express builds on top of Connect and therefore on the idea that you can reuse middleware that performs certain basic tasks. This means you get an expressive API for your web applications, without sacrificing a rich ecosystem of reusable components that sit on top of the HTTP stack.

To see the expressiveness hands-on, write a small application powered entirely by Express to search the Twitter API.

A SIMPLE EXPRESS APP

This app, albeit simple, is by definition dynamic. When the user requests "tweets" for their search term, you need to produce HTML that contains them. Instead of concatenating strings that make up that HTML manually in our request handlers, you'll be leveraging a simple template language that will split the logic of the *controller* from the *view*.

The first step will be to ensure we include the module requirements that satisfy these needs.

CREATING THE MODULE

Create `package.json` as usual, but this time add two extra dependencies: `ejs`, the template engine for this example, and superagent, to simplify the HTTP requests for the Twitter searches.

```
{
    "name": "express-tweet"
  , "version": "0.0.1"
  , "dependencies": {
        "express": "2.5.9"
      , "ejs": "0.4.2"
      , "superagent": "0.3.0"
    }
}
```

Please notice that even though I'm using Express 2 for this example, the code should be completely compatible with Express 3 (under development at the time of this writing).

The next step after defining the meta data for the project will be to create the templates that produce the HTML you need.

HTML

Unlike you did in the previous applications, you are going to use a simple template language to avoid having HTML code directly in the application logic (what is normally called *controllers* or *route handlers*). This template language is called EJS (or embedded js), and is similar to embedding PHP in HTML.

You start by defining `index.ejs` inside the `views/` folder. The templates can live anywhere, but for the sake of project structure, put them in a separate directory.

The first template gets served for the default route (the home page). It prompts the user to submit a search term to crawl Twitter:

```
<h1>Twitter app</h1>
<p>Please enter your search term:</p>
<form action="/search" method="GET">
  <input type="text" name="q">
```

```
    <button>Search</button>
</form>
```

The other template is the search results, `search.ejs`. Highlight the current term and then walk through the results (if any) or otherwise display a message:

```
<h1>Tweet results for <%= search %></h1>
<% if (results.length) { %>
  <ul>
    <% for (var i = 0; i < results.length; i++) { %>
    <li><%= results[i].text %> - <em><%= results[i].from_user %></em></li>
    <% } %>
  </ul>
<% } else { %>
  <p>No results</p>
<% } %>
```

As you can see, all we did was embed JavaScript code between the special `<%` and `%>` EJS tags. In order to print out variables, you need to add extra `"="` after `<%`.

SETUP

As usual, you define your dependencies in a `server.js` file:

```
var express = require('express')
```

After requiring Express, you want to initialize your web server with it. Express provides a shortcut method `createServer` just like Connect that returns an Express HTTP server. Add the following line:

```
var app = express.createServer()
```

Unlike other popular web frameworks, Express doesn't require configuration or a specific filesystem structure. It's flexible enough to let you customize every single aspect of its functionality.

For this app, specify the template engine (so that you don't have to include it every time you reference your views) and where your views files (templates) are located. The method you called earlier, `express.createServer`, augments HTTP servers with a configuration system. You can call `set` to change configuration flags. Add these afterwards:

```
app.set('view engine', 'ejs');
app.set('views', __dirname + '/views');
app.set('view options', { layout: false });
```

The third parameter `view options` defines configuration options that are passed to every template when rendering a view. The value `layout` is set to `false` here, to match what will become a default with Express 3.

If you wanted to obtain a configuration setting, you would call `app.set` with just one flag. For example, if you wanted to print out the value of the setting `views`, you call it like this:

```
console.log(app.set('views'));
```

Moving forward, you'll leverage additional methods Express adds to expressively define routes, something that you've done a lot quite a bit in Chapter 7 and Chapter 8.

DEFINING ROUTES

Instead of defining middleware that checks the properties `method` and `url` manually every time, you can use Express to *progressively* define routes by calling the function corresponding to the HTTP method you want to handle and then supplying the URL and the handler middleware.

The methods Express adds to the server are `get`, `put`, `post`, `del`, `patch`, and `head`, matching HTTP verbs GET, PUT, POST, DELETE, PATCH, and HEAD, respectively. The following are examples of route definitions with them:

```
app.get('/', function (req, res, next) {});
app.put('/post/:name', function (req, res, next) {});
app.post('/signup', function (req, res, next) {});
app.del('/user/:id', function (req, res, next) {});
app.patch('/user/:id', function (req, res, next) {});
app.head('/user/:id', function (req, res, next) {});
```

The first parameter is the route, and the second is the route handler. Route handlers work just like middleware.

Note that routes can take a special format to define variables within them. In the example above `/user/:id`, `id` can take different values and the route will still match: for example `/user/2`, `/user/3`, and so on. You'll learn more about them later in the chapter.

For now, you should first define your home page route: Add the following to `server.js`:

```
app.get('/', function (req, res) {
  res.render('index');
});
```

The complete code for server.js should look like this so far:

```
/**
 * Module requirements.
 */
```

```
var express = require('express')
  , search = require('./search')

/**
 * Create app.
 */

var app = express.createServer();

/**
 * Configuration
 */

app.set('view engine', 'ejs');
app.set('views', __dirname + '/views');
app.set('view options', { layout: false });

/**
 * Routes
 */

app.get('/', function (req, res) {
  res.render('index');
});

/**
 * Listen
 */
app.listen(3000);
```

Express adds a method called `render` to the response; it acts as shortcut to

1. Initializing the template engine
2. Reading the view file and passing it to the template engine
3. Getting the resulting HTML and sending it as a response

Because you specified the `view engine` to be `ejs` in the previous step, you don't need to reference `index.ejs`.

As shown in Figure 9-1, test the route (don't forget to call `listen`).

Figure 9-1: The route handler / renders the index view.

For the second route, call a function named `search` (which you define in a separate module):

```
app.get('/search', function (req, res, next) {
  search(req.query.q, function (err, tweets) {
    if (err) return next(err);
    res.render('search', { results: tweets, search: req.query.q });
  });
});
```

Next, add the search dependency after `express`:

```
var express = require('express')
  , search = require('./search')
```

Notice that if an error is passed by the `search` function, you pass it to `next`. When you learn more about error handling later in the chapter you'll understand why, but for now assume that Express takes care of informing the user of the error.

In this route, you also call `render`, but you pass an object as second parameters. The contents of that object get *exposed* to the view. Notice how you pass `tweets` and `search`, both of which get referenced directly in `search.ejs`. You call this object the `locals` object because its keys become *local to the template*.

SEARCH

The search module exposes a simple function to query the Twitter Search API. The file this module will reside in, `search.js`, goes in the same directory as `server.js` for this example.

In the function call search above, you passed it the search term, and the function callback passed back an error (if any), and an array of tweets.

To write a module that does this, you start defining its dependencies. In this case, you're only going to need superagent:

```
var request = require('superagent')
```

Since the HTTP request made to the Twitter web service we make is essential to the functioning of your application, you want to make sure the search module does proper error handling.

For example, if the Twitter API is down or malfunctioning, you want to pass an error object so that ultimately the user sees an error page (for example, showing HTTP status code error 500).

```
/**
 * Search function.
 *
 * @param {String} search query
 * @param {Function} callback
 * @api public
 */

module.exports = function search (query, fn) {
  request.get('http://search.twitter.com/search.json')
    .data({ q: query })
    .end(function (res) {
      if (res.body && Array.isArray(res.body.results)) {
        return fn(null, res.body.results);
      }
      fn(new Error('Bad twitter response'));
    });
};
```

Similar to the other superagent examples, you want to make a GET request, sending the querystring data field q with the search term. The URL superagent hit for the search term hello world will be something like `http://search.twitter.com/search.json?q=hello+world`.

In the response handler, you're actively making sure that the request works and satisfies our expectations completely. Instead of looking at HTTP status codes and verifying you got 200 instead of something else, it's smarter to ask the question: did I get an array of tweets as part of the response?

If you remember from Chapter 7, if superagent gets a JSON response, it will automatically decode it and place its contents as part of the res.body variable. Since the Twitter API responds with a JSON object with a key results containing an array of tweets, the following snippet from the code above is all you need for error handling:

```
if (res.body && Array.isArray(res.body.results)) {
    return fn(null, res.body.results);
}
```

RUN

Run the server and point your browser to `http://localhost:3000` (see Figure 9-2) and try out a search term (see Figure 9-3).

Figure 9-2: An example filling out a search term and submitting it.

Figure 9-3: The results of querying the search term.

It works! After making the search to Twitter, you got back an array of tweets. It eventually made its way to the template `search.ejs`, which generated the dynamic list of tweets.

After the HTML was produced by the render functionality of Express, the `/search` route successfully served the complete page to the user as shown in Figure 9-3.

After this simple example, it's time to analyze some of the Express features you used in depth, and learn new ones.

SETTINGS

One of the interesting features Express provides that proves necessary for any type of web application is the ability to manage environments and settings.

For example, during production you can make a performance enhancement and let express cache the templates so that they get served faster. However, if you enable this feature during development, you would need to restart Node every time you make a change to a template to test the result.

Express lets you set this environment by calling `configure`:

```
app.configure('production', function () {
  app.enable('view cache');
});
```

In this case, `app.enable` is the equivalent to calling `app.set` like you saw in the simple Express example above for the views `config` flag.

```
app.set('view cache', true);
```

To know whether a configuration flag is enabled you can also call `app.enabled`. `app.disable` and `app.disabled` are also available.

When the environment variable `NODE_ENV` is set to `production`, the callback we defined with `app.configure` gets executed.

To test it, run

```
$ NODE_ENV=production node server
```

If node `NODE_ENV` is defined, the environment defaults to development:

```
app.configure('development', function () {
  // gets called in the absence of NODE_ENV too!
});
```

Some other useful built-in settings are

- `case sensitive routes`: Enable case-sensitive routing. By default, when you define a route as follows:

  ```
  app.get('/my/route', function (req, res) {}
  ```

  Express will match that route for `/my/route` and `/MY/ROUTE`. By enabling this, routes will match if the cases match.

- strict routing: When enabled trailing slashes are no longer ignored. For example, the previous example route matches the URLs /my/route and /my/route/. If strict routing is enabled, however, only /my/route would match, since that's how it was defined with app.get.

- jsonp callback: Enable res.send() / res.json() transparent jsonp support. JSONP is a technique for serving cross-domain JSON that consists in wrapping the response with the callback provided by the user.

- When JSONP is requested, the URL would look like this: /my/route?callback=myCallback. Express can automatically detect the callback parameter and wrap the response with the myCallback text. To enable this behavior, call app.enable('jsonp callback'). Please note that this only applies when you call res.send or res.json in a route, which are described later in the chapter.

TEMPLATE ENGINES

To use ejs in the preceding example, you must take two steps:

1. You install the ejs module through NPM.
2. You declare the view engine as ejs.

In the same way many other templates are commonly used with Express:

- Haml
- Jade
- CoffeeKup
- jQuery Templates for node

Express tries to call require with the extension name of the template or the configured view engine.

For example, you can call

```
res.render('index.html')
```

In this case, Express tries to require the html engine. Because it can't find one, the call results in an error.

You can map extensions to known template engines by using the app.register API. For example, to map html extensions to the jade template engine, run

```
app.register('.html', require('jade'));
```

Jade is one of the most popular template languages, and definitely worth learning. To find out more about it, refer to its website http://jade-lang.org.

ERROR HANDLING

It's natural in the Node environment to pass around error objects as the result of non-blocking I/O callbacks. In our example in this chapter, we expected the possibility of an `Error` object when we performed the Twitter API search.

What you normally want to do with them in the context of Express routes is pass these error objects to next. By default, Express will show an error page and send the status code 500.

Most web applications however will want to customize error pages, or even set up custom backend reporting.

You can define special handlers with app.error that act as middleware for errors:

```
app.error(function (err, req, res, next) {
  if ('Bad twitter response' == err.message) {
    res.render('twitter-error');
  } else {
    next();
  }
});
```

Notice that in that example I'm inspecting the error message to decide whether the middleware will handle the error or not, and call next otherwise.

You can set up multiple `.error` handlers that have different actions. For example, the last error handler can send a `500 Internal Server Error` and render a generic error page:

```
app.error(function (err, req, res) {
  res.render('error', { status: 500 });
});
```

If you call next and another handler is not available, the default Express error handler will kick in.

CONVENIENCE METHODS

Express provides a series of extensions to Node's `Request` and `Response` objects that greatly simplify different tasks.

The extensions to the `Request` object are

- `header`: This extension allows for easily retrieving a header as a function in a way that is not case sensitive:

  ```
  req.header('Host')
  req.header('host')
  ```

- accepts: This extension analyzes the Accept header of the request according to the supplied value and returns true or false:

```
req.accepts('html')
req.accepts('text/html')
```

- is: This extension is similar to accepts, but it checks the Content-Type header:

```
req.is('json')
req.is('text/html')
```

The extensions to the Response object are

- header: This extension takes one argument to check whether a header has been set for the response:

```
res.header('content-type')
```

Or two arguments to set a header:

```
res.header('content-type', 'application/json')
```

- render: You have learned most of the usage of render already. In the previous example, however, you might have noticed you passed the status local. This is a special type of local that, when set, also sets the *status code* of the response.
  - In addition, you can supply a third parameter to render to obtain the HTML without sending it automatically as the response.

```
res.render('template', function (err, html) {
  // do something with html
});
```

- send: This magic method acts based on the *type* of the supplied argument.
  - Number: Sends a status code:

```
res.send(500);
```

  - String: Sends HTML:

```
res.send('<p>html</p>');
```

  - Object/Array: Serializes it into JSON, setting the appropriate Content-Type header:

```
res.send({ hello: 'world' }); res.send([1,2,3]);
```

- json: This extension is similar to send for most situations. It explicitly sends a value as JSON.

```
res.json(5);
```

You want to use this method when the type of the value is unknown. res.send relies on type checking for an object to decide whether to call JSON.stringify on it. If a number is supplied, it assumes you want to send a status code and finish the response. res.json, however, would pass the number through JSON.stringify.

Since most of the time you'll want to encode objects, res.send is still the most common choice.

- `redirect`: Redirect offers a helper for sending the 302 (Moved Temporarily) status code and the Location header. The following:

  ```
  res.redirect('/some/other/url')
  ```

  is effectively equivalent to:

  ```
  res.header('Location', '/some/other/url');
  res.send(302);
  ```

  which in turn is equivalent to the following native Node.JS:

  ```
  res.writeHead(302, { 'Location': '/some/other/url' });
  ```

- `redirect` also takes a custom status code as its second parameter. For example, if you want to send Moved Permanently instead you would set it to 301:

  ```
  res.redirect('/some/other/url', 301)
  ```

- `sendfile`: This extension is similar in spirit to the Connect `static` middleware, but it is used for individual files:

  ```
  res.sendfile('image.jpg')
  ```

Beyond our usage of routes in the simple example app, there's a lot more to them that can be really useful for larger web applications.

ROUTES

Routes can define custom parameters:

```
app.get('/post/:name', function () {
  // . . .
})
```

In this case, the variable `name` is populated inside the `req.params` object. For example, say you point your browser to `'/post/hello-world'`, the object `req.params` gets populated accordingly:

```
app.get('/post/:name', function () {
  // req.params.name == "hello-world"
})
```

You can make parameters optional by appending a question mark (?) symbol after them. In the previous route, if you point your browser to `/post`, there won't be a match. The route is defined by the requirement of a parameter:

```
app.get('/post/:name?', function (req, res, next) {
  // this will match for /post and /post/a-post-here
})
```

Routes that include parameters like these compile down to regular expressions internally. That means for more advanced route matching you can also pass a `RegExp` object directly. For example, if you wanted to make that route match only for alphanumeric characters and dashes, you could use the following:

```
app.get(/^\/post\/([a-z\d\-]*)/, function (req, res, next) {
  // req.params contains the matches set by the RegExp capture groups
})
```

In the same spirit as middleware, you can use `next` to control the *flow* of route matching. Even when a route is executed, you can still force Express to continue matching the request against other defined routes.

For example, make a route that accepts only parameters that start with an `'h'`:

```
app.get('/post/:name', function (req, res, next) {
  if ('h' != req.params.name[0]) return next();
  // . . .
});
```

This fine-grained route flow control solves a variety of situations gracefully thanks to its flexibility.

For example, many web applications allow routes such as `/home` and `/about`, but they also want to have *permalinks* that point to *dynamic* content, such as vanity URLs.

After you define all your routes, you can define one that captures vanity usernames and makes a database call. If the username is not found, you can `next` and send a `404`; otherwise, you render his profile:

```
app.get('/home', function (req, res) {
  // . . .
});

app.get('/:username', function (req, res, next) {
  // if you got here, no prior application routes matched
  getUser(req.params.username, function (err, user) {
    if (err) return next(err);

    if (exists) {
      res.render('profile')
    } else {
      next();
    }
  });
});
```

Express takes the concept of middleware you're already familiar with and expands on it. Read on to learn more about it.

MIDDLEWARE

Because Express is built on top of Connect, when you create an Express server, you can use it to enable Connect-compatible middleware. For example, to serve images under an `images/` folder, you can leverage the static middleware like this:

```
app.use(express.static(__dirname + '/images'));
```

Or if you wanted to leverage connect sessions, you would do it just like we did for Connect:

```
app.use(express.cookieParser());
app.use(express.session());
```

Notice that you can access Connect middleware directly as part of the Express requirement. There's no need to `require('connect')` or add connect as a dependency to your `package.json` file. Middleware are easily accessible to you.

More interestingly, Express also allows for middleware that gets appended *only* after a certain route matched, as opposed to *every request*.

Imagine a situation in which you want to check that the user is authenticated, but only for certain protected routes. In this case, you can define a `secure` middleware that sends the status code `403 Not Authorized` if the `req.session.logged_in` is not true:

```
function secure (req, res, next) {
  if (!req.session.logged_in) {
    return res.send(403);
  }

  next();
}
```

Then you can apply it to routes:

```
app.get('/home', function () {
  // accessible to everyone
});

app.get('/financials', secure, function () {
  // secure!
});

app.get('/about', function () {
  // accessible to everyone
});

app.get('/roadmap', secure, function () {
  // secure!
});
```

You can define more than one middleware function for each route:

```
''app.post('/route', a, b, c, function () { });
```

In some situations, you want to call `next` from route middleware in such a way that the rest of the middleware for that route gets skipped, and Express resumes processing *at the next route*.

For example, if instead of sending `403`, you want to let Express check other routes, you could use the following approach:

```
function secure (req, res, next) {
  if (!req.session.logged_in) {
    return next('route');
  }

  next();
}
```

By calling `next('route')`, you ensure the current route gets skipped.

As applications grow and the number of routes and middleware increases, it's useful to have some code organization strategies in mind. The next section describes the most fundamental ways of achieving this.

ORGANIZATION STRATEGIES

The first rule for any Node.JS application, including Express web apps, is to always be modular. Node.JS gives us a very powerful code organization strategy through the simple `require` API.

For example, consider an application that has three distinct sections /blog, /pages, and /tags, each with other routes under their hierarchy. For example, /blog/search, /pages/list, or /tags/cloud.

A successful organization strategy would be to maintain a server.js file with the *route map* and then include the route handlers as modules blog.js, pages.js, and tags.js. First, you define the dependencies and initialize the app, include middleware, and so on:

```
var express = require('express')
  , blog = require('./blog')
  , pages = require('./pages')
  , tags = require('./tags')

// initialize app
var app = express.createServer();

// here you would include middleware, settings, etc
```

Then you define what I refer to as the route map, which is simply laying out all the URLs that you want to handle in a single place:

```
// blog routes
app.get('/blog', blog.home);
app.get('/blog/search', blog.search);
app.post('/blog/create', blog.create);

// pages routes
app.get('/pages', pages.home);
app.get('/pages/list', pages.list);

// tags routes
app.get('/tags', tags.home);
app.get('/tags/search', tags.search);
```

Then, for each specific file you would leverage exports. Consider the example for `blog.js`:

```
exports.home = function (req, res, next) {
  // home
};

exports.search = function (req, res, next) {
  // search functionality
};
```

Modules offer great flexibility. You could take this to a next level and divide modules by methods. For example:

```
exports.get = {};
exports.get.home = function (req, res, next) {})
exports.post = {};
exports.post.create = function (req, res, next) {})
```

The other way in which applications can be decoupled is what's known as *app mounting*. You can export an entire Express app as a module (which you could also obtain from NPM), and *mount it* to your existing application, making the routes match seamlessly.

Consider the example of an application that needs a blog. You can define a blog with all its routes `/`, `/categories`, and `/search`, and export that as `blog.js`:

```
var app = module.exports = express.createServer();
app.get('/', function (req, res, next) {});
app.get('/categories', function (req, res, next) {});
app.get('/search', function (req, res, next) {});
```

Notice that the routes are defined in absolute terms, without a prefix. Then, in your main app, all you have to do is require it and pass it to `app.use`:

```
app.use(require('./blog'));
```

With this, all the blog routes immediately become available to another application. In addition, you can set a prefix for them:

```
app.use ('/blog', require('./blog'));
```

Now the routes `/blog/`, `/blog/categories`, and `/blog/search` will seamlessly be handled by the other express application, which can have its own completely separate set of dependencies, middleware, configuration, and more.

SUMMARY

In this chapter you learned how to leverage Express, the most popular Node.JS web framework.

The main benefit you'll see from your usage and implementation of Express is that it's simple, largely unopinionated but flexible, and it builds on top of other battle-tested and clean abstractions like Connect.

Unlike other web frameworks and libraries, Express can be easily molded to fit different needs, structures, and patterns. You learned how to use it with minimal implementation overhead in the first application example, just like the Node.JS Hello World.

As a matter of fact, you might have noticed that Express tries to stay close to the Node.JS core API and _extend_ it, as opposed to creating a new world on top of it. That's why route handlers still receive the native Node request and response objects, the same we received in the first HTTP server we wrote. You learned and appreciated the usefulness of these extensions, and how for example they make writing APIs that respond with JSON a breeze with `res.send`.

Finally, you learned how to put different pieces together to create maintainable code. Again, the main strategy of staying close to the Node.JS core APIs pays off: leveraging `require` is one of the most powerful tools for superior code organization.

10 WEBSOCKET

SO FAR, MOST website and web application developers are accustomed to communicating exclusively with a server by making HTTP requests that are followed by HTTP responses.

The model of *requesting a resource* by specifying its URL, `Content-Type`, and other attributes that you saw in previous chapters works well if you keep in mind the use case that the World Wide Web was crafted to solve. The web was created to deliver documents that were heavily interlinked to each other. URLs have paths because documents typically have hierarchies in file systems. And each level of hierarchy can contain indexes with hyperlinks.

Consider the following, for example:

```
GET /animals/index.html
GET /animals/mammals/index.html
GET /animals/mammals/ferrets.html
```

With time, however, the web became more and more interactive. The traditional web that was about retrieving entire documents every time the user clicked is less common nowadays, especially with all the tools that HTML5 makes available. You can now create very sophisticated web applications that often have completely deprecated desktop application counterparts, games, text editors, and more.

AJAX

The Web 2.0 marked the uprise of the *web application*. One of its key ingredients was AJAX, which translated into a snappier user experience for a fundamental reason: you no longer had to retrieve an entire HTML document every time the user interacted with the server.

For example, if you are updating your profile on a social networking application, you can make an asynchronous POST request and get a simple OK in return. Then with one of the readily available JavaScript frameworks, you can alter the view to represent the user action.

Alternatively, when you click Remove on a table, you can send a DELETE request and erase the row (`<tr>`) element without having the browser fetch a lot of unnecessary data, images, scripts, and stylesheets and then rerender the entire page.

In essence, AJAX was important because it allowed you to get rid of a lot of *data transfer and rendering overhead* that you didn't need for *many of the things that web applications were trying to do with web applications.*

In recent times, however, many applications have been transferring data in ways in which the traditional HTTP request+response model results in significant overhead. Consider the example of the application you are going to build in this chapter. Say you want to show where the cursors of every visitor of your website are in real time. Every time a visitor moves her mouse, you send her coordinates.

Say you use jQuery to send AJAX requests. The first idea that comes to mind is using $ .post to send a POST request with the cursor location every time the mousemove event is triggered, as shown here:

```
$(document).mousemove(function (ev) {
  $.post('/position', { x: ev.clientX, y: ev.clientY });
});
```

This code, despite looking straightforward, has a fundamental problem: you have no control over the order in which the server receives requests.

When your code makes a request, the browser can send it through any of its available sockets because browsers open multiple sockets to the target server to enhance performance. For example, while an image is being downloaded, an AJAX request can still be sent. If the browser operates with only one socket, this is impossible and websites are extremely slow to interact with.

If three requests are made in parallel through three different sockets, you have no guarantee of the order in which they are received. As a result, you need to adjust your code to send only one request at a time and wait for the response to send the next one:

```
var sending = false;

$(document).mousemove(function (ev) {
  if (sending) return;
  sending = true;
  $.post('/position', { x: ev.clientX, y: ev.clientY }, function () {
    sending = false;
  });
});
```

Now consider what the TCP traffic would look like using Firefox as an example:

Request

```
POST / HTTP/1.1
Host: localhost:3000
User-Agent: Mozilla/5.0 (Macintosh; Intel Mac OS X 10.7; rv:8.0.1) Gecko/20100101
  Firefox/8.0.1
Accept: */*
Accept-Language: en-us,en;q=0.5
Accept-Encoding: gzip, deflate
Accept-Charset: ISO-8859-1,utf-8;q=0.7,*;q=0.7
Content-Type: application/x-www-form-urlencoded; charset=UTF-8
X-Requested-With: XMLHttpRequest
Referer: http://localhost:3000/
Content-Length: 7
Pragma: no-cache
Cache-Control: no-cache

x=6&y=7
```

Response

```
HTTP/1.1 200 OK
Content-Type: text/plain
Content-Length: 2
Connection: keep-alive

OK
```

As you can see, a great amount of text surrounds a minimal amount of data. A lot of unneeded headers *for this particular use case* are sent back and forth, and they greatly outweigh how much data we're sending.

Even if you could remove some of those headers, do you really need a response in this case? If you're sending something as volatile and unimportant as the position of a mouse, you don't really need to wait for an OK to send more.

The ideal case for this particular web application starts to resemble raw TCP (like that in the chat application in Chapter 6) more than it resembles HTTP. Ideally, you would want to write the positions to a socket sequentially with minimal *framing* (that is, the data that surrounds the data you care about).

If you think in terms of `telnet`, ideally you would like the browser to send

```
x=6&y=7 \n
x=10&y=15 \n
. . .
```

Now, thanks to HTML5, you have a solution: WebSocket. WebSocket is the TCP of the web, a low-level bidirectional socket that gives control of the communication back to you.

HTML5 WEBSOCKET

When you discuss WebSocket, you're talking about two distinct parts: the WebSocket API implemented by browsers, and the WebSocket Protocol implemented by servers. Both have been designed and developed in conjunction with other technologies as part of the HTML5 initiative and movement, but are not a formal part of the HTML5 specification. The former is being standardized by the W3C, and the latter has been standardized by the IETF as RFC 6455.

The API as it's implemented by the browser looks like this:

```
var ws = new WebSocket('ws://host/path');
ws.onopen = function () {
  ws.send('data');
}
ws.onclose = function () {}
ws.ondata = function (ev) {
  alert(ev.data);
}
```

The simplicity of its API is, not coincidentally, reminiscent of the TCP client you wrote in Chapter 6. As you can see, unlike `XMLHttpRequest` (AJAX), it's not oriented around requests and responses, but messages sent with the `send` method. You can send and receive messages in UTF-8 or binary encoding very easily, through the `data` event, and learn about the connection being opened or closed through the `open` and `close` events.

Connection must first be established with a *handshake*. The handshake looks like a normal HTTP request, but after the server responds to it, the client and server begin exchanging data with minimal framing:

Request

```
GET /ws HTTP/1.1
Host: example.com
Upgrade: websocket
Connection: Upgrade
Sec-WebSocket-Version: 6
Sec-WebSocket-Origin: http://pmx
Sec-WebSocket-Extensions: deflate-stream
Sec-WebSocket-Key: x3JJHMbDL1EzLkh9GBhXDw==
```

Response

```
HTTP/1.1 101 Switching Protocols
Upgrade: websocket
Connection: Upgrade
Sec-WebSocket-Accept: HSmrc0sMlYUkAGmm5OPpG2HaGWk=
```

WebSockets are still based on HTTP, which means it's fairly easy to implement the protocol on top of existing servers. The main difference is that as soon as the handshake is complete, a minimalistic TCP-like socket is available to you.

To better understand these concepts, let's write an example app.

AN ECHO EXAMPLE

The first example will consist of a server and a client exchanging simple `ping` and `pong` strings. When the client sends a ping, you'll record the time, and measure how many milliseconds it takes for the server to respond.

SETTING IT UP

For this example, you use `websocket.io`, which I created while working at LearnBoost.

It's important to keep in mind that `websocket.io` handles only the WebSocket requests. All the other requests in your website or application are still handled by a regular web server, which is why you also include `express` in your `package.json file`:

```
"name": "ws-echo"
  , "version": "0.0.1"
  , "dependencies": {
        "express": "2.5.1"
      , "websocket.io": "0.1.6"
  }
}
```

The server simply responds to messages by echoing them back to the browser. The browser measures how long it takes for the server to respond.

SETTING UP THE SERVER

The first thing you need to do is initialize `express` and attach `websocket.io` to it so that it can handle the WebSocket requests:

```
var express = require('express')
  , wsio = require('websocket.io')

/**
 * Create express app.
 */

var app = express.createServer();

/**
 * Attach websocket server.
 */

var ws = wsio.attach(app);

/**
 * Serve your code
 */

app.use(express.static('public'));

/**
 * Listening on connections
 */

ws.on('connection', function (socket) {
  // . . .
});

/**
 * Listen
 */

app.listen(3000);
```

Now focus on the `connection` handler. I explicitly designed `websocket.io` to closely resemble how you would implement a `net.Server`. Because you want to echo back messages, all you need to do is listen on the `message` event and `send` it back.

```
ws.on('connection', function (socket) {
  socket.on('message', function (msg) {
```

```
      console.log(' \033[96mgot:\033[39m ' + msg);
      socket.send('pong');
    });
});
```

SETTING UP THE CLIENT

Now you're ready to move onto the code, which goes into the `public` folder:

index.html

```
<!doctype html>
<html>
  <head>
    <title>WebSocket echo test</title>
    <script>
      var lastMessage;

      window.onload = function () {
        // create socket
        var ws = new WebSocket('ws://localhost:3000');
        ws.onopen = function () {
          // send first ping
          ping();
        }
        ws.onmessage = function (ev) {
          console.log(' got: ' + ev.data);
          // you got echo back, measure latency
          document.getElementById('latency').innerHTML = new Date - lastMessage;
          // ping again
          ping();
        }
        function ping () {
          // record the timestamp
          lastMessage = +new Date;
          // send the message
          ws.send('ping');
        };
    </script>
  </head>
  <body>
    <h1>WebSocket Echo</h1>
    <h2>Latency: <span id="latency"></span>ms</h2>
</body>
</html>
```

If you look at the HTML, it's fairly self-explanatory. It just sets up a placeholder to display the latency (which is the number of milliseconds that a message takes to complete a round trip).

The JavaScript code is relatively straightforward also. You keep track of the last message timestamp:

```
var lastMessage
```

Initializing `WebSocket` opens the connection:

```
var ws = new WebSocket('ws://localhost:3000');
```

You register the connection as open and send the first message to the server:

```
ws.onopen = function () {
  ping();
}
```

When the server replies, you measure the latency and ping again:

```
ws.onmessage = function () {
  console.log(' got: ' + ev.data);
  // you got echo back, measure latency
  document.getElementById('latency').innerHTML = new Date - lastMessage;
  // ping again
  ping();
}
```

Finally, let's define the `ping` function, which tracks the timestamp to measure the response against (so that we can determine the *latency*), and sends a simple string:

```
function ping () {
  // record the timestamp
  lastMessage = +new Date;
  // send the message
  ws.send('ping');
};
```

RUNNING THE SERVER

Now you run the server:

```
$ node server.js
```

Then you point the browser to http://localhost:3000 (see Figure 10-1). Make sure you test with a modern web browser that supports WebSocket, like Chrome 15+ or IE 10+. If unsure, go to http://websocket.org and look at the "Does your browser support WebSocket?" box.

You successfully created a single-user realtime application. Check the terminal output and your web browser's console for a log of the messages exchanged. In most modern computers, it will take on average between 1 and 5 milliseconds to exchange this message. As an exercise, try writing this same example leveraging AJAX and Express routes, and compare how long it takes to complete a `ping-pong` cycle.

Figure 10-1: The time it takes for a packet to go to the server and back to the client

For the next example, you'll write an application where the server's role is to connect multiple users on a single screen.

MOUSE CURSORS

You are going to display the image of a cursor representing the position of all the connected users in the screen.

Through this example, you learn the concept of *broadcasting*, which consists of one user relaying a message to everyone but himself.

SETTING UP THE EXAMPLE

The requirements for this project are the exact same as for the previous example. In your `package.json` include:

```
{

    "name": "ws-cursors"
  , "version": "0.0.1"
  , "dependencies": {
      "express": "2.5.1"
    , "websocket.io": "0.1.6"
    }

}
```

SETTING UP THE SERVER

The basic server setup is equivalent to the previous app. You serve static HTML with express, and you attach a websocket.io server to it in your server.js:

```
var express = require('express')
  , wsio = require('websocket.io')

/**
 * Create express app.
 */

var app = express.createServer();

/**
 * Attach websocket server.
 */

var ws = wsio.attach(app);

/**
 * Serve your code
 */

app.use(express.static('public'))

/**
 * Listening on connections
 */

ws.on('connection', function (socket) {
  // . . .
});

/**
 * Listen
 */

app.listen(3000);
```

In this case, however, you want to take a different action when a user connects. You want to keep track of everyone's positions in memory in a simple object. You also keep track of the total number of clients that have connected so that you can give each client a unique ID. That ID identifies the client's position in the positions object:

```
var positions = {}
  , total = 0

ws.on('connection', function (socket) {
  // . . .
});
```

When a user first connects, you want to send everyone's positions to him as the first message. That way, when the user first loads the page, he can see everyone who is connected.

To that end, you encode the `positions` object as JSON:

```
ws.on('connection', function (socket) {
  // you give the socket an id
  socket.id = ++total;

  // you send the positions of everyone else
  socket.send(JSON.stringify(positions));
});
```

When a client sends a message, you assume he's sending his position as JSON (as an object with x and y coordinates). You then store it in the `positions` object:

```
socket.on('message', function (msg) {
  try {
    var pos = JSON.parse(msg);
  } catch (e) {
    return;
  }

  positions[socket.id] = pos;
});
```

Finally, when the user disconnects, you clear his position:

```
socket.on('close', function () {
  delete positions[socket.id];
});
```

What is missing here? Broadcasting, of course. When a position is received, you want to send it to everyone else. And when the socket closes, you want to notify everyone else that the user disconnected so his cursor is removed from the screen.

You declare a `broadcast` function to go through the rest of the clients and send them a message. Include it right after you register the ws `connection` listener:

```
function broadcast (msg) {
  for (var i = 0, l = ws.clients.length; i < l; i++) {
    // you avoid sending a message to the same socket that broadcasts
    if (ws.clients[i] && socket.id != ws.clients[i].id) {
      // you call 'send' on the other clients
      ws.clients[i].send(msg);
    }
  }
}
```

Because you have *two* distinct types of data to send, you send a small JSON packet with a `type` identifier.

When you relay a position, you send an object that looks like this:

```
{
    type: 'position'
  , pos: { x: <x>, y: <y> }
  , id: <socket id>
}
```

When a user disconnects, you send

```
{
    type: 'disconnect'
  , id: <socket id>
}
```

Therefore,

```
socket.on('message', function () {
  // . . .
  broadcast(JSON.stringify({ type: 'position', pos: pos, id: socket.id }));
});
```

And upon `close`, you send

```
socket.on('close', function () {
  // . . .
  broadcast(JSON.stringify({ type: 'disconnect', id: socket.id }));
});
```

Now you're done with the server and can move on to the client.

SETTING UP THE CLIENT

For the client, you start with a simple HTML document and an `onload` handler for the window in your index.html:

```
<!doctype html>
<html>
  <head>
    <title>WebSocket cursors</title>
    <script>
      window.onload = function () {
        var ws = new WebSocket('ws://localhost');
        // . . .
      }
    </script>
```

```
  </head>
  <body>
    <h1>WebSocket cursors</h1>
  </body>
</html>
```

For this task, you want to concentrate on the two main events: `open` and `message`.

When the connection first opens, you attach a `mousemove` handler to start relaying the cursor position to others:

```
ws.onopen = function () {
  document.onmousemove = function (ev) {
    ws.send(JSON.stringify({ x: ev.clientX, y: ev.clientY }));
  }
}
```

When a message is received, as you saw in the previous section, it can signal either someone's cursor moving or someone disconnecting:

```
// we instantiate a variable to keep track of initialization for this client
var initialized;

ws.onmessage = function (ev) {
    var obj = JSON.parse(ev.data);

  // the first message is the position of all existing cursors
  if (!initialized) {
    initialized = true;
    for (var id in obj) {
      move(id, obj[id]);
    }
  } else {
    // other messages can either be a position change or
    // a disconnection
    if ('disconnect' == obj.type) {
      remove(obj.id);
    } else {
      move(obj.id, obj.pos);
    }
  }
}
```

You then declare the functions `move` and `remove`.

For the `move` function, you first want to make sure the element for the cursor exists. You look for a DOM element with the ID `cursor-{id}`. If the element is missing, you create the image element and set the image URL and a basic style to make it float around.

Then you adjust its position on the screen:

```
function move (id, pos) {
  var cursor = document.getElementById('cursor-' + id);

  if (!cursor) {
    cursor = document.createElement('img');
    cursor.id = 'cursor-' + id;
    cursor.src = '/cursor.png';
    cursor.style.position = 'absolute';
    document.body.appendChild(cursor);
  }

  cursor.style.left = pos.x + 'px';
  cursor.style.top = pos.y + 'px';
}
```

For removing, you simply detach the element from the DOM:

```
function remove (id) {
  var cursor = document.getElementById('cursor-' + id);
  cursor.parentNode.removeChild(cursor);
}
```

RUNNING THE SERVER

As in the other example, all you need to do is run the server and point your browser to it. Make sure to open multiple tabs (shown in Figure 10-2) to fully experience the real-time interaction.

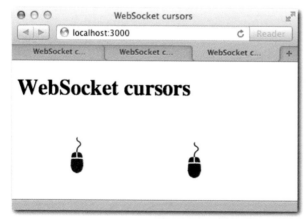

Figure 10-2: Several clients connected, relaying their cursor positions in real time.

cursor.png courtesy of http://thenounproject.com

THE CHALLENGES AHEAD

Even though you got the basic example functioning, these applications need some more work to become ready for real-world usage.

CLOSE DOESN'T MEAN DISCONNECT

When a `close` event fires on a WebSocket server or client, it means something specific: the TCP connection was appropriately close. In the real world, however, this is not always the case. Your computer can shut down unexpectedly, a network error can occur, or you spill a glass of water on your motherboard. In a lot of scenarios, `close` might never fire!

The solution for this problem is to rely on timeouts and heartbeats. For your application to handle these scenarios, you need to send dummy messages every number of seconds to make sure the client is alive and otherwise consider him forcefully disconnected.

JSON

As examples get more complicated, the variety of messages that the server and clients exchange increases.

The second example here relied heavily on encoding and decoding JSON packets manually. Because this is a common pattern in applications, that work should be done for you as part of another abstraction.

RECONNECTIONS

What happens if the client temporarily disconnects? Most applications try to get the user reconnected automatically. In these examples, if a disconnection occurs, the only way to reconnect is to refresh the browser.

BROADCASTING

Broadcasting is a common pattern in real-time applications where interaction with other clients is expected. You shouldn't need to define your own broadcasting mechanism manually.

WEBSOCKETS ARE HTML5: OLDER BROWSERS DON'T SUPPORT THEM

WebSocket is a recent technology. Many browsers, proxies, firewalls, and antivirus software are still not ready to work completely with this new protocol and way of communicating. A solution for older browsers is needed.

THE SOLUTION

Fortunately, all these problems have solutions. In the next chapter, you work with a module called `socket.io` whose goal is to fix all the aforementioned issues while retaining the simplicity and speed of WebSocket-based communication.

SUMMARY

You now understand the fundamentals of the WebSocket API and the WebSocket protocol, and how you can use Node.JS to leverage it for very fast message exchange. In the first example you familiarized yourself with its most basic usage.

You created a multi-user application that exhibits the strengths of WebSocket: its minimal framing allows for sending lots of short messages that arrive to other clients as fast as possible.

Finally, I described the weaknesses in terms of API and browser support that we can improve upon thanks to the socket.io framework, described in the next chapter.

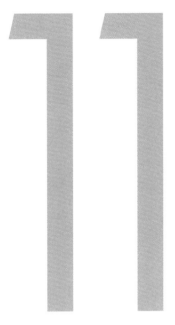

SOCKET.IO

AS MENTIONED PREVIOUSLY, getting WebSocket ready for your applications takes more than a simple implementation.

Socket.IO is a project I created that aims to solve the most common deficiencies of the simple implementation. It provides a great deal of flexibility while retaining a simple API:

Server API

```
io.listen(app);
io.sockets.on('connection', function
(socket) {
  socket.emit('my event', { my: 'object' });
});
```

Browser/Client API

```
var socket = io.connect();
socket.on('my event', function (obj) {
  console.log(obj.my);
});
```

TRANSPORTS

One of the most appealing features about Socket.IO is that communication is based on *transports*, not all of which are WebSocket, which means Socket.IO works on a large variety of browsers and devices, all the way from IE6 to iOS.

For example, you can utilize AJAX as a method for real-time communication when using a technique called *long polling*. Basically, this technique consists of making serial AJAX calls, but if the server doesn't have any data to send you, the connection stays open for 20–50 seconds so that no extra data transfer due to HTTP request/response headers occurs.

Socket.IO automatically leverages complex and convoluted techniques such as long polling for you, without making the API any more complicated than WebSocket.

In addition, even if WebSocket is supported by the browser but blocked by proxies or firewalls, Socket.IO can still handle that situation gracefully.

DISCONNECTED VERSUS CLOSED

Another fundamental feature that Socket.IO brings to the table is timeouts. As discussed in Chapters 6 and 10, an application that relies on perfectly closed TCP connections is not ready for real-world usage.

Throughout your use of Socket.IO in this chapter, you listen on `connect` events instead of `open`, and `disconnect` instead of `close`. The reason is that Socket.IO provides *reliable* events. If the client stops transmitting data but doesn't properly close the connection after a certain amount of time elapses, Socket.IO considers him disconnected.

This approach allows you to focus on the core of your application logic instead of all the possible different hiccups of networks.

Socket.IO also takes care of reconnecting when the connection is lost, which happens automatically by default.

EVENTS

So far you saw that typical communication on the web has been oriented around retrieving (requesting) documents (resources) over HTTP. The real-time web, however, is about the transmission of *events*.

Even though Socket.IO still allows you to transmit simple text back and forth like WebSocket, it also enables you to *emit* and *listen* on events that send JSON data back and forth In the following example you can see Socket.IO acting as as reliable WebSocket:

```
io.sockets.on('connection', function (socket) {
  socket.send('a');
  socket.on('message', function (msg) {
```

```
      console.log(msg);
   });
});
```

If you were to re-imagine the cursor example from Chapter 10 with Socket.IO, the application code would be greatly simplified:

Client code

```
var socket = io.connect();

socket.on('position', move);

socket.on('remove', remove);
```

Notice that instead of having to parse the incoming strings of a single event (message), we can channel data according to its meaning within the applications. Events can receive any number of parameters in any of the types JSON encodes: `Number`, `Array`, `String`, `Object`, and so on.

NAMESPACES

Another powerful feature that Socket.IO offers is the ability to separate a single connection into *namespaces* that are isolated from each other.

Sometimes your application requires separation of logic into distinct parts, but for performance or speed reasons it's still desirable to leverage the same connection. Considering you can't make assumptions about how fast the clients are or how capable their browsers are, it's usually a good idea to not rely on too many open connections simultaneously.

Therefore, Socket.IO allows you to listen on the `connection` event of multiple namespaces:

```
io.sockets.on('connection');
io.of('/some/namespace').on('connection')
io.of('/some/other/namespace').on('connection')
```

Even though you'll get different connection objects, when you connect from the browser like in the following example, a single transport (like a WebSocket connection) will be used:

```
var socket = io.connect();
var socket2 = io.connect('/some/namespace');
var socket3 = io.connect('/some/other/namespace');
```

In some cases, modules or parts of your application are written in such a way that for the sake of abstraction are completely isolated from the rest. Some part of your client side JavaScript codebase might be completely unaware of another that's executing in parallel.

For example, you could build a social network that displays a real time chat program alongside a farming game. Even though they could both share some common data, such as the identity of the authenticated user, it would be a good idea to write them in a way that they both assume complete control of a socket.

That socket, thanks to the namespaces (also called *multiplexing*) feature, does not necessarily have to be its own allocated actual TCP socket. Socket.IO takes care of channeling data through the same resource (the chosen transport for that user) and passing the data to the appropriate callbacks.

Now that you've learned the major differences between Socket.IO and WebSocket, you're ready for the first example application, a chat program.

A CHAT PROGRAM

SETTING UP THE PROGRAM

In the same fashion as `websocket.io`, you make `socket.io` attach itself to a regular `http.Server` that can still handle the requests and responses for your application:

package.json

```
{
    "name": "chat.io"
  , "version": "0.0.1"
  , "dependencies": {

        "express": "2.5.1"
      , "socket.io": "0.9.2"
    }
}
```

As usual, once you create the `package.json` file make sure to run `npm install` to fetch all the dependencies.

SETTING UP THE SERVER

As with `websocket.io`, you set up a normal Express app with the `static` middleware:

server.js

```
/**
 * Module dependencies.
 */

var express = require('express')
  , sio = require('socket.io')
```

```
/**
 * Create app.
 */

app = express.createServer(
    express.bodyParser()
, express.static('public')
);

/**
 * Listen.
 */

app.listen(3000);
```

Now it's time to attach `socket.io`. You call `sio.listen` in the same fashion as you do with `websocket.io`:

```
var io = sio.listen(app);
```

Now you can set up the connection's listener:

```
io.sockets.on('connection', function (socket) {
  console.log('Someone connected');
});
```

For now, you can simply output to the console whenever someone connects. Because Socket. IO is a custom API, you have to load the Socket.IO client on the browser.

SETTING UP THE CLIENT

Because you added the static middleware for the `public` folder, you need to create a file `index.html` inside.

This time, for the sake of convenience, keep the chat logic separate from the markup, into its own file called `chat.js`.

One of the handy aspects of Socket.IO is that when it appends itself to `http.Server`, all the communication that happens to URLs that begin with `/socket.io` are intercepted.

Socket.IO therefore also takes care of exposing the client code to the browser out of the box. Consequently, you don't have to worry about obtaining and serving the file manually.

Notice that in the following example you create a `<script>` tag that references `/socket.io/socket.io.js`:

index.html

```
<!doctype html>
<html>
  <head>
    <title>Socket.IO chat</title>
    <script src="/socket.io/socket.io.js"></script>
    <script src="/chat.js"></script>
    <link href="/chat.css" rel="stylesheet" />
  </head>
  <body>
    <div id="chat">
      <ul id="messages"></ul>
      <form id="form">
        <input type="text" id="input" />
        <button>Send</button>
      </form>
    </div>
  </body>
</html>
```

For now, `chat.js` is going to connect to make sure the client loaded properly. If everything goes well, you should be see the output `Someone connected` in the console.

chat.js

```
window.onload = function () {
  var socket = io.connect();
}
```

All the functions and classes exposed by the Socket.IO client are contained in the `io` namespace.

`io.connect` is similar to `new WebSocket`, but smarter. In this case, because you are not passing any arguments to it, it attempts to connect to the same host that is loading the page, which is a desirable behavior for this example.

You run this application normally with

```
$ node server
```

Then you point your browser to `http://localhost:3000`. You should see the output from the Socket.IO logger regarding what's going on underneath the hood; for example, you can see what transport in particular this client is using (see Figure 11-1).

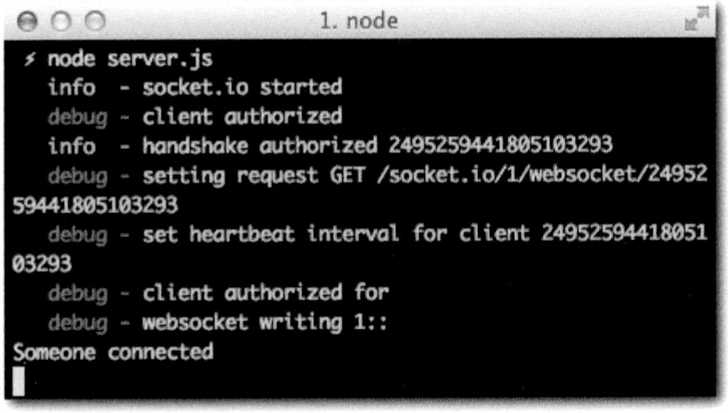

Figure 11-1: Debug output from socket.io along with the message you print with console.log

If you connect from a modern browser, as in this example, Socket.IO is likely able to connect and then upgrade the connection to WebSocket.

Socket.IO always tries to find a method for connection that is faster for the user and performs best for your server, but it always ensures a connection despite adverse conditions.

EVENTS AND BROADCASTING

Now that you have successfully connected, it's time to identify the fundamental pieces of the Socket.IO server.

Broadcasting upon join

Whenever a user connects, you want to notify everyone else that she did. Because this is going to be a special message not sent by anyone in particular, you can call this an *announcement* and style it accordingly.

The first thing to do from the client perspective is to ask what the user's name is.

Because you want to disallow any interaction with the chat until the user is actually connected, you need to hide the chat:

chat.css

```
/* … */
#chat { display: none }
```

Then you show it upon connection. To this end, you are going to listen on the `connect` event on the created socket (within the `window.onload` function you defined earlier):

chat.js

```
socket.on('connect', function () {
  // send a join event with your name
  socket.emit('join', prompt('What is your nickname?'));

  // show the chat
  document.getElementById('chat').style.display = 'block';
});
```

On the server, you are going to listen on the `join` event to notify all others that the user connected. Replace the previous io.sockets connection handler with the following:

server.js

```
// ...
io.sockets.on('connection', function (socket) {
  socket.on('join', function (name) {
    socket.nickname = name;
    socket.broadcast.emit('announcement', name + ' joined the chat.');
  });
});
```

Focus your attention on `socket.broadcast.emit`. `broadcast` is called a *flag*, which alters the behavior of the function that follows it.

In this case, if you simply call `socket.emit`, you echo back the message. But what you really want to do is *broadcast* that message to everyone else, which is what adding the flag accomplishes.

On the client, you are going to listen on the announcement event and create an element in the list of messages in the DOM. Add this at the bottom of the `connect` handler:

chat.js

```
socket.on('announcement', function (msg) {
  var li = document.createElement('li');
  li.className = 'announcement';
  li.innerHTML = msg;
  document.getElementById('messages').appendChild(li);
});
```

Broadcasting chat messages

Next, you can give users the ability to write a message that gets sent to everyone else.

When a user enters data into the form and submits it, you are going to emit a `text` event with its content:

chat.js

```
var input = document.getElementById('input');
document.getElementById('form').onsubmit = function () {
  socket.emit('text', input.value);

  // reset the input
  input.value = '';
  input.focus();

  return false;
}
```

Because obviously the user wrote the message, you don't want the server to send it back to himself. So you call the function `addMessage` immediately to display the message as soon as it's sent:

chat.js

```
function addMessage (from, text) {
  var li = document.createElement('li');
  li.className = 'message';
  li.innerHTML = '<b>' + from + '</b>: ' + text;
  document.getElementById('messages').appendChild(li);
}
document.getElementById('form').onsubmit = function () {
  addMessage('me', input.value);
  // . . .
}
```

You want to do the same thing when you receive messages from others. Here, you can simply pass the reference to the `addMessage` function and ensure that from the server side you broadcast the message with the right parameters:

chat.js

```
// …
socket.on('text', addMessage);
```

server.js

```
socket.on('text', function (msg) {
  socket.broadcast.emit('text', socket.nickname, msg);
});
```

The code so far for each file should roughly look as follows:

chat.js

```javascript
window.onload = function () {
  var socket = io.connect();
  socket.on('connect', function () {
    // send a join event with your name
    socket.emit('join', prompt('What is your nickname?'));

    // show the chat
    document.getElementById('chat').style.display = 'block';

    socket.on('announcement', function (msg) {
      var li = document.createElement('li');
      li.className = 'announcement';
      li.innerHTML = msg;
      document.getElementById('messages').appendChild(li);
    });
  });

  function addMessage (from, text) {
    var li = document.createElement('li');
    li.className = 'message';
    li.innerHTML = '<b>' + from + '</b>: ' + text;
    document.getElementById('messages').appendChild(li);
  }

  var input = document.getElementById('input');
  document.getElementById('form').onsubmit = function () {
    addMessage('me', input.value);
    socket.emit('text', input.value);

    // reset the input
    input.value = '';
    input.focus();

    return false;
  }

  socket.on('text', addMessage);
}
```

server.js

```javascript
/**
 * Module dependencies.
 */

var express = require('express')
```

```
  , sio = require('socket.io')

/**
 * Create app.
 */

app = express.createServer(
    express.bodyParser()
  , express.static('public')
);

/**
 * Listen.
 */

app.listen(3000);

var io = sio.listen(app);

io.sockets.on('connection', function (socket) {
  socket.on('join', function (name) {
    socket.nickname = name;
    socket.broadcast.emit('announcement', name + ' joined the chat.');
  });

  socket.on('text', function (msg) {
    socket.broadcast.emit('text', socket.nickname, msg);
  });
});
```

If you run `server.js`, you should now have a completely functioning real time chat application, like the one shown in Figure 11-2..

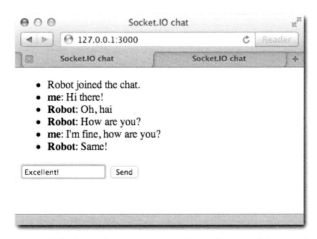

Figure 11-2: The chat application in action. Here chatting from multiple browser tabs.

Next up, you'll learn about callbacks for events, and how they can help you add a new feature.

ENSURING RECEPTION

In the chat example, you call `addMessage` immediately upon the user pressing Enter, therefore creating the illusion that everyone else is seeing the message at that exact instant.

And just like WebSocket, Socket.IO does not *enforce* responses for each message you send. Sometimes, however, the need for confirmation that a message was received arises. Socket.IO calls this type of confirmation an *acknowledgment*.

To implement acknowledgments, all you have to do is pass a function whenever you're emitting an event.

First, you're going to return a reference to the element you create in the `addMessage` function so that you can append a CSS class to it after the message is confirmed as received. Then you can display a nice icon next to it.

/chat.js

```
function addMessage (from, text) {
  // ...
  return li;
}
```

Next, you add the callback. Socket.IO can also receive *data* along with these acknowledgments. For this example, you can send a timestamp indicating when the message was received:

/chat.js

```
document.getElementById('form').onsubmit = function () {
  var li = addMessage('me', input.value);
  socket.emit('text', input.value, function (date) {
    li.className = 'confirmed';
    li.title = date;
  });
```

On the server side, Socket.IO appends a callback as the last parameter of the event:

/server.js/

```
// ...
socket.on('text', function (msg, fn) {
  // ...
  // confirm the reception
  fn(Date.now());
});
```

Now, when the server acknowledges that it received your message, a class will be added and the `title` attribute will be set for the appended list item. This brings the best of both worlds: the application has maximum responsiveness since it shows the message as soon as you press Enter, but you can still give feedback to the user through CSS (for example, by adding an icon next to the message, such as the encircled check mark in Figure 11-3.

Figure 11-3: In this example I set a CSS background after the acknowledgement is received.

A DJ-BY-TURNS APPLICATION

How cool would it be if you empowered the users of your chat application to be DJs?

- The server starts by selecting a DJ.
- The DJ is given the ability to query an API, get search results, and select a song. He can then broadcast the song to others.
- When the DJ leaves, he leaves the spot open for the next user to be elected DJ.

EXTENDING THE CHAT

The foundations of the chat application are solid enough to add this functionality to it.

The first thing to do is select a DJ if none is selected. Since you also want to keep track of the current song, you'll define two state variables: `currentSong` and `dj`.

Since the DJ can change, you'll define an `elect` function that performs the DJ selection task and announcements. When the `join` event is emitted, a DJ can be elected or the current song (`currentSong`) is relayed to the user. Later, when you implement search, `currentSong` is going to be populated with an object.

server.js

```
var io = sio.listen(app)
, currentSong
  , dj

function elect (socket) {
  dj = socket;
  io.sockets.emit('announcement', socket.nickname + ' is the new dj');
  socket.emit('elected');
  socket.dj = true;
  socket.on('disconnect', function () {
    dj = null;
    io.sockets.emit('announcement', 'the dj left - next one to join becomes dj');
  });
}

io.sockets.on('connection', function (socket) {
  socket.on('join', function (name) {
    socket.nickname = name;
    socket.broadcast.emit('announcement', name + ' joined the chat.');
    if (!dj) {
      elect(socket);
    } else {
      socket.emit('song', currentSong);
    }
  });
  // …
});
```

The `elect` function does the following:

1. Mark the current user as the DJ
2. Emit an announcement to everyone that a new DJ is ready.
3. Let the user know that she has been elected by emitting an `elected` event.
4. Upon the user being disconnected, mark the DJ spot as available so that the next connection becomes the DJ.

In the client, add the song selection interface to the markup, under the chat form:

index.html

```
<div id="playing"></div>
<form id="dj">
  <h3>Search songs</h3>
  <input type="text" id="s" />
  <ul id="results"></ul>
  <button type=submit>Search</button>
</form>
```

INTEGRATING WITH THE GROOVESHARK API

Grooveshark (http://grooveshark.com) offers a simple and handy API for your purposes; it's called TinySong.

TinySong allows a search like this:

```
GET http://tinysong.com/s/Beethoven?key={apiKey}&format=json
```

And it returns results like these:

```
[
  {
    "Url": "http:\/\/tinysong.com\/7Wm7",
    "SongID": 8815585,
    "SongName": "Moonlight Sonata",
    "ArtistID": 1833,
    "ArtistName": "Beethoven",
    "AlbumID": 258724,
    "AlbumName": "Beethoven"
  },
  {
    "Url": "http:\/\/tinysong.com\/6Jk3",
    "SongID": 564004,
    "SongName": "Fur Elise",
    "ArtistID": 1833,
    "ArtistName": "Beethoven",
    "AlbumID": 268605,
    "AlbumName": "Beethoven"
  },
  {
    "Url": "http:\/\/tinysong.com\/8We2",
    "SongID": 269743,
    "SongName": "The Legend Of Lil' Beethoven",
    "ArtistID": 7620,
    "ArtistName": "Sparks",
    "AlbumID": 204019,
    "AlbumName": "Sparks"
  }
]
```

You therefore expose a Socket.IO event called `search` that leverages the `superagent` module to query the API and return the results.

Add the superagent module to package.json and the module dependencies:

server.js

```
var express = require('express')
  , sio = require('socket.io')
  , request = require('superagent')
```

package.json

```
  , "dependencies": {
        "express": "2.5.1"
      , "socket.io": "0.9.2"
      , "superagent": "0.4.0"
    }
```

Notice that you have to include your own API key as part of the URL, which you can get on the website http://tinysong.com:

Define the `apiKey` as follows:

server.js

```
var io = sio.listen(app)
  , apiKey = '{ your API key }'
  , currentSong
  , dj
```

And then define the search event:

```
socket.on('search', function (q, fn) {
    request('http://tinysong.com/s/' + encodeURIComponent(q)
        + '?key=' + apiKey + '&format=json', function (res) {
        if (200 == res.status) fn(JSON.parse(res.text));
    });});
```

Notice that I'm manually parsing the JSON response. This is due to a `TinySong` not currently sending the right `Content-Type` response header, which makes superagent's automatic JSON parsing not be enabled.

To make things more fun in the application, you're going to make the search available to everyone, but only the `Select` functionality available to the DJ.

In the `chat.css` file, add these two lines:

```
#results a { display: none; }
form.isDJ #results a { display: inline; }
```

Then you're going to add the logic to make the search, get the results back through a Socket. IO callback and relay the song choice to everyone.

In the chat.js file, add the following:

```
// search form
var form = document.getElementById('dj');
var results = document.getElementById('results');
form.style.display = 'block';
form.onsubmit = function () {
  results.innerHTML = '';
  socket.emit('search', document.getElementById('s').value, function (songs) {
    for (var i = 0, l = songs.length; i < l; i++) {
      (function (song) {
        var result = document.createElement('li');
        result.innerHTML = song.ArtistName + ' - <b>' + song.SongName + '</b> ';
        var a = document.createElement('a');
        a.href = '#';
        a.innerHTML = 'Select';
        a.onclick = function () {
          socket.emit('song', song);
          return false;
        }
        result.appendChild(a);
        results.appendChild(result);
      })(songs[i]);
    }
  });
  return false;
};

socket.on('elected', function () {
  form.className = 'isDJ';
});
```

Most of the code is centered around DOM manipulation. Since the server relays all the songs from the TinyURL API, you are free to render it however you want. In this case I decided to show the song's band next to the song's name (ArtistName and SongName keys, respectively).

When the elected event is received, you change form's className to reveal the links to select a given song.

Upon clicking the Select link, you send a song event to the server, whose job is simply going to be marking the current song and broadcasting it. In server.js add the following event:

server.js

```
socket.on('song', function (song) {
  if (socket.dj) {
    currentSong = song;
    socket.broadcast.emit('song', song);
  }
});
```

Now that users have the ability to search and relay songs, all that's left to add is the ability to play them. That's what we reserved the <div id=playing> element for.

PLAYING

Just like you did with the addMessage function, you're going to define one to mark the current song being played.

Add the following code to chat.js. It simply renders the song's band and title next to the text Now Playing, and it injects an iframe that points to the Url field that TinySong gave you to play the song.

```
var playing = document.getElementById('playing');
function play (song) {
  if (!song) return;
  playing.innerHTML = '<hr><b>Now Playing: </b> '
    + song.ArtistName + ' ' + song.SongName + '<br>';

  var iframe = document.createElement('iframe');
  iframe.frameborder = 0;
  iframe.src = song.Url;
  playing.appendChild(iframe);
};
```

You want to use, once again, this function in two situations: as soon as the DJ selects a song (for himself), and when the song event is relayed to a regular user by the DJ.

For the second case, you simply pass the new play function as the callback to the song event in chat.js:

```
socket.on('song', play);
```

For the DJ to start listening immediately, you want to call play as soon as he selects it. Go back to the onclick handler where you emit the song event to the server and add call play, so that the handler looks as follows:

```
a.onclick = function () {
  socket.emit('song', song);
```

```
            play(song);
            return false;
        }
```

And you're done!. If you recall from the initial addition to the `join` event on the server-side, the `song` event gets emitted if there's a `currentSong` on the server side. This means that the song will start playing not just for users that were connected at the time of its selection by the DJ, but also new users joining the room after they select their nickname (see Figure 11-4).

The final code for the complete Chat + DJ application should look roughly as follows:

server.js

```
var express = require('express')
  , sio = require('socket.io')
  , request = require('superagent')

app = express.createServer(
    express.bodyParser()
  , express.static('public')
);

app.listen(3000);

var io = sio.listen(app)
  , apiKey = '{ your API key }'
  , currentSong
  , dj

function elect (socket) {
  dj = socket;
  io.sockets.emit('announcement', socket.nickname + ' is the new dj');
  socket.emit('elected');
  socket.dj = true;
  socket.on('disconnect', function () {
    dj = null;
    io.sockets.emit('announcement', 'the dj left - next one to join becomes dj');
  });
}

io.sockets.on('connection', function (socket) {
  socket.on('join', function (name) {
    socket.nickname = name;
    socket.broadcast.emit('announcement', name + ' joined the chat.');
    if (!dj) {
      elect(socket);
    } else {
      socket.emit('song', currentSong);
    }
  });
```

continued

server.js   (continued)

```
  socket.on('song', function (song) {
    if (socket.dj) {
      currentSong = song;
      socket.broadcast.emit('song', song);
    }
  });

  socket.on('search', function (q, fn) {
    request('http://tinysong.com/s/' + encodeURIComponent(q)
      + '?key=' + apiKey + '&format=json', function (res) {
      if (200 == res.status) fn(JSON.parse(res.text));
    });
  });

  socket.on('text', function (msg) {
    socket.broadcast.emit('text', socket.nickname, msg);
  });
});
```

chat.js

```
window.onload = function () {
  var socket = io.connect();
  socket.on('connect', function () {
    // send a join event with your name
    socket.emit('join', prompt('What is your nickname?'));

    // show the chat
    document.getElementById('chat').style.display = 'block';

    socket.on('announcement', function (msg) {
      var li = document.createElement('li');
      li.className = 'announcement';
      li.innerHTML = msg;
      document.getElementById('messages').appendChild(li);
    });
  });

  function addMessage (from, text) {
    var li = document.createElement('li');
    li.className = 'message';
    li.innerHTML = '<b>' + from + '</b>: ' + text;
    document.getElementById('messages').appendChild(li);
  }

  var input = document.getElementById('input');
  document.getElementById('form').onsubmit = function () {
    addMessage('me', input.value);
    socket.emit('text', input.value);
```

```
  // reset the input
  input.value = '';
  input.focus();

  return false;
}

socket.on('text', addMessage);

// plays a song
var playing = document.getElementById('playing');
function play (song) {
  if (!song) return;
  playing.innerHTML = '<hr><b>Now Playing: </b> '
    + song.ArtistName + ' ' + song.SongName + '<br>';

  var iframe = document.createElement('iframe');
  iframe.frameborder = 0;
  iframe.src = song.Url;
  playing.appendChild(iframe);
};
socket.on('song', play);

// search form
var form = document.getElementById('dj');
var results = document.getElementById('results');
form.style.display = 'block';
form.onsubmit = function () {
  results.innerHTML = '';
  socket.emit('search', document.getElementById('s').value, function (songs) {
    for (var i = 0, l = songs.length; i < l; i++) {
      (function (song) {
        var result = document.createElement('li');
        result.innerHTML = song.ArtistName + ' - <b>' + song.SongName + '</b> ';
        var a = document.createElement('a');
        a.href = '#';
        a.innerHTML = 'Select';
        a.onclick = function () {
          socket.emit('song', song);
          play(song);
          return false;
        }
        result.appendChild(a);
        results.appendChild(result);
      })(songs[i]);
    }
  });
  return false;
};
```

continued

chat.js (continued)

```
socket.on('elected', function () {
  form.className = 'isDJ';
});
}
```

index.html

```html
<!doctype html>
<html>
  <head>
    <title>Socket.IO chat</title>
    <script src="/socket.io/socket.io.js"></script>
    <script src="/chat.js"></script>
    <link href="/chat.css" rel="stylesheet" />
  </head>
  <body>
    <div id="chat">
      <ul id="messages"></ul>
      <form id="form">
        <input type="text" id="input" />
        <button>Send</button>
      </form>
      <div id="playing"></div>

      <form id="dj">
        <h3>Search songs</h3>
        <input type="text" id="s" />
        <ul id="results"></ul>
        <button>Search</button>
      </form>
    </div>
  </body>
</html>
```

Figure 11-4: The DJ+Chat application in action

SUMMARY

Socket.IO is a really simple but extremely powerful API to build applications that communicate data back-and-forth really fast, in real time. Socket.IO gives you the confidence that this data exchange happens not only as fast as possible, but also that it works on every browser and lots of mobile devices.

During this chapter you learned how to structure a really simple application that takes advantage of some of the API sugar it provides. You leveraged events as a way of organizing the different type of information that's sent back and forth between users and the server.

A fundamental part of writing real time applications is broadcasting. You learned how to convey an event to everyone in the server, but also how to have one person convey something to everyone else. You used this technique, for example, to enable a DJ to announce what song is currently playing to everyone else.

One thing to keep in mind is that a lot of the functionality is contained in the client side: you need to have code ready to restructure the interface according to the variety of events that can happen. Since this chapter focuses solely on Socket.IO, I made sure to stay away from templating libraries or higher-level frameworks that can be leveraged on the client-side and worked on top of the DOM APIs directly, but in the real world this can get quite complicated as the application grows.

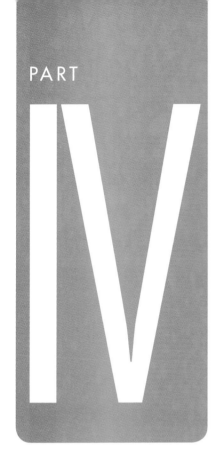

PART

IV

DATABASES

12

MONGODB

MONGODB IS A *document-oriented, schema-less* database that has been shown to fit in really well with Node.JS applications and cloud deployments.

One of its most interesting features is that unlike MySQL or PostgreSQL, which store data in *tables* that are generally fixed in their design (*schema*), MongoDB can store documents *of any kind* in collections (*schema-less*).

For example, say you create a table that holds the user profiles of a web application:

First	Last	Email	Twitter
Guillermo	Rauch	rauchg@gmail.com	rauchg

When you build your application, you *decide* your users' information will be structured around this particular design. You expect to have one or more of the following: first name, last name, email, and Twitter ID.

As applications evolve, business needs change, or as time passes and new needs arise, you might need to add or remove some of those columns.

The fundamental problem, however, with the way most traditional (SQL) databases are optimized to work is that it's very *expensive* to make changes to the table design, both operationally and in terms of performance.

Every time you need to make a change to that design, in MySQL, for example, you need to run a command to add a column:

```
$ mysql
  > ALTER TABLE profiles ADD COLUMN . . .
```

And the same occurs if you remove one or more columns.

With MongoDB, you can think of your data as *documents* that are flexible in their design. And, as it happens, these documents are stored in a format that resembles JSON *very closely* (or *completely, for most purposes*):

```
{
    "name": "Guillermo"
  , "last": "Rauch"
  , "email": "rauchg@gmail.com"
  , "age": 21
  , "twitter": "rauchg"
}
```

Another important characteristic of MongoDB that sets it apart from most NoSQL databases that are key-value is that documents can have arbitrary *depth*.

For example, instead of adding all the possible social networks as keys of your document, you can store them as a data structure within:

```
{
    "name": "Guillermo"
  , "last": "Rauch"
```

```
  , "email": "rauchg@gmail.com"
  , "age": 21
  , "social_networks": {
        "twitter": "rauchg"
      , "facebook": "rauchg@gmail.com"
      , "linkedin": 27760647
    }
}
```

As you can see, you are also free to combine *data types*. Here, `twitter` and `facebook` are both strings, but `linkedin` is a number. When you obtain that document from Node.JS, the data types you get are truthful to the stored ones.

As this chapter unfolds, it examines most of the commonly used capabilities of MongoDB and looks at the best patterns to achieve the most *long-term flexibility* and *maximum performance* (through indexing). You also learn ways to query documents in different ways and simplify its usage through Mongoose, a Node.JS module I co-created with Nathan White that brings some of the features of traditional database ORMs (Object-Relational Mappers) to the MongoDB and JavaScript world. A term that's increasingly common to refer to this type of project is ODM: Object Document Mapper.

INSTALLATION

It's important for this chapter that you install the latest version of MongoDB available in the 2.x branch.

You can obtain MongoDB through the downloads area of the website: www.mongodb.org/downloads. In addition, you might want to take a quick look at the Quickstart guide available for every platform we cover in this book here: www.mongodb.org/display/DOCS/Quickstart

You can make sure it's running by executing the `mongo` client, which should look like Figure 12-1.

Figure 12-1: The MongoDB shell

If you are not able to access MongoDB, review your installation and ensure that the MongoDB server (`mongod`) is running by looking at your system's process manager.

ACCESSING MONGODB: A USER AUTHENTICATION EXAMPLE

The most essential way of accessing MongoDB documents through Node.JS is with a *driver*. What is normally called a driver in Node.JS is a basic API that understands the *protocol* of the network access layer of the database and how to *encode and decode* the data that it stores.

The project of choice is called node-mongodb-native, created by Christian Amor Kvalheim. You can find it on the Node Package Manager (NPM) with the name mongodb.

For the first example, you create a simple Express application that stores users' information in MongoDB and allows you to log in and sign up.

SETTING UP THE APPLICATION

You create your `package.json` with the dependencies for the project. In this case, they're simply `express` and `mongodb`. In addition, for the templates, you use `jade`:

```
{
    "name": "user-auth-example"
  , "version": "0.0.1"
  , "dependencies": {
        "express": "2.5.8"
      , "mongodb": "0.9.9"
      , "jade": "0.20.3"
    }
}
```

CREATING THE EXPRESS APP

You start by requiring your dependencies as you normally do using `require`:

```
/**
 * Module dependencies
 */

var express = require('express')
  , mongodb = require('mongodb')
```

This application deals with *form processing*, so you are going to implement the `bodyParser` middleware.

Because you also want to authenticate users and retain that information, you also leverage the session middleware (which depends on the `cookieParser` Connect middleware, as explained in Chapter 8).

```
/**
 * Set up application.
```

```
 */

app = express.createServer()

/**
 * Middleware.
 */

app.use(express.bodyParser());
app.use(express.cookieParser());
app.use(express.session({ secret: 'my secret' }));
```

Because the template engine of choice for this example is `jade`, you set the `view engine` Express configuration flag:

```
/**
 * Specify your views options.
 */

app.set('view engine', 'jade');

// the following line won't be needed in express 3


app.set('view options', { layout: false });
```

By default, the folder where the views are located is `views/`. You create it and create a layout template that surrounds all your views called layout.jade:

```
doctype 5
html
  head
    title MongoDB example
  body
    h1 My first MongoDB app
    hr
    block body
```

Even though it's not the scope of this chapter, it's important to learn a few things about jade, as it's one of the most prevalent template engines in the Node.JS world:

- Instead of using complicated nested XML or HTML tags, jade leverages indentation (by default of two spaces, you should refrain from using tabs). Therefore this code:

  ```
  p
      span Hello world
  ```

  Is equivalent to `<p><span>Hello world</span></p>`.

- Instead of writing `<h1>My first MongoDB app</h1>` you wrote the tag name first followed by its content `h1 My First MongoDB app`.

You used `doctype` 5 to automatically insert the HTML5 doctype

- You used a special keyword `block` so that other files can fill in that block. That's why you call this file the *layout*. Other special keywords include `if` and `else`

- Attributes look like HTML and JavaScript mixed together, and it's easy to embed variables (or locals, as express calls the variables exposed from a controller):

  ```
  a(href=#, another=attribute, dynamic=someVariable) My link
  ```

- You can embed variables in the content with the interpolation syntax

  ```
  p Welcome back, #{user.name}
  ```

You then define the routes. You have a homepage route (`/`) plus signup (`/signup`) and login (`/login`) routes:

```
/**
 * Default route
 */

app.get('/', function (req, res) {
  res.render('index', { authenticated: false });
});

/**
 * Login route
 */

app.get('/login', function (req, res) {
  res.render('login');
});

/**
 * Signup route
 */

app.get('/signup', function (req, res) {
  res.render('signup');
});
```

In the homepage route (`/`), you pass a local `authenticated` with the value of `false`. You populate this variable after you implement the login functionality.

You leverage it in the `index` template:

index.jade

```
extends layout
block body
if (authenticated)
  p Welcome back, #{me.first}
  a(href="/logout") Logout
```

```
else
  p Welcome new visitor!
  ul
    li: a(href="/login") Login
    li: a(href="/signup") Signup
```

The signup and login views (see Figure 12-2) are simple semantic forms:

signup.jade

```
extends layout
block body
form(action="/signup", method="POST")
  fieldset
    legend Sign up
    p
      label First
      input(name="user[first]", type="text")
    p
      label Last
      input(name="user[last]", type="text")
    p
      label Email
      input(name="user[email]", type="text")
    p
      label Password
      input(name="user[password]", type="password")
    p
      button Submit
    p
      a(href="/") Go back
```

login.jade

```
extends layout
block body
form(action="/login", method="POST")
  fieldset
    legend Log in
    p
      label Email
      input(name="user[email]", type="text")
    p
      label Password
      input(name="user[password]", type="password")
    p
      button Submit
    p
      a(href="/") Go back
```

You finally make the application listen:

```
/**
 * Listen
 */

app.listen(3000);
```

And if you point your browser, you should be able to navigate through all the routes with ease.

Figure 12-2: The /signup route

CONNECTING TO MONGODB

Before you proceed to *find* documents (for login) and *insert* documents (for signup), you need to connect to the MongoDB server and select the database.

And you want to do so even before you make the server listen. Because the logic of the application depends completely on the database, it wouldn't make sense to allow requests to come in before you're ready to query data for them.

Because you're using the MongoDB driver directly, the API is verbose. The goal, however, is to expose the MongoDB collection API as app.users so that any route can access it easily.

You first initialize the server by creating a mongodb.Server and supplying an IP and port:

```
/**
 * Connect to the database.
 */

var server = new mongodb.Server('127.0.0.1', 27017)
```

You then tell the driver to connect to the database. For this example, call it `my-website`. In MongoDB, if a certain name you pick doesn't exist, it creates the database for you.

```
new mongodb.Db('my-website', server).open(function (err, client) {
```

If you can't connect, you want to abort the process:

```
  // don't allow the app to start if there was an error
  if (err) throw err;
```

You print out if you succeed:

```
  console.log('\033[96m  + \033[39m connected to mongodb');
```

Then you set up the collection:

```
  // set up collection shortcuts
  app.users = new mongodb.Collection(client, 'users');
```

And finally you make Express ready to take in connections:

```
  // listen
  app.listen(3000, function () {
    console.log('\033[96m  + \033[39m app listening on *:3000');
  });
});
```

If you run the application (always ensuring your database is running as well), the output should now look like this:

```
$ node server.js
  +  connected to mongodb
  +  app listening on *:3000
```

If you go to the `mongo` client again and run `show log global`, you should , as illustrated in Figure 12-3, see your connection!

```
$ mongo
> show log global;
[. . .]
{date} [initandlisten] connection accepted from 127.0.0.1:53649 #16
```

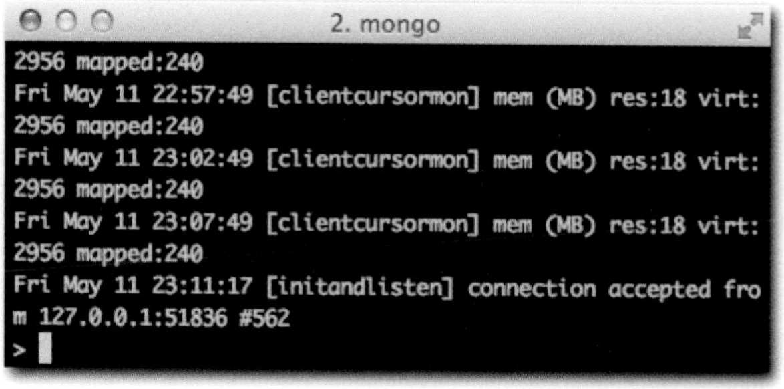

Figure 12-3: As you can see in the last log line, Mongo gets a connection from your local web server

CREATING DOCUMENTS

The API for insertion is simple. You simply call `Collection#insert` by supplying the document and a callback. As with most callbacks in Node, the first parameter is an error, and in this case, the second one is an array of the inserted documents:

```
collection.insert({ my: 'document' }, function (err, docs) {
  // . . .
});
```

An additional `options` object is an optional second parameter, which you look at later.

If you look at the signup form again, you can see that the input names follow this format: `user[field]`. For example:

```
input(name="user[name]", type="text")
```

When `bodyParser` encounters that format, as you can see, it exposes the field as `req.body.user.name`.

This functionality is particularly handy for you because you can insert the document directly into MongoDB. For the sake of this example, skip data validation (which is very important).

The signup processing route is thus very simple:

```
/**
 * Signup processing route
 */

app.post('/signup', function (req, res, next) {
  app.users.insert(req.body.user, function (err, doc) {
    if (err) return next(err);
    res.redirect('/login/' + doc[0].email);
  });
});
```

If an error occurs, you want to make sure to `next` it so that you can display an `"Error 500"` page. Although infrequent, errors occur and it's important that the application always deals with them.

A common gotcha is to forget to `return` after taking care of the error. That mistake could end up producing unexpected behavior in the application. For example, in this situation if an error occurs, the `doc` variable is `undefined`, and the code throws an uncaught exception.

After a successful insertion, you redirect to the login route supplying the email.

In the login route, you capture this *parameter* and expose it to the view:

```
/**
 * Login route
 */

app.get('/login/:signupEmail', function (req, res) {
  res.render('login', { signupEmail: req.params.signupEmail });
});
```

In the view, you display a message:

```
if (signupEmail)
  p Congratulations on signing up! Please login below.
```

Then you prepopulate the email input:

```
input(name="user[email]", type="text", value=signupEmail)
```

Now launch the application and try signing up! If you launch the `mongo` client and run the `find` command on the new collection, you should see the document(s) you created:

```
 Brian: in the mongo client things appear like this$ mongo my-website
> db.users.find()
{ "first" : "A", "last" : "B", "email" : "a@b.com", "password" : "d", "_id" : Object
  Id("4ef2cbd77bb50163a7000001") }
```

Notice that the document looks identical to what you expected, with minimal effort on your part. In addition, Mongo adds an `_id` field automatically that lets you uniquely identify your document. Handy!

FINDING DOCUMENTS

Now that you have created a document, you can look it up in the `/login` route. Essentially, you want to retrieve the document that matches an email and password combination.

In MongoDB, no fixed schema determines a collection, so every time you know you are going to *query* a collection in a particular way, making sure it's properly indexed is a good idea. If a certain key is not indexed, especially if it's found within a nested structure, it could result in a *tablescan* lookup and a performance decrease in your application.

MongoDB has a command called `ensureIndex` that, as the name implies, you can call regardless of whether an index exists to ensure it's there before querying. You can do so at the initialization step of the application.

After setting `app.users`, you then should add two `ensureIndex` calls:

```
client.ensureIndex('users', 'email', function (err) {
  if (err) throw err;
  client.ensureIndex('users', 'password', function (err) {
    if (err) throw err;

    console.log('\033[96m  + \033[39m ensured indexes');

    // listen
    app.listen(3000, function () {
      console.log('\033[96m  + \033[39m app listening on *:3000');
    });
  });
});
```

If you relaunch the app, you notice the extra log:

```
$ node server.js
+   connected to mongodb
+   ensured indexes
+   app listening on :3000
```

You can now start querying!

```
/**
 * Login process route
 */

app.post('/login', function (req, res) {
  app.users.findOne({ email: req.body.user.email, password: req.body.user.password
  }, function (err, doc) {
    if (err) return next(err);
    if (!doc) return res.send('<p>User not found. Go back and try again</p>');
    req.session.loggedIn = doc._id.toString();
    res.redirect('/');
  });
});
```

In the same way as the `insert` command, the `findOne` command takes a MongoDB query document.

You store the `_id` as part of the session so that you can retrieve this user in subsequent routes he visits. Notice that you're explicitly storing it as a string, which for a MongoDB ObjectId this is a hexadecimal representation.

Finally, you also can implement the `/logout` route, which simply clears the session. Remember, you can freely alter the `req.session` object, and after you produce a response (a redirect in this case), Express saves it down automatically.

```
/**
 * Logout route.
 */

app.get('/logout', function (req, res) {
  req.session.loggedIn = null;
  res.redirect('/');
});
```

In this case, you preserve the session and set the ID to `null`. Alternatively, if you want to wipe the session entirely, you can call `req.session.regenerate()`.

AUTHENTICATION MIDDLEWARE

It's likely that most applications you develop will require access to the authenticated user in more than one place.

If you take a look at `index.jade` again, the expectation there is that you can access the object `me` to access the document matching the logged-in user and that you can verify whether the user is authenticated through the `authenticated` local:

```
if (authenticated)
  p Welcome back, #{me.name}
  a(href="/logout") Logout
```

You can thus define middleware that exposes both variables automatically for you to any template you render. Now you can leverage the `res.local` Express API:

```
/**
 * Authentication middleware.
 */

app.use(function (req, res, next) {
  if (req.session.loggedIn) {
    res.local('authenticated', true);
    app.users.findOne({ _id: { $oid: req.session.loggedIn } }, function (err, doc) {
      if (err) return next(err);
      res.local('me', doc);
      next();
    });
```

```
  } else {
    res.local('authenticated', false);
    next();
  }
});
```

Notice that in the `findOne` call you're passing the `$oid` modifier. This allows you to send a string instead of an actual `ObjectId` object. If you recall from before, you made sure to store `loggedIn` as a string by calling the `toString` method.

Remember to remove the `{ authenticated: false }` test value you set up earlier in the index route, which should now look like this (see Figure 12-4):

```
app.get('/', function (req, res) {
  res.render('index');
});
```

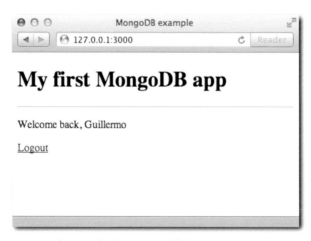

Figure 12-4: The screen after the user successfully logs in

The previous application didn't take into consideration a few fundamental features that real-world applications require. The following three sections discuss those features.

VALIDATION

What happens if the user submits a form that's too large? In the previous example, he could potentially insert a large document right into the database.

In addition, you might want to ensure that the `email` field is actually an `email` field prior to storing it and that the password is at least six characters long and a string and not a `Date` or `Number`.

You also don't want to repeat these rules every time you create, update, or query your database.

Mongoose solves this problem by allowing you to define schemas in your application layer that enforce certain properties but that are still flexible and easily modifiable. They are called *models*.

ATOMICITY

Say you're writing a blogging engine on top of Express and MongoDB. Naturally, one of the sections of the application allows you to edit the title and content of the post and maybe another allows you to edit and remove tags.

MongoDB document-oriented design fits this situation perfectly. In the `posts` collection, you might imagine a document that looks like this:

```
{
    "title": "I just bought Smashing Node.JS"
  , "author": "John Ward"
  , "content": "I went to the bookstore and picked up. . ."
  , "tags": ["node.js", "learning", "book"]
}
```

Now say at the exact same time, user A is trying to edit the title of the document and user B is trying to *add* a tag.

If both users send an `update` operation with a copy of the entire document each, only one copy prevails. One of the two users is unable to make his change.

If you want to ensure the *atomicity* of an operation, MongoDB exposes different operators such as `$set` and `$push`:

```
db.blogposts.update({ _id: <id> }, { $set: { title: 'My title' } })
db.blogposts.update({ _id: <id> }, { tags: { $push: "new tag" })
```

Mongoose solves this problem by detecting the changes you make to a document and altering only the specific properties affected. And if you're operating on an array (including arrays of documents), atomicity is still retained.

SAFE MODE

When you use the driver, as mentioned earlier, you can optionally supply a hash of options to operations:

```
app.users.insert({ }, { <options> })
```

One of those options is called `safe`, which enables the safe mode of making changes to the database.

By default, MongoDB does not notify you right away if an error occurs after an operation. The driver needs to make a special call called db.getLastError after the operation is executed to find out whether the data is altered successfully.

The reasoning behind this is that in many applications, speed is more important than knowing whether a particular operation failed. For example, if you keep a collection of logs, missing some of them isn't the end of the world, but maximizing performance is desired.

Mongoose, by default, enables safe mode for all operations, and you can still turn it off if required.

INTRODUCING MONGOOSE

As usual, the first thing you want to do to start working with Mongoose is to define it in your package.json as a dependency and then to require it:

```
var mongoose = require('mongoose')
```

The first simplification that Mongoose makes over the raw driver is that it assumes most applications work with a single database, which makes getting started significantly easier. To connect, you simply call mongoose.connect with a mongodb:// URI:

```
mongoose.connect('mongodb://localhost/my_database');
```

In addition, with mongoose it doesn't matter *when* the connection is actually established, as it will buffer commands and send them to MongoDB as soon as it connects. This means you don't have to listen on a connection callback. You can connect and start querying in the following line.

DEFINING A MODEL

Models are simply instances of the Schema class. When you specify a field, you simply use the JavaScript native constructor that matches the desired type:

```
var Schema = mongoose.Schema
  , ObjectId = Schema.ObjectId;

var PostSchema = new Schema({
    author    : ObjectId
  , title     : String
  , body      : String
  , date      : Date
});
```

These types are:

- Date
- String

- Number
- Array
- Object

In addition, MongoDB has a specific type `ObjectId`, which you can reference as `Schema.ObjectId`.

In the example of this blog post, you can store the `ObjectId` of the user who created the blog post.

Mongoose accepts different options for any given key. When you want to supply options, you need to reference the aforementioned constructors as a `type` key in an object. As an example, if you want a key to be automatically populated with a default, you would pass the `default` and `type` options as follows:

```
var PostSchema = new Schema({
    author    : ObjectId
  , title     : { type: String, default: 'Untitled' }
  , body      : String
  , date      : Date
});
```

After creating the `Schema`, you register a `Model` with `mongoose`:

```
var Post = mongoose.model('BlogPost', PostSchema);
```

Mongoose sets your collection name to `blogposts` for this case, unless you specify otherwise via the third parameter. It always lowercases and pluralizes the name of your model, by convention.

If you want to retrieve the `Model` later, you can call `mongoose.model` with just one parameter:

```
var Post = mongoose.model('BlogPost');
```

You can then operate on it. If you want to create a blog post, all you need to do is use the `new` operator:

```
new Post({ title: 'My title' }).save(function (err) {
  console.log('that was easy!');
});
```

It's important to note that the `Schema` is just a simple abstraction that describes what your model looks like and how it works. The interaction with the data occurs in the model, not the `Schema`.

Therefore, when it comes to querying, you execute the static `Post.find` (or others, which are listed below) as opposed to initializing a `Post` with the `new` keyword.

DEFINING NESTED KEYS

For the sake of organization, sometimes it's useful to organize keys within substructures:

```
var BlogPost = new Schema({
    author     : ObjectId
  , title      : String
  , body       : String
  , meta       : {
      votes  : Number
    , favs   : Number
  }
});
```

In MongoDB, you use *dot notation* to operate on these properties. If you want to `find` by number of votes, for example, you define your query like this:

```
db.blogposts.find({ 'meta.votes': 5 })
```

DEFINING EMBEDDED DOCUMENTS

In MongoDB, documents can be big and deep. This means that if you have a document for your blog post, you can include the comments inside it instead of in a separate collection:

```
var Comments = new Schema({
    title      : String
  , body       : String
  , date       : Date
});

var BlogPost = new Schema({
    author     : ObjectId
  , title      : String
  , body       : String
  , buf        : Buffer
  , date       : Date
  , comments   : [Comments]
  , meta       : {
      votes  : Number
    , favs   : Number
  }
});
```

Mongoose also naturally allows you to define the types that you expect for that field.

SETTING UP INDEXES

As I mentioned before, indexes are a key ingredient to ensuring fast queries in a MongoDB database.

In order to set up an index for any given key, pass an option `index` with the Boolean value `true` to it.

As an example, if you want to index by the `title` key, and set the `uid` key as unique:

```
var BlogPost = new Schema({
    author      : ObjectId
  , title       : { type: String, index: true }
  , uid         : { type: Number, unique: true }
});
```

To set up more complicated indexes (like compound indexes), you can leverage the static `index` method:

```
BlogPost.index({ key: -1, otherKey: 1 });
```

MIDDLEWARE

In most applications of respectable size, sometimes the same data is altered in different ways and places.

Centralizing the interaction with your database around a model interface is a useful way of avoiding code repetition.

Mongoose aids with this goal by introducing *middleware*. Middleware in Mongoose works in a similar fashion to Express middleware. You can define methods that are executed prior to distinct actions: `save` and `remove`.

For example, say you want to email an author when his blog post is removed:

```
Blogpost.pre('remove', function (next) {
  emailAuthor(this.email, 'Blog post removed!');
  next();
});
```

You can define middleware multiple times per action to perform any sort of operation, especially asynchronous ones.

INSPECTING THE STATE OF THE MODEL

Many times, you want to perform actions that depend on what changes have been made to the particular instance of a model you're interacting with:

```
Blogpost.pre('save', function (next) {
  if (this.isNew) {
    // doSomething
  } else {
    // doSomethingElse
```

```
  }
});
```

You can also access what keys have been altered by referencing `this.dirtyPaths`.

QUERYING

All the common operations are exposed to the `Model` instance:

- `find`
- `findOne`
- `remove`
- `update`
- `count`

Mongoose also adds `findById`, which takes an `ObjectId` and matches it against the `_id` property of your document.

EXTENDING QUERIES

If you don't supply a callback to a particular `Query`, you can keep mutating it until you call `run`:

```
Post.find({ author: '4ef2cbffb1d9807fa7000001' })
  .where('title', 'My title')
  .sort('content', -1)
  .limit(5)
  .run(function(err, post) {
    // . . .
  })
```

SORTING

To sort, simply supply the key and its direction:

```
query.sort('key', 1)
query.sort('some.key', -1)
```

MAKING SELECTIONS

If you have large documents and want to select only certain keys, you can call `Query#select`.

For example, if you want to show a list of blog posts with links, you don't need to retrieve all the fields (some of which could be really large):

```
Post.find()
  .select('field', 'field2')
```

LIMITING

If you want to limit the number of results to a certain ceiling, call `Query#limit`:

```
query.limit(5)
```

SKIPPING

To skip a certain number of documents, you use

```
query.skip(10);
```

This capability is useful in combination with `Model#count` to do pagination:

```
Post.count(function (err, totalPosts) {
  var numPages = Math.ceil(totalPosts / 10);
});
```

POPULATING KEYS AUTOMATICALLY

In the `BlogPost` model example, you store the ID of the user who owns it as the `author` property.

Many times, upon querying a blog post, you also want to retrieve the associated user. You can supply the `ref` property to an `ObjectId` type:

```
var BlogPost = new Schema({
    author     : { type: ObjectId, ref: 'Author' }
  , title      : String
  , body       : String
  , meta       : {
      votes : Number
    , favs  : Number
  }
});
```

You can later query documents that autopopulate the author! Simply call `populate` for each key that you want to populate:

```
BlogPost.find({ title: 'My title' })
  .populate('author')
  .run(function (err, doc) {
    console.log(doc.author.email);
  })
```

CASTING

Because Mongoose knows in advance what data types to expect, it always tries to *cast* types for you.

For example, assume you have an `age` property, and you indicate in your `Schema` that it's a `Number`. If someone posts a regular form on your website, chances are that if no JSON or custom logic is involved, you receive a string instead of a number. Mongoose takes advantage of the fact that you are dealing with a dynamic language and has no problem converting `'21'` (as `String`) to `21` (as `Number`) prior to its storage.

The same occurs for the `ObjectId`. In the previous example, you had to leverage the `$oid` modifier to make the query with a ObjectID string successful, but this is something far too common to be so verbose. If you pass `"4ef2cbd77bb50163a7000001"` to Mongoose, it is cast automatically to `ObjectId("4ef2cbd77bb50163a7000001")`

In addition, if a value type mismatch occurs but the casting fails, Mongoose raises a validation error and prevents the document from being stored. This behavior ensures ease of use while preserving consistent and clean storage of your documents.

A MONGOOSE EXAMPLE

Just like you did with the node http module, improved upon by Connect and later Express, you're going to see what Mongoose brings to the table in terms of expressiveness by refactoring the previous application.

To kick it off, you'll create a new `package.json` with the mongoose dependency.

SETTING UP THE APPLICATION

Your new `package.json` file should look like this:

```
{
    "name": "mongoose-example"
  , "version": "0.0.1"
  , "dependencies": {
        "express": "2.5.2"
      , "mongoose": "2.5.10"
    }
}
```

Try out that it works successfully by running `npm install`, as usual. Next up, you'll work on refactoring the main server code.

REFACTORING

Copy your `server.js` file and `views` from the previous example in this chapter to get started.

The first thing you'll want to do is replace the requirement for the `mongodb` module for `mongoose`, since it's no longer present in the `package.json` file. Internally, `mongoose` leverages the `mongodb` module for us.

The top part of your `server.js` file should now look like this:

```
/**
 * Module dependencies.
 */

var express = require('express')
  , mongoose = require('mongoose')
```

Now you're going to focus on the bottom part of the file, where the connection to the database occurs

```
/**
 * Connect to the database.
 */

var server = new mongodb.Server('127.0.0.1', 27017)
// . . .
```

As mentioned before, mongoose greatly simplifies how you connect to a database, access collections, set up indexes and much more. This will translate in the following simplification for the last part of the `server.js` file:

```
/**
 * Connect to the database.
 */

mongoose.connect('mongodb://127.0.0.1/my-website');
app.listen(3000, function () {
  console.log('\033[96m  + \033[39m app listening on *:3000');
});
```

Next up, you're going to define the model that will replace the reference to `app.users` and set up the indexes you were previously setting up in that section.

SETTING UP MODELS

Models can be defined with Mongoose anywhere in the file. It doesn't matter whether Mongoose has connected yet or not.

At the end of the file, append the model definition:

```
/**
 * Define model.
 */

var Schema = mongoose.Schema

var User = mongoose.model('User', new Schema({
```

```
    first: String
  , last: String
  , email: { type: String, unique: true }
  , password: { type: String, index: true }
}));
```

Now, start leveraging it by looking at the occurrences for `app.users`. The first one is in the authentication middleware. Replace the `$oid` search with the convenient Mongoose method `findById`:

```
app.use(function (req, res, next) {
  if (req.session.loggedIn) {
    res.local('authenticated', true);
    User.findById(req.session.loggedIn, function (err, doc) {
      if (err) return next(err);
      res.local('me', doc);
      next();
    });
  } else {
    res.local('authenticated', false);
    next();
  }
});
```

In the login POST route, you want to once again leverage the model method. In this case, `findOne`:

```
app.post('/login', function (req, res) {
  User.findOne({ email: req.body.user.email, password: req.body.user.password },
function (err, doc) {
    if (err) return next(err);
    if (!doc) return res.send('<p>User not found. Go back and try again');
    req.session.loggedIn = doc._id.toString();
    res.redirect('/');
  });
});
```

As I mentioned before, models can be used statically (as shown in those two examples), but are also constructors.

The POST signup route should thus look as follows:

```
app.post('/signup', function (req, res, next) {
  var user = new User(req.body.user).save(function (err) {
    if (err) return next(err);
    res.redirect('/login/' + user.email);
  });
});
```

Notice that you don't need a callback with the document anymore. You can simply refer to the instance we create from within the callback (`user.email` is used instead of `doc[0].email`).

The refactor is now complete! If you run `server.js`, everything should run smoothly, but the codebase is significantly cleaner and easier to iterate on and reason about.

SUMMARY

In this chapter you were introduced to one of the most popular databases in the Node.JS world: MongoDB.

You learned the basics of how document databases work, and explored the utilization of the MongoDB driver in Node.JS.

You noticed how natural it is to work with data in this way, and how well it maps to how data is usually sent back and forth between a browser and the web server.

By refactoring our first example, you now appreciate the significant advantages introduced by a framework that introduces the notion of models, among other very convenient APIs.

13 MYSQL

DESPITE THE INTRODUCTION and increasing popularity of NoSQL, SQL databases are still empowering the majority of applications today.

Node.JS has a rich ecosystem of modules designed to work with SQL databases, especially the one that is the focus of this chapter: MySQL.

In the same fashion as Chapter 12 on MongoDB, here you first learn how to leverage the raw power of the driver (a project called node-mysql).

With node-mysql, you write your own SQL queries to interact with the database.

In addition to the driver, you're going to learn how to use an Object-Relational Mapper (ORM) for MySQL called node-sequelize. As you'll see, an ORM gives you a mapping between JavaScript instances of a model and data contained in your MySQL database, making it easier to work with relationships, data sanitization, and much more.

NODE-MYSQL

To learn how to use node-mysql, you create a few simple models for a shopping cart application.

SETTING IT UP

As usual, you start your application with `express`, `jade`, and in this case `node-mysql`:

package.json

```
{
    "name": "shopping-cart-example"
  , "version": "0.0.1"
  , "dependencies": {
        "express": "2.5.2"
      , "jade": "0.19.0"
      , "mysql": "0.9.5"
    }
}
```

THE EXPRESS APP

Next, you create a simple Express app with the following routes:

- `/`: displays all the items and an item creation form.
- `/item/<id>`: shows a particular item and its user reviews.
- `/item/<id>/review` (POST): creates a review.
- `/item/create` (POST): creates an item.

From the index and item routes you're going to render simple templates. Notice that I configured the express `view options` to exclude a layout, which matches the behavior of Express 3. Template layouts are going to be leveraged directly through jade.

server.js

```
/**
 * Module dependencies.
 */

var express = require('express')

/**
 * Create app.
 */
```

```
app = express.createServer();

/**
 * Configure app.
 */

app.set('view engine', 'jade');
app.set('views', __dirname + '/views');
app.set('view options', { layout: false });


/**
 * Main route
 */

app.get('/', function (req, res, next) {
  res.render('index');
});

/**
 * Item creation route.
 */

app.post('/create', function (req, res, next) {
});

/**
 * Item route.
 */

app.get('/item/:id', function (req, res, next) {
  res.render('item');
});

/**
 * Item review creation route.
 */

app.post('/item/:id/review', function (req, res, next) {
});

/**
 * Listen.
 */

app.listen(3000, function () {
  console.log(' - listening on http://*:3000');
});
```

CONNECTING TO MYSQL

The next step is to add the node-mysql dependency:

server.js

```
var express = require('express')
  , mysql = require('mysql')
```

To initialize the connection, you call `createClient` in a similar way to the Node API for creating a `net` client.

In a similar way to what Mongoose does for mongodb, node-mysql accepts commands before it connects to MySQL, buffers them (that is, keeps them around in memory), and after the connection is established, sends them all to MySQL.

You therefore don't need to listen on a connection callback or event, and you simply initialize the client with your settings. Add the following after the configuration section of the app:

server.js

```
/**
 * Connect to MySQL
 */

var db = mysql.createClient({
    host: 'localhost'
  , database: 'cart-example'
});
```

If you set a user and password for your database, make sure to include them as the `user` and `password` options passed to the `createClient` API. For more advanced usage, reference to the documentation of node-mysql available at http://github.com/felixge/node-mysql.

INITIALIZING THE SCRIPT

Prior to using a SQL database from the application, you almost always need to set up the necessary database and tables.

To make this reusable, you create a simple node script called `setup.js` that runs the necessary CREATE TABLE commands.

Because the connection parameters are the same as the ones used for the application, you first need to abstract out the configuration as a `config.json` file:

config.json

```json
{
    "host": "localhost"
  , "database": "cart-example"
}
```

Note that valid JavaScript is not necessarily valid JSON. For this example, you add quotation marks around all keys and ensure all values are surrounded with double quotation marks instead of single quotation marks.

Starting with Node 0.6, you can use `require` to load JSON files without relying on JSON. parse and `fs#readFileSync`. You then edit the dependencies:

server.js

```js
/**
 * Module dependencies.
 */

var express = require('express')
  , mysql = require('mysql')
  , config = require('./config')

// . . .
```

In the connection line, you replace the object with the `config` reference:

server.js

```js
var db = mysql.createClient(config);
```

You are now ready to create the setup script. It depends only on `mysql` and the config because it is meant to be executed only from the command-line interface.

setup.js

```js
/**
 * Module dependencies.
 */

var mysql = require('mysql')
  , config = require('./config')
```

You initialize the client next, making sure not to include the `database` field of the `config`, as it's not created yet:

setup.js

```
/**
 * Initialize client.
 */
delete config.database;
var db = mysql.createClient(config);
```

The API that `node-mysql` exposes for executing queries is simple: `client.query`
`(<sql>, <callback>)`. The API for closing the connection is `client.end`.

Because you are dealing with essentially a single TCP connection, the server receives all the
commands you send out in the order you write them. This means that you don't need to nest
callbacks to ensure proper order of execution:

```
// this is unnecessary!
db.query('CREATE TABLE. . .', function (err) {
  db.query('CREATE TABLE. . .', function (err) {
    db.query('CREATE TABLE. . .', function (err) { });
  });
});
```

Because you still should make sure errors that occur are reported to the user, you can listen
on the `db` error event:

```
db.on('error', function () {
  // handle error
});
```

For the terminal program, however, the desired behavior when an error occurs is to display
the error and its stack trace to the user and abort execution. As you might recall from
Chapter 4, when an `error` is emitted on an `EventEmitter` for which there are no listeners
(that is, the event goes unhandled), Node throws the error to ensure the programmer is aware
of the program's potential point of failure instead of silently avoiding it. As a result, you don't
really need to attach an error handler for this particular program, and Node takes care of
notifying the user of the unhandled error.

First, you need to create the database and tell MySQL it's the one to keep using:

setup.js

```
/**
 * Create database.
 */

db.query('CREATE DATABASE IF NOT EXISTS `cart-example`');
  db.query('USE `cart-example`');
```

setup.js

```
/**
 * Create tables.
 */

db.query('DROP TABLE IF EXISTS item');
 db.query('CREATE TABLE item (' +
  'id INT(11) AUTO_INCREMENT,' +
  'title VARCHAR(255),' +
  'description TEXT,' +
  'created DATETIME,' +
  'PRIMARY KEY (id))');
db.query('DROP TABLE IF EXISTS review');
db.query('CREATE TABLE review (' +
  'id INT(11) AUTO_INCREMENT,' +
  'item_id INT(11),' +
  'text TEXT,' +
  'stars INT(1),' +
  'created DATETIME,' +
  'PRIMARY KEY (id))');
```

setup.js

```
/**
 * Close client.
 */

db.end();
```

As you saw in Chapter 3, Node exits the process when it has nothing left to do in the event loop. By connecting to the MySQL server, you open a file descriptor, for which Node's event loop waits on notifications. When you call end, the file descriptor gets closed, therefore ending the life of the program.

Code like this is therefore redundant:

setup.js

```
db.end(function () {
  process.exit();
});
```

You are now ready to test the script:

```
$ node setup.js
```

You can then check with the mysql client that the database and tables are created (see Figure 13-1):

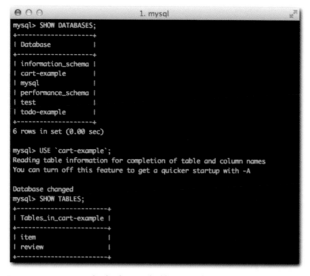

Figure 13-1: Inspecting the database and tables created with setup.js with MySQL command-line client

```
$ mysql
> show databases;
. . .
> use cart-examples;
. . .
> SHOW TABLES;
. . .
```

CREATING DATA

Next, you create a simple layout in the views directory. This file, as you can see, contains a special jade `block body` declaration, that other views will be filling in.

views/layout.jade

```
doctype 5
html
  head
    title My shopping cart
  body
    h1 My shopping cart
    #cart

block body
```

The index file displays all items as a list and a form to create a new product:

views/index.jade

```
extends layout
block body
h2 All items
if (items.length)
  ul
    each item in items
      li
        h3: a(href="/item/#{item.id}")= item.title
        = item.description
else
  p No items to show

h2 Create new item

form(action="/create", method="POST")
  p
    label Title
    input(type="text", name="title")
  p
    label Description
    textarea(name="description")
  p
    button Submit
```

Since you're looping through an `items` array by checking for the `length` property, make sure to fill it in the / route with an empty one for now, as shown below. The items array will of course come for the database later on:

server.js

```
app.get('/', function (req, res, next) {
  res.render('index', { items: [] });
});. . .
```

And for the item view, you also include the item and its reviews and a form to submit a review:

views/item.jade

```
extends layout

block body
  a(href="/") Go back

  h2= item.title
  p= item.description
```

continued

views/item.jade   (continued)

```
h3 User reviews

if (reviews.length)
  each review in reviews
    .review
      b #{review.stars} stars
      p= review.text
    hr
else
  p No reviews to show. Write one!

form(action="/item/#{item.id}/review", method="POST")
  fieldset
    legend Create review
    p
      label Stars
      select(name="stars")
        option 1
        option 2
        option 3
        option 4
        option 5
    p
      label Review
      textarea(name="text")
    p
      button(type="submit") Send
```

Notice that in the form `action` attribute you leveraged the jade *interpolation* feature. By using #{} you can include a variable within some other string in a safe way (so that HTML entities get escaped). If you wanted to include a string without escaping, use !{} instead.

Before you start selecting data, you need to be able to insert it to simplify the testing of the app.

Add the `bodyParser` middleware to process POST requests after the app configuration:

server.js

```
/**
 * Middleware.
 */

app.use(express.bodyParser());
```

And then you complete the /create route:

---

server.js

```
/**
 * Item creation route.
 */

app.post('/create', function (req, res, next) {
  db.query('INSERT INTO item SET title = ?, description = ?',
    [req.body.title, req.body.description], function (err, info) {
      if (err) return next(err);
      console.log(' - item created with id %s', info.insertId);
      res.redirect('/');
    });
});
```

This code has two interesting aspects. The first one is that db.query allows for replacing ? tokens in the query with properly escaped data. By replacing tokens, the code avoids concatenation and ensures that your app is not vulnerable to SQL injection attacks. If you include ? in a query, you pass an array of values to replace as the second parameter.

The other interesting aspect is the info object. In this case, to get the ID of the inserted item, you look for insertId in it. This property is always present provided an error doesn't occur. If an error does occur, you want to interrupt all flow and next it.

The review creation route is similar:

```
/**
 * Item review creation route.
 */

app.post('/item/:id/review', function (req, res, next) {
  db.query('INSERT INTO review SET item_id = ?, stars = ?, text = ?',
    [req.params.id, req.body.stars, req.body.text], function (err, info) {
      if (err) return next(err);
      console.log(' - review created with id %s', info.insertId);
      res.redirect('/item/' + req.params.id);
    });
});
```

You test by running the app and creating an item (illustrated in Figure 13-2).

Figure 13-2: Filling the form to create an item in the main route

Upon doing so, you should Figure 13-3 see in the console.

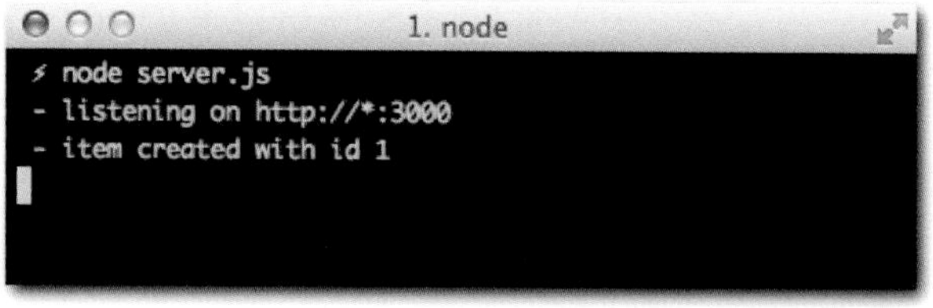

```
⚡ node server.js
- listening on http://*:3000
- item created with id 1
```

Figure 13-3: The console after an item is created reveals the id of the inserted row

FETCHING DATA

Retrieving data from MySQL is equally as straightforward with node-mysql. When the command you're executing is a SELECT one, the callback you get contains an array of result objects, and an object describing the properties of the returned fields. You're going to focus on the former only for the scope of this chapter.

This maps really well to what we're expecting in the template index.jade, since we're looping through the array items and looking up the id, title, and description properties.

Therefore, all we need to do is check for an error and pass the results to the view:

```
/**
 * Main route
 */
```

```
app.get('/', function (req, res, next) {
  db.query('SELECT id, title, description FROM item', function (err, results) {
res.render('index', { items: results });
  });
});
```

Once your / route looks like this, you should be able to relaunch your application and see a list of the items you created previously.

As for the item route, which we link to from that list, you want to retrieve the item, make sure it exists, and fetch the reviews along with it. If the item does not exist, you want to send a 404 status code.

To avoid making the code hard to follow, break the logic into functions that are defined in the logical order they're executed:

server.js

```
/**
 * Item route.
 */

app.get('/item/:id', function (req, res, next) {
  function getItem (fn) {
    db.query('SELECT id, title, description FROM item WHERE id = ? LIMIT 1',
    [req.params.id], function (err, results) {
      if (err) return next(err);
      if (!results[0]) return res.send(404);
      fn(results[0]);
    });
  }

  function getReviews (item_id, fn) {
    db.query('SELECT text, stars FROM review WHERE item_id = ?',
    [item_id], function (err, results) {
      if (err) return next(err);
      fn(results);
    });
  }

  getItem(function (item) {
    getReviews(item.id, function (reviews) {
      res.render('item', { item: item, reviews: reviews });
    });
  });
});
```

Figure 13-4 shows the completed application. You can now browse the items, submit reviews for them, and see them reflect in the interface.

Figure 13-4: The completed application in action

SEQUELIZE

In the preceding example, you experienced some of the gotchas of working with SQL databases.

The first one is that the process of setting up the tables is manual (therefore time consuming), and the table definitions are not part of the project itself. The application doesn't know that an item has a title property that allows a maximum of 255 characters. If it did, you could, for example, perform automatic validation of user input with error messages.

The solution to this problem is elegantly packaged for you by sequelize: you can define schemas and models and can also leverage synchronization features to create tables for use based on those definitions. The `setup.js` part of the preceding example is therefore completely removed.

Because the schemas are part of the application, you can also use them to leverage type conversion or casting. If you want to insert an item with specific data, you can pass a Java-Script `Date` object instead of having to manually compose the date format that MySQL expects.

Last but not least is associations. In the preceding example, you manually retrieved the reviews for an item, but you could also retrieve them automatically.

To apply the different concepts and features that sequelize brings to the table, create a simple TODO list application. TODO tasks can be grouped as projects. You can add, create, and remove projects, and you can add, create, and remove tasks for a given project.

SETTING UP SEQUELIZE

Because sequelize uses the node-mysql driver internally, the dependencies list looks like this:

package.json

```
{
    "name": "todo-list-example"
  , "version": "0.0.1"
  , "dependencies": {
        "express": "2.5.2"
      , "jade": "0.19.0"
      , "sequelize": "1.3.7"
    }
}
```

SETTING UP THE EXPRESS APP

This particular application deviates a little bit from the traditional style and introduces some AJAX interaction for creating and removing items. You can make the application more RESTful by introducing the usage of the DELETE method. If you're not familiar with REST, it's a set of principles that introduce a broader usage of the protocol constructs that HTTP makes available to us, such as methods like PATCH or DELETE or status codes that are normally not utilized.

The routes look as follows:

- / (GET): retrieves projects.
- /projects (POST): creates projects.
- /project/:id (DELETE): deletes a project.
- /project/:id/tasks (GET): retrieves tasks.
- /project/:id/tasks (POST): adds tasks.
- /task/:id (DELETE): removes a task.

```
/**
 * Module dependencies.
 */

var express = require('express')
```

```
/**
 * Create app.
 */

app = express.createServer();

/**
 * Configure app.
 */

app.set('view engine', 'jade');
app.set('views', __dirname + '/views');
app.set('view options', { layout: false });

/**
 * Main route
 */

app.get('/', function (req, res, next) {
  res.render('index');
});

/**
 * Project deletion route.
 */

app.del('/project/:id', function (req, res, next) {
});

/**
 * Project creation route.
 */

app.post('/projects', function (req, res, next) {
});

/**
 * Show tasks for project.
 */

app.get('/project/:id/tasks, function (req, res, next) {
});

/**
 * Add task for project.
 */

app.post('/project/:id/tasks, function (req, res, next) {
});

/**
 * Item route.
```

```
 */

app.del('/task/:id', function (req, res, next) {
});
/**
 * Listen.
 */

app.listen(3000, function () {
  console.log(' - listening on http://*:3000');
});
```

You define a simple layout again, this time with jQuery to make AJAX requests easy:

views/layout.jade

```
doctype 5
html
  head
    title TODO list app
    script(src="http://code.jquery.com/jquery-1.7.2.js")
    script(src="/js/main.js")
  body
    h1 TODO list app
    #todo
      block body
```

Notice that the layout loads a `main.js` file, which is going to contain all the client side logic (that deals with, for example, the AJAX submission of requests).

The projects and tasks lists behave in the same way because you perform the same operations on them: `add` and `delete`:

views/index.jade

```
extends layout

block body
  h2 Projects

  #list
    ul#projects-list
      each project in projects
        li
          a(href="/project/#{project.id}/items")= project.title
          a.delete(href="/project/#{project.id}") x

    form#add(action="/projects", method="POST")
      input(type="text", name="title")
```

button(type="submit") Addviews/tasks.jade

```
h2 Tasks for project #{project.title}

#list
  ul#tasks-list
    each task in tasks
      li
        span= task.title
        a.delete(href="/task/#{task.id} ") x

  form#add(action="/project/#{project.id}/tasks", method="POST")
    input(type="text", name="title")
    button Add
```

CONNECTING SEQUELIZE

Now you're ready to add sequelize to your dependencies:

server.js

```
/**
 * Module dependencies.
 */

var express = require('express')
  , Sequelize = require('sequelize')
```

You then initialize the main class. You can do this directly underneath the module dependencies, or after the application settings, for the sake of clarity.

server.js

```
/**
 * Instantiate sequelize.
 */

var sequelize = new Sequelize('todo-example', 'root')
```

The Sequelize constructor takes the following parameters:

- database (String)
- username (String) - required
- password (String) - optional
- other options (Object) - optional
  - host (String)
  - port (Number)

You can create the database from the command line as follows. Remember to replace `root` with your MySQL user in the Sequelize constructor and the command below:

```
$ mysqldmin -u root -p create todo-exmaple
```

DEFINING MODELS AND SYNCHRONIZING

To define a model, you call `sequelize.define`. You can do this directly after requiring sequelize. The first parameter is the name that identifies the model, and the second is an object of properties.

server.js
```
var Project = sequelize.define('Project', {
    title: Sequelize.STRING
  , description: Sequelize.TEXT
  , created: Sequelize.DATE
});
```

As you can see, you map keys to the following sequelize types. Next to each of them, you can see the MySQL type they map to:

- `Sequelize.STRING` // VARCHAR(255)
- `Sequelize.BOOLEAN` // TINYINT(1)
- `Sequelize.TEXT` // TEXT
- `Sequelize.DATE` // DATETIME
- `Sequelize.INTEGER` // INT

In addition to passing the types, you can supply options by passing an object. For example, to set a default value, you pass

```
title: { type: Sequelize.STRING, defaultValue: 'No title' }
```

You then set the task model:

server.js
```
/**
 * Define task model.
 */

var Task = sequelize.define('Task', {
    title: Sequelize.STRING
});
```

Finally, you set a `hasMany` association:

---

server.js

```
/**
 * Set up association.
 */

Task.belongsTo(Project);
  Project.hasMany(Task);
```

Sequelize takes care of setting up the appropriate columns, primary keys, and indexes to make the relationships.

The implication of a `belongsTo` association is that each `Task` has a field pointing to the project it belongs to. The other implication is that the instances of the task model have a method called `getProject` to easily access the parent project.

As for `hasMany`, the result will be that when you access Project instances later on by calling `find`, they will have a method `getTasks` to easily access the project's tasks.

The other relationship type supported by sequelize which you won't use for this example is `hasOne`: the symmetrical opposite of `belongsTo`.

Finally, you need to make sure the schema is synchronized to the database without having to manually run `CREATE TABLE` commands:

```
/**
 * Synchronize.
 */

sequelize.sync();
```

During development, you are bound to change the tables a lot. You can tell sequelize to always drop the existing table and create it again to ensure that changes are always reflected by supplying the option `{ force: true }`.

---

server.js

```
sequelize.sync();
```

CREATING DATA

For both the projects and tasks lists, you want to attach a jQuery listener when the form is submitted.

When you send the AJAX call, you expect a JSON response with the model instance data.

From that, you append an item to the DOM.

Before proceeding, you need to add a static middleware to serve the `public/js` directory (which you should create as well). Since you're going to POSTing data from jQuery, you also want the `bodyParser` middleware.

server.js

```
/**
 * Middleware
 */

app.use(express.static(__dirname + '/public'));
app.use(express.bodyParser());
```

public/js/main.js

```
$(function () {
  $('form').submit(function (ev) {
    ev.preventDefault();
    var form = $(this);
    $.ajax({
        url: form.attr('action')
      , type: 'POST'
      , data: form.serialize()
      , success: function (obj) {
          var el = $('<li>');
          if ($('#projects-list').length) {
            el
              .append($('<a>').attr('href', '/project/' + obj.id
+ '/tasks').text(obj.title + ' '))
              .append($('<a>').attr('href', '/project/' + obj.id)
.attr('class', 'delete').text('x'));
          } else {
            el
              .append($('<span>').text(obj.title + ' '))
              .append($('<a>').attr('href', '/task/' + obj.id)
.attr('class', 'delete').text('x'));
          }
          $('ul').append(el);
        }
    });
form.find('input').val(''); // clear the input
  });
});
```

The code is simple. You capture the submission of any form in the website, and you ajaxify it:

1. You capture the submission of the form

2. You prevent the default behavior by calling `preventDefault`. That is, you prevent the browser from attempting to POST the form automatically, since you're going to do it with the AJAX request.

3. You call jQuery's `$.ajax` to make a POST request with the form serialized as a query string as the body (which you achieve by passing the result of `form.serialize` as the `data` property).

When the JSON comes back, you reconstruct the item to inject to the list of projects or tasks. If it's a project, you insert a link to the tasks list and a delete link. If it's a task, you simply inject a span and a delete link.

You now populate the `.post` routes in the Express application. You leverage the `.build` method exposed in each model:

server.js

```
/**
 * Project creation route.
 */

app.post('/projects', function (req, res, next) {
  Project.build(req.body).save()
    .success(function (obj) {
      res.send(obj);
    })
    ..error(next)
});

/**
 * Add task for project.
 */

app.post('/project/:id/tasks', function (req, res, next) {
    res.body.ProjectId = req.params.id;
  Task.build(req.body).save()
    .success(function (obj) {
      res.send(obj);
    })
    .error(next)
});
```

It's very important to keep in mind that you should only pass the entire request body like this (such as `pass req.body`) when there are no security implications from the user being able to set *any* field in your database, as in the case of this example application. Even if you only create a few inputs in a form, never forget that the user can forge any type of request manually.

As you saw in Chapter 9, the `res.send` method from Express allows you to send JSON easily.

When you call `.save` on a model instance, as shown below, sequelize can either emit a `success` event with the built object or `failure` with an error. Even though the following code is valid within sequelize:

```
Task.build(req.body).save()
    .on('success', function (obj) {
       res.send(obj);
     })
    .on('failure', next)
```

It's much easier to add the event handlers through the convenience `success` and `error` methods:

```
  Task.build(req.body).save()
    .success(function (obj) {
       res.send(obj);
     })
    .error(next)
```

Notice that in order to make sure the relationship between a task and a project is preserved, I add the field `ProjectId` to the `Task` object I create with `Task.build`. Back when you set up the `belongsTo` relationship in the model, sequelize automatically added the `ProjectId` field to the schema definition.

RETRIEVING DATA

Each sequelize model exposes simple methods for retrieving one or multiple instances from a given table.

If you call `Model#find`, you can supply a primary key directly and then listen on the `success` and `failure` events:

```
/**
 * Main route
 */

app.get('/', function (req, res, next) {
  Project.findAll()
    .success(function (projects) {
      res.render('index', { projects: projects });
    })
    .error(next);
});
```

Because you set up the project – tasks association previously, you can leverage the getTasks method to expose both the project and tasks to the view for the /project/:id/items route:

server.js

```
app.get('/project/:id/tasks', function (req, res, next) {
  Project.find(Number(req.params.id))
    .success(function (project) {
      project.getTasks().on('success', function (tasks) {
        res.render('tasks', { project: project, tasks: tasks });
      })
    })
    .error(next)
});
```

Also notice that when you leverage the find method of the model instance you need to convert the parameter to a Number. This is important for sequelize to know that it has to perform a primary key lookup.

Let's now focus on the remaining routes: projects and tasks deletion.

REMOVING DATA

Next, you use event delegation to capture any link with the class delete and send a DELETE request. Add the following code right after the $(form).submit handler:

public/js/main.js

```
$('ul').delegate('a.delete', 'click', function (ev) {
  ev.preventDefault();
  var li = $(this).closest('li');
  $.ajax({
      url: $(this).attr('href')
    , type: 'DELETE'
    , success: function () {
        li.remove();
      }
  });
});
```

Delegation allows you to capture the click of any anchor that contains the class delete, regardless of whether you added it dynamically or it was already in the DOM.

Notice that upon clicking an anchor with the class name delete, you look for the parent li item, and then upon success of the AJAX call, you remove it.

You then define the deletion routes:

```
/**
 * Project deletion route.
 */

app.del('/project/:id', function (req, res, next) {
  Project.find(Number(req.params.id)).success(function (proj) {
    proj.destroy()
      .success(function () {
        res.send(200);
      })
      .error(next);
  }).error(next);
});

/**
 * Item deletion route.
 */

app.del('/task/:id', function (req, res, next) {
  Task.find(Number(req.params.id)).success(function (task) {
    task.destroy()
      .success(function () {
        res.send(200);
      })
      .error(next)
  }).error(next);
});
```

As you can see, you first fetch the task or project *instance*, and once it is retrieved you call `destroy` to remove it. If the `destroy` command succeeds, a status code 200 is sent back to the browser.

Similarly, if you wanted to modify the property of a retrieved item you would call the method `updateAttributes`. The following snippet would change the title of a given task instance:

```
task.updateAttributes({
  title: 'a new title'
});
```

Figure 13-5 shows the completed app. You can browse projects and tasks, add new ones asynchronously and delete them at will.

Figure 13-5: Creating a new task for a project

WRAPPING UP

There's still a lot more functionality contained within sequelize. Just like Mongoose does for MongoDB, Sequelize can add a validation layer in between MySQL and the data your application supplies to the models, which is really useful in addition to being able to define types.

You can set up validations by passing the `validate` option in the field definition within your model. The type goes under the key `type`.

For example, if you wanted to only allow uppercase letters as part of your tasks, your model definition would look as follows:

```
var Task = sequelize.define('Task', {
    title: { type: Sequelize.STRING, isUppercase: true }
});
```

To set up custom validations, simply pass an arbitrary name and validation function. For a complete list of built-in validators, refer to the official Sequelize documentation on validators: http://sequelizejs.com/?active=validations#validations.

It's also possible to expand Models with your own class and instance methods:

```
var Task = sequelize.define('Task', {
    title: { type: Sequelize.STRING, isUppercase: true }
  , classMethods: {
      staticMethod: function(){}
    }
  , instanceMethods: {
      instanceMethod: function(){}
    }
});
```

The `staticMethod` in the example above would be called as follows:

```
Task.staticMethod()
```

The `instanceMethod` would become available to instances that are selected:

```
Task.find(4).success(function (task) {
  task.instanceMethod();
});
```

SUMMARY

MySQL is still one of the most powerful and reliable open-source databases available. Regardless of what new trends emerge, the fact that MySQL is still a great choice for building a variety of applications is unlikely to change.

Throughout this chapter, you learned the excellent MySQL Node.JS driver. You had to write SQL by hand to set up the database, tables and then query it.

For the purpose of developing web applications, ORMs are usually a very useful weapon to have. In the second example of this chapter, you didn't write a single query, and you manipulated the dataset by operating on model classes and instances, thanks to Sequelize.

Even though you must be careful to always select the right tool for the job, you now have a good understanding of what projects you can leverage to work with MySQL really effectively from Node.JS.

14

REDIS

NOW THAT YOU have successfully leveraged two major databases with Node.JS—MongoDB and MySQL—it's time learn about Redis.

Redis is a database, but it would be more accurately described as a datastructure server, a definition that resonates more with MongoDB than MySQL.

Instead of interacting with rows in tables or documents in collections, you always access data in Redis through keys. As a result, you can think of Redis as a key-value store like the following JavaScript object:

```
{
    'key': 'some value'
  , 'key.2': 'some other value'
}
```

But because it's a datastructure server, the value is not always a simple string. The following are the fundamental data types that you can assign to keys in Redis:

- string
- list
- set
- hash
- sorted set

A fundamental difference between Redis and MongoDB, however, is that Redis document structure is always *flat*. Even though a key, for example, can contain something that resembles a JavaScript object very closely—a *hash*—that hash can't contain nested data structures like it could in MongoDB.

Another fundamental difference is how you persist data. Redis is designed to be an extremely fast **in-memory** store with configurable persistence to disk. It's important to remember persistence to disk matters because anything stored in memory is volatile and susceptible to be lost upon a system crash or reboot.

What this means is that Redis usage and configuration should be carefully reviewed prior to its deployment for sensitive information systems (such as those involving financial transactions). Even though Redis stores its working dataset (that is, all the data you work with and query) in memory, it does have different strategies for ensuring a copy of it stays in the hard drive. The problem is that its *default* configuration and behavior is not as well suited for sensitive systems as MySQL could be, for example. That's why Redis is commonly regarded as "not durable,, but such a categorization is not truly informative.

If you're planning to deploy Redis for the first time, I encourage you to review the different options related to persistence in the official website: http://redis.io/topics/persistence. In summary, you can think of Redis as a single, big, flat (key-value) JavaScript object, where the values can be special data structures (a hash, a set, a string, and so on) It's designed for lookup and write speed (it keeps everything in memory). How safe the data is after writing to it is configurable, but it could be a bad choice for certain types of systems if used out of the box.

INSTALLING REDIS

Redis is officially distributed as a tarball with its complete source code and supported under Mac OS X and Linux. If you're familiar with compiling software, you can head directly to http://redis.io/download and download the latest stable version.

For the Mac, however, the easiest way to install Redis is with `homebrew`:

```
$ brew install redis
```

Or with `ports`:

```
$ sudo port install redis
```

These two package managers will set it up to load upon bootup, unlike when you install it from the source code. To make it run when compiling, you can run the following command:

```
$ nohup redis-server &
```

For Windows, there's unofficial ports that are well maintained. Refer to the URL above for the latest up-to-date information about Windows support.

THE REDIS QUERY LANGUAGE

To start learning the Redis query language (the equivalent of SQL in the Redis world, in other words), first make sure the server is running; then execute

```
$ redis-cli
```

As when you execute `node`, `redis-cli` takes you to a prompt that's not unlike establishing a `telnet` connection to the Redis server. In other words, the commands that you're about to execute are almost the same as those the Node client executes when it establishes a TCP connection to Redis.

The first command to execute is `KEYS`. Commands in Redis are not case sensitive, but by convention they usually are uppercase.

Like function calls, commands can take an arbitrary number of arguments. If you execute the `KEYS` command without arguments, Redis comes back with an error:

```
redis 127.0.0.1:6379> KEYS
(error) ERR wrong number of arguments for 'keys' command
```

The `KEYS` command takes a pattern to match keys against and returns them. You supply * to match all keys:

```
redis 127.0.0.1:6379> KEYS *
(empty list or set)
```

Because the Redis installation is new here, it comes back with no results.

You now use the `SET` command to assign a string to a key. Redis returns `OK`:

```
redis 127.0.0.1:6379> SET my.key test
OK
```

Running `GET my.key` should return the value you just stored:

```
redis 127.0.0.1:6379> GET my.key
"test"
```

And executing `KEYS *` again should reflect the new key:

```
redis 127.0.0.1:6379> KEYS *
1) "my.key"
```

The majority of Redis commands depend on which data type you're working with. You use `GET` and `SET` to operate with strings, but somewhat unintuitively, you can't use `GET` to "get" a hash.

DATA TYPES

One of the fundamental benefits of Redis's simple design is that the developer can easily predict performance. The database is not a black box, but simply a process that holds some known data structures in memory that you can access from other programs through a simple protocol.

If you look for the command `HEXISTS` in the official Redis documentation manual, you can see that one of the sections contemplated is time complexity.

In the case of the `HEXISTS` command, the time complexity is $O(1)$, or *constant time*. This means that running the `HEXISTS` command takes the same amount of time *always*, no matter the size of the dataset.

If you look at the `SMEMBERS` command, the time complexity is $O(n)$, or *linear time,* and it varies according to the size of the set. This means that the amount of time Redis takes to complete the response is directly proportional to how much data you're holding in that particular key.

Because the Redis object model is roughly equivalent to a big, flat JSON object, the easiest way to understand the different data types is to think of their JavaScript counterparts. For each data type, the following sections provide examples of their rough equivalents in the JS world.

STRINGS

Strings in Redis contemplate both the `Number` and `String` data type in JavaScript.

In addition to using `SET` and `GET`, you can increment and decrement numbers:

```
redis 127.0.0.1:6379> SET online.users 0
OK
redis 127.0.0.1:6379> INCR online.users
(integer) 1
redis 127.0.0.1:6379> INCR online.users
(integer) 2
```

HASHES

In the Redis world, hashes are the equivalent of subobjects. Those subobjects are limited to keys and values that are *strings*, unlike in MongoDB.

Say you want to store a user profile in Redis that looks like this:

```
{
    "name": "Guillermo"
  , "last": "Rauch"
  , "age": "21"
}
```

Because both keys and values are strings (or integers), it's a suitable data structure for a hash.

In Redis, as mentioned earlier, everything is accessed by a unique key in a big object. To store the profiles, then, you need to include the user ID as part of the key to uniquely identify it. The Redis database looks somewhat like this:

```
{
    "profile:1": { name: "Guillermo", "last": "Rauch", . . . }
  , "profile:2": { name: "Tobi", "last": "Rauch", . . . }
}
```

The use of the colon (`:`) in this case is completely up to you. You could use a dot, an underscore, or nothing. The fundamental premise is that each key remains unique to avoid collisions when interacting with the documents and that it contains enough information for you to access it easily from your application.

The basic command for operating with hashes is `HSET`:

```
redis 127.0.0.1:6379> HSET profile.1 name Guillermo
(integer) 1
```

This command is equivalent to simply setting a key in JavaScript:

```
obj['profile.1'].name = 'Guillermo';
```

To retrieve all keys and values for a given hash, you use HGETALL and supply the key:

```
redis 127.0.0.1:6379> HGETALL profile.1
1) "name"
2) "Guillermo"
```

Redis returns a list composed of alternating keys and values:

```
redis 127.0.0.1:6379> HSET profile.1 last Rauch
(integer) 1
redis 127.0.0.1:6379> HGETALL profile.1
1) "name"
2) "Guillermo"
3) "last"
4) "Rauch"
```

To delete a key in the hash, you can call HDEL:

```
redis 127.0.0.1:6379> HSET profile.1 programmer 1
(integer) 1
redis 127.0.0.1:6379> HGETALL profile.1
1) "name"
2) "Guillermo"
3) "last"
4) "Rauch"
5) "programmer"
6) "1"
redis 127.0.0.1:6379> HDEL profile.1 programmer
(integer) 1
redis 127.0.0.1:6379> HGETALL profile.1
1) "name"
2) "Guillermo"
3) "last"
4) "Rauch"
```

In JavaScript, the preceding command is equivalent to using the delete operator in a hash:

```
delete obj['profile.1'].programmer
```

You can check for the existence of a certain field with HEXISTS:

```
redis 127.0.0.1:6379> HEXISTS profile.1 programmer
(integer) 0
```

This command is equivalent to checking whether a value is not undefined:

```
'undefined' != typeof obj['profile.1'].programmer
```

LISTS

A Redis list is the equivalent of a JavaScript array of strings.

The two fundamental operations you can perform in Redis are RPUSH (push to the right, or tail of the list) and LPUSH (push to the left, or head of the list).

You operate on lists similarly to the way you do with hashes:

```
redis 127.0.0.1:6379> RPUSH profile.1.jobs "job 1"
(integer) 1
redis 127.0.0.1:6379> RPUSH profile.1.jobs "job 2"
(integer) 2
```

You can then access a specified range of the array:

```
redis 127.0.0.1:6379> LRANGE profile.1.jobs 0 -1
1) "job 1"
2) "job 2"
```

LPUSH is also intuitively similar:

```
redis 127.0.0.1:6379> LPUSH profile.1.jobs "job 0"
(integer) 3
redis 127.0.0.1:6379> LRANGE profile.1.jobs 0 -1
1) "job 0"
2) "job 1"
3) "job 2"
```

RPUSH is the equivalent of pushing to an array in JavaScript:

```
obj['profile.1.jobs'].push('job 2');
```

LPUSH is the equivalent of unshifting:

```
obj['profile.1.jobs'].unshift('job 2');
```

The LRANGE command returns a range of items in the list. It's similar but not identical to an array slice in JavaScript. In particular, if the second argument is -1, it returns *all* the values of the list.

SETS

Sets lie somewhere in between a list and a hash. They share the property of hashes that each item in a set (or key in a hash) is unique and unrepeatable. As with keys in a hash, operating on members of a set happens in constant time (that is, no matter how big the set, removing, adding, or looking up members of a set takes the same amount of time).

Like lists and unlike hashes, a set holds only single values (strings) without keys. But sets also have their own unique and interesting properties. Redis allows you to compute the intersections between sets, unions, the retrieval of random members, and so on.

To add a member to a set, you use `SADD`:

```
redis 127.0.0.1:6379> SADD myset "a member"
(integer) 1
```

To retrieve all members in a set, you use `SMEMBERS`:

```
redis 127.0.0.1:6379> SMEMBERS myset
1) "a member"
```

Calling `SADD` again with the same value does nothing:

```
redis 127.0.0.1:6379> SADD myset "a member"
(integer) 0
redis 127.0.0.1:6379> SMEMBERS myset
1) "a member"
```

To remove an item from a set, you use `SREM`:

```
redis 127.0.0.1:6379> SREM myset "a member"
(integer) 1
```

SORTED SETS

Sorted sets share all the characteristics of Redis sets, but as the name implies, they are sortable. Their use cases in the Redis world are notably more rare and advanced.

REDIS AND NODE

Because JavaScript already has all these data structures readily available to you (or easily achievable) and operating with them doesn't require the existence of a protocol and server, how is Redis useful to you?

One of the fundamental reasons is that if you shut down the Node process, the data you are holding in memory goes away with it.

In Chapter 9, you saw how to leverage Redis to store user session data. If you store it in each Node process, you have two fundamental disadvantages:

- The application could never be powered by more than one process As applications grow and a single process is not able to sustain all the load or traffic, you need to scale an application to *multiple processes or computers.*

- You lose session data each time you reload your application: for example, upon deploying new code.

Redis also has other important advantages, such as interoperability between programming languages, eventual persistence, and other features that are not so easily attainable without writing a complete data store solution.

IMPLEMENTING A SOCIAL GRAPH WITH NODE-REDIS

For a sample application with Redis and Node, you can leverage the power of sets and intersections to create a social graph of *follows* and *followers*, very much like Twitter.

Setting up the application

The Redis client of choice comes from a project called node_redis (https://github.com/mranney/node_redis) The NPM project name is simply `redis`:

package.json

```
{
    "name": "sample-social-graph"
  , "version": "0.0.1"
  , "dependencies": {
        "redis": "0.7.1"
    }
}
```

Connecting to redis

`node-redis` obeys a design that's similar to the MySQL client you already looked at in Chapter 13.

First, you `require` the module and then initialize a client with `createClient`:

```
/**
 * Module dependencies.
 */

var redis = require('redis')

/**
 * Create client.
 */

var client = redis.createClient();
```

The client exposes all the commands as simple functions. For example, say you want to use SET:

```
client.set('my key', 'my value', function (err) {
  // . . .
});
```

The same applies to all other commands, such as SMEMBERS or HEXISTS.

Defining the model

The basic premise is that you can create different Redis sets for follows and followers for each user, including IDs as part of the key:

```
user:<id>:follows
user:<id>:followers
```

When one user (id "1") follows another (id "2"), you want to execute two operations:

```
- Add user id "2" to the user:1:follows
- Add user id "1" to the user:2:followers
```

In addition, you store the user profile as a hash:

```
user:<id>:data
```

You start by defining the basic model:

```
/**
 * User model
 */

function User (id, data) {
  this.id = id;
  this.data = data;
}
```

Each instance of a User contains an id that identifies that user and the data of the user account.

You then expose a static method find for populating a User instance from Redis:

```
User.find = function (id, fn) {
  client.hgetall('user:' + id + ':data', function (err, obj) {
    if (err) return fn(err);
    fn(null, new User(id, obj));
  });
};
```

Creating and modifying users

It's desirable for the model to be able to find a user, change some of his data, and save it back into Redis. And you should also be able to run new User, set some data, and save it into Redis.

Thankfully, operating on hashes from Node is simpler than it would be with Redis commands. The functions `hgetall` and `hmset` operate with native JavaScript objects, therefore making this possible:

```
client.hmset('somehash', { a: 'key', another: 'key' });
```

The equivalent of this command in the Redis command-line interface (CLI) would be

```
HMSET somehash "key" "value" "anotherkey" "anothervalue"
```

And when you are retrieving with `hgetall`, the second parameter is a JavaScript object:

```
client.hgetall('somehash', function (err, obj) {
  // obj.a == 'key'
});
```

You therefore can add a `save` method to the model that executes `hmset` to enable the creation and modification of user records:

```
User.prototype.save = function (fn) {
  if (!this.id) {
    this.id = String(Math.random()).substr(3);
  }

  client.hmset('user:' + this.id + ':data', this.data, fn)
};
```

Defining graph methods

The basic two operations that you want to perform for a given user are to follow and unfollow another:

```
User.prototype.follow = function (user_id, fn) {
  client.multi()
    .sadd('user:' + user_id + ':followers', this.id)
    .sadd('user:' + this.id + ':follows', user_id)
    .exec(fn);
};

User.prototype.unfollow = function (user_id, fn) {
  client.multi()
    .srem('user:' + user_id + ':followers', this.id)
    .srem('user:' + this.id + ':follows', user_id)
    .exec(fn);
};
```

Notice that unlike the previous example, this one calls `client.multi`. Calling `multi` tells the Redis client that all the commands executed up until `exec` is called are part of a transaction and should all be executed together.

If you modify a `followers` list, but something happens afterward and the `follows` alteration fails, you could end up with inconsistent and fault-prone data. You therefore need to execute both commands as part of a transaction.

Finally, you also want to be able to retrieve the IDs of follows and followers:

```
User.prototype.getFollowers = function (fn) {
  client.smembers('user:' + this.id + ':followers', fn);
};

User.prototype.getFollows = function (fn) {
  client.smembers('user:' + this.id + ':follows', fn);
};
```

Computing intersections

Besides follows and followers, you also can compute a third type of relationship: friendship.

You can say two users are friends if they follow each other. In other words, if a user ID appears both in the *follows* and *followers* sets of a given user, that user is a friend.

Adding the `getFriends` method is therefore as easy as calling the `SINTER` command to compute the intersection between the two sets:

```
User.prototype.getFriends = function (fn) {
  client.sinter('user:' + this.id + ':follows', 'user:' + this.id + ':followers',
  fn);
};
```

Testing it out

To test the model, you are going to create a few users that would be representative of those created through a web application.

The first step is to compile the model you worked on above into its own file for reusability, so that you can `require` it easily. Notice that I added the appropriate `module.exports` line:

model.js

```
/**
 * Module dependencies.
 */

var redis = require('redis')

/**
 * Module exports
```

```
 */

module.exports = User;

/**
 * Create client.
 */

var client = redis.createClient();

/**
 * User model
 */

function User (id, data) {
  this.id = id;
  this.data = data;
}

User.prototype.save = function (fn) {
  if (!this.id) {
    this.id = String(Math.random()).substr(3);
  }

  client.hmset('user:' + this.id + ':data', this.data, fn)
};

User.prototype.follow = function (user_id, fn) {
  client.multi()
    .sadd('user:' + user_id + ':followers', this.id)
    .sadd('user:' + this.id + ':follows', user_id)
    .exec(fn);
};

User.prototype.unfollow = function (user_id, fn) {
  client.multi()
    .srem('user:' + user_id + ':followers', this.id)
    .srem('user:' + this.id + ':follows', user_id)
    .exec(fn);
};

User.prototype.getFollowers = function (fn) {
  client.smembers('user:' + this.id + ':followers', fn);
};

User.prototype.getFollorws = function (fn) {
  client.smembers('user:' + this.id + ':follows', fn);
};
```

continued

model.js (continued)

```
User.prototype.getFriends = function (fn) {
  client.sinter('user:' + this.id + ':follows', 'user:' + this.id + ':followers',
  fn);
};

User.find = function (id, fn) {
  client.hgetall('user:' + id + ':data', function (err, obj) {
    if (err) return fn(err);
    fn(null, new User(id, obj));
  });
};
```

Make sure to run `npm install redis` so that the only dependency for this example is installed, and also check that Redis is running by running `redis-cli`.

The next step is to create the testing file and require the model. In the same directory, `test. js` should look like this:

test.js

```
/**
 * Module dependencies
 */

var User = require('./model')
```

If you execute the test file right now with `node test`, you will notice it hangs and doesn't exit by itself. This is because the model establishes the connection to Redis.

Next, you want to create a few testing users. To organize the code properly and avoid too many nested callbacks, I defined a `create` function that receives an object of emails and user data. For this example, the email address of the user is going to be its unique id within Redis.

test.js

```
/**
 * Module dependencies
 */

var User = require('./model')

/**
 * Create test users
 */
```

```
var testUsers = {
    'mark@facebook.com': { name: 'Mark Zuckerberg' }
  , 'bill@microsoft.com': { name: 'Bill Gates' }
  , 'jeff@amazon.com': { name: 'Jeff Bezos' }
  , 'fred@fedex.com': { name: 'Fred Smith' }
};

/**
 * Create users function
 */

function create (users, fn) {
  var total = Object.keys(users).length;
  for (var i in users) {
    (function (email, data) {
      var user = new User(email, data);
      user.save(function (err) {
        if (err) throw err;
        --total || fn();
      });
    })(i, users[i]);
  }
}

/**
 * Create test users.
 */

create(testUsers, function () {
  console.log('all users created');
  process.exit();
});
```

If you execute `node test` now, it should add the four users and exit. You can use `redis-cli` to verify everything is as expected:

```
redis-cli
redis 127.0.0.1:6379> KEYS *
1) "user:fred@fedex.com:data"
2) "user:jeff@amazon.com:data"
3) "user:bill@microsoft.com:data"
4) "user:mark@facebook.com:data"
redis 127.0.0.1:6379> HGETALL "user:fred@fedex.com:data"
1) "name"
2) "Fred Smith"
```

Notice that the HGETALL command I executed is essentially what the User.find function does: it retrieves the data available for a given user based on his id.

To prevent misleading results, every time you execute `node test` to verify your progress, I suggest you wipe the Redis database clean to make sure data created by different tests don't interfere. You can do that with the following command:

```
redis-cli FLUSHALL
```

Notice that the `HGETALL` command I executed is essentially what the `User.find` function does: it retrieves the data available for a given user based on his id.

Now that the users are created successfully, you want to retrieve the actual `User` objects based on each email, so that you can set up the relationships through the methods we created in the model. This process is normally called `hydration`, so you set up a `hydrate` method and use it from the `create` callback:

---

test.js

```
/**
 * Hydrate users function
 */

function hydrate (users, fn) {
  var total = Object.keys(users).length;
  for (var i in users) {
    (function (email) {
      User.find(email, function (err, user) {
        if (err) throw err;
        users[email] = user;
        --total || fn();
      });
    })(i);
  }
}

/**
 * Create test users.
 */

create(testUsers, function () {
  hydrate(testUsers, function () {
    console.log(testUsers);
  });
});
```

If, as shown in Figure 14-1, you run the test again, you will notice that the `testUsers` object is now populated with the `User` objects (which contain `id` and `data` properties, as you set them in the `User` constructor above).

```
{ 'mark@facebook.com': { id: 'mark@facebook.com', data: { name: 'Mark Zuckerberg' }
  },
  'bill@microsoft.com': { id: 'bill@microsoft.com', data: { name: 'Bill Gates' } },
  'jeff@amazon.com': { id: 'jeff@amazon.com', data: { name: 'Jeff Bezos' } },
  'fred@fedex.com': { id: 'fred@fedex.com', data: { name: 'Fred Smith' } } }
```

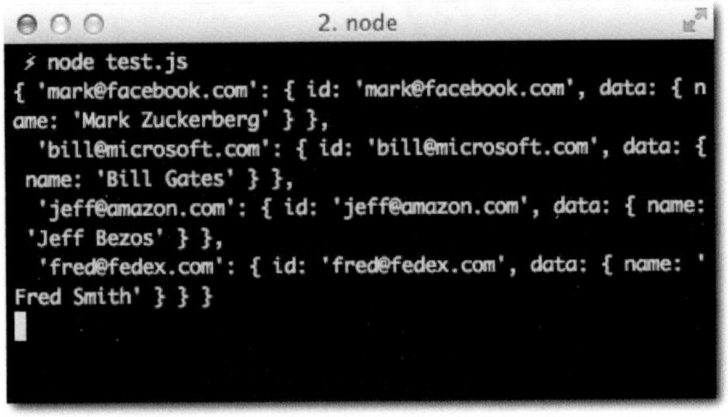

Figure 14-1: JSON output of created users

After hydrating, you can now play with the different methods available:

test.js

```
create(testUsers, function () {
  hydrate(testUsers, function () {
    testUsers['bill@microsoft.com'].follow('jeff@amazon.com', function (err) {
      if (err) throw err;
      console.log('+ bill followed jeff');

      testUsers['jeff@amazon.com'].getFollowers(function (err, users) {
        if (err) throw err;
        console.log("jeff's followers", users);

        testUsers['jeff@amazon.com'].getFriends(function (err, users) {
          if (err) throw err;
          console.log("jeff's friends", users);

          testUsers['jeff@amazon.com'].follow('bill@microsoft.com'
          , function (err) {
            if (err) throw err;

            console.log('+ jeffed follow bill');
```

continued

test.js (continued)

```
            testUsers['jeff@amazon.com'].getFriends(function (err, users) {
              if (err) throw err;

              console.log("jeff's friends", users);
              process.exit(0);
            });
          });
        });
      });
    });
  });
});
```

In Figure 14-2 you can see Redis intersection in action, as the console output reflects.

```
2. bash
⚡ node test.js
+ bill followed jeff
jeff's followers [ 'bill@microsoft.com' ]
jeff's friends □
+ jeffed follow bill
jeff's friends [ 'bill@microsoft.com' ]
⚡ ▮
```

Figure 14-2: Followers and friends in the social graph

SUMMARY

Redis is in my opinion one of the most important up and coming databases, which is why I spent the initial part of this chapter teaching you about its fundamentals.

Since it acts as a datastructure server, it can not only be used as a regular database but also be used as the glue to provide interoperability between small programs.

For example, in Chapter 9 you learned how to make sure sessions would stick around after reloading a Node process with `connect-redis`. Node could of course hold those same data structures in memory as well, but by separating the data into a different process that you can connect to over TCP with a simple protocol, you gain freedom and independence: your programs can be stopped and started at will, and the data will still remain accessible.

A surprising number of programs and web applications have very simple data models, and the datasets usually fit very well in memory. For those scenarios, I recommend you always consider Redis due to its simplicity, reliability, and ease of use from Node.JS. A testament to this is the very example covered in this chapter: you wrote an entire model that covers an important aspect of social applications today with just the Redis driver!

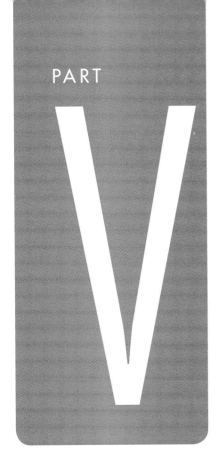

V TESTING

15

CODE
SHARING

IN THE INTRODUCTION of the book, I referred to one of the most appealing aspects of Node.JS: the fact that JavaScript, the language it empowers, is the only language supported by browsers.

Even though so far you have been writing code in JavaScript alone, which reduces the mental overhead of having to switch contexts between languages when working on web applications, you haven't taken advantage of the unique opportunity of writing code *once* and running it *everywhere*.

This chapter analyzes what use cases are optimal for code sharing and how to solve common language compatibility problems. You also learn how you can write modular code with the best practices of Node that can be *compiled* to run in the browser without bloat by using `browserbuild`.

WHAT CAN BE SHARED?

The easiest way to answer whether a certain piece of code can be shared between the browser and server is to break down this question into two questions:

- Is it worthwhile to run the codebase in both environments?
- Do the APIs it depends on exist in both environments? If not, can they easily be replaced or added (also known as *shimming*)?

Answering the first question is normally easy, and the answer itself depends exclusively on your program and project. Answering the second question can be a little trickier.

In Chapter 2, you saw that certain APIs that you commonly associate with JavaScript are not a formal part of the language but a *standard* API added on top of it by browsers. Examples of these APIs are XMLHttpRequest, WebSocket, the DOM, the 2d Canvas API, and so on.

Although no XMLHttpRequest API is available as part of the core Node.JS offering, you can completely shim its API and make it work on top of the normal Node.JS HTTP client APIs. A project in NPM called xmlhttprequest does exactly this.

In other cases, certain modules interact only with native APIs, and those are normally the easiest to write in such a way that they run in both environments.

Examples of these are

- **Date manipulation toolkits:** They normally simply extend or work with the Date object API.
- **Template engines:** They usually take a String, parse it with regular expressions or for loops, generate (compile) a function, which outputs a String.
- **Math and crypto libraries:** They normally depend exclusively on Number and Math.
- **OOP frameworks:** They provide syntax sugar for writing classes in JavaScript. In other words, they provide different APIs to make writing object-oriented code in JavaScript more similar to classical OOP languages.

WRITING COMPATIBLE JAVASCRIPT

The first challenge you need to solve is executing JavaScript code that has been written with the Node.JS module system, which is not available in the browser.

EXPOSING MODULES

The first challenge you face is the lack of a module global in the browser environment. Even if your file doesn't rely on required dependencies, the way that a certain file becomes useful to other parts of a Node program is by leveraging module.exports or exports.

Assume you want to write a simple function that sums two numbers:

---

add.js

```
module.exports = function (a, b) {
  return a + b;
}
```

In Node, you can simply leverage the function by calling `require('./add')` from another file. In the browser, you most likely want to expose the module as a *global variable* add.

To avoid modifying the existing code, you can simulate `module.exports` for the browser by prefixing the code with a fake object:

```
if ('undefined' == typeof module) {
  module = { exports: {} };
}
```

At the end of the module, after the object is populated, you can expose it to the `window`:

```
if ('undefined' != typeof window) {
  window.add = module.exports;
}
```

Unlike in Node.JS, in the browser, files get evaluated in the global scope. Therefore, you would be introducing a global `module` variable to the rest of the program that you don't want.

Wrapping your module in a self-invoking function is therefore a good idea:

```
(function (module) {
  module.exports = function (a, b) {
    return a + b;
  }

  if ('undefined' != typeof window) {
    window.add = module.exports;
  }
})('undefined' == typeof module ? { module: { exports: {} } } : module);
```

Ta-da! The module can still be required:

```
$ node
> require('./add')(1,2)
3
```

And you can include it in the DOM:

add.html

```
<script src="add.js"><script>
<script>
  console.log(add(1,2));
</script>
```

SHIMMING ECMA APIS

The next challenge you usually face is the reliance on modern JavaScript features not available to all browsers and JavaScript engines.

Sometimes the v8 engine in Node is even more up to date than that which has been shipped by the Google Chrome browser to millions of computers. In other cases, such as `Function#bind`, otherwise-modern engines like the JavaScriptCore VM that empowers Safari still miss certain implementations. You have to pay special care to what features are used if you intend your code to run everywhere.

There are two distinct approaches to adding missing functionality: the pure shimming of a missing implementation by extending the native `prototype` or the use of utility functions.

Extending prototypes

Say a particular module you're writing and intend to run in Node and browsers uses `Function#bind`:

```
var myfn = fn.bind(this);
```

Because `bind` is not available everywhere, you can add it if it's missing:

```
if (!Function.prototype.bind) {
  Function.prototype.bind = function () {
    // code that replicates bind behavior
  }
}
```

A project called `es5-shim` goes above and beyond by implementing all the missing ECMA-standard APIs in a cross-browser way whenever possible. You can find it at https://github.com/kriskowal/es5-shim.

The obvious advantage of this technique is that you can include the shim and mostly not worry about changing your code.

The disadvantage is that the evaluation of your library in the browser affects prototypes used or extended by others, which is more obtrusive than it could be.

Utilities

Another approach is defining simple functions that receive the native object as an argument, try to leverage existing implementations if present, or re-implement the functionality otherwise.

An example of a missing API in many browsers that you commonly use in Node is `Object.keys`.

You can then create a utility as follows:

```
var keys = Object.keys || function (obj) {
  var ret = [];
  for (var i in obj) {
    if (Object.prototype.hasOwnProperty.call(obj, i)) {
      ret.push(i);
    }
  }
  return ret;
};
```

The advantages of this technique are that it works everywhere, it's not obtrusive, and it makes clear to the developer what areas are *simulated* instead of *native,* which can aid in detecting performance loopholes in certain browsers.

On the downside, you have to be careful about remembering to leverage the utility instead of the original.

In addition, the resulting code sometimes looks more convoluted. If you're trying to achieve compatibility with old versions of IE where `Array#forEach` and `Array#map`/ `Array#filter` are missing, you might use code like this:

```
arr.filter(function () {}).map(function(){ }).forEach(function () {})
```

However, this code looks less clear when utilities are leveraged:

```
each(map(filter(arr, function() {}), function () {}), function (){})
```

SHIMMING NODE APIS

Certain Node APIs such as `EventEmitter` are likely to be leveraged by your own custom classes. Fortunately, the community has written versions of Node APIs that work in all environments.

EventEmitter

Implementations of the node `EventEmitter` can be found at https://github.com/Wolfy87/EventEmitter and https://github.com/tmpvar/node-eventemitter.

assert

The assert module has been ported to the browser: https://github.com/Jxck/assert.

SHIMMING BROWSER APIS

In many situations, you want Node to run APIs that some or all browsers natively expose.

XMLHttpRequest

The node-XMLHttpRequest project (found at https://github.com/driverdan/node-XMLHttpRequest) brings the shimmed API to Node by simply requiring it:

```
var XMLHttpRequest = require('xmlhttprequest')
```

DOM

A complete and tested implementation of DOM levels I, II, and III exists at https://github.com/tmpvar/jsdom.

WebSocket

The WebSocket client API (https://github.com/einaros/ws) is available to Node as well:

```
var WebSocket = require('ws')
```

node-canvas

The canvas 2D context for image manipulation is available to Node thanks to node-canvas: https://github.com/learnboost/node-canvas.

CROSS-BROWSER INHERITANCE

A common need in modules is to make a class inherit from another. In Chapter 2, you learned about .__proto__, which is a proprietary extension and also impossible to shim directly.

A simple alternative is declaring a utility function as follows:

```
/**
 * Inheritance utility.
 *
 * @param {Function} constructor
```

```
 * @param {Function} constructor you inherit from
 * @api private
 */

function inherits (a, b) {
  function c () {};
  c.prototype = b.prototype;
  a.prototype = new c;
};
```

You can then leverage it for both Node and browsers:

```
function A () {}
function B () {}

inherits(A, B);
// instead of A.prototype.__proto__ = B.prototype
```

PUTTING IT ALL TOGETHER: BROWSERBUILD

Wrapping your modules with self-invoking functions and performing `typeof` checks all over the place can be a daunting experience.

I created a project called `browserbuild` whose basic premise is to empower you to write modules in Node style (that is, that leverage `require`, `module.exports`, and `exports` and are broken into multiple files). By simply running a command, you can compile a browser version.

Browserbuild makes it possible to write the add example you wrote above in Node style, and then generate the version you would include in the HTML as `<script>` through a compilation process.

Browserbuild is available as an NPM module that sets up a `browserbuild` command-line script. To install it globally on your computer, you can run the following:

```
npm install -g browserbuild
browserbuild --version
```

The second command should output the installed version of browserbuild. The version I'll use for this section is 0.4.8.

Alternatively, you can install it in the working directory and leverage it through the `.bin` directory locally:

```
npm install browserbuild
./node_modules/browserbuild/.bin/browserbuild --version
```

A BASIC EXAMPLE

For this example you're going to write a module that depends on a logging utility.

First, write the main file main.js:

main.js

```
var log = require('./log'):

module.exports = function () {
log('Executed my module');
}
```

This is the equivalent of that main file in an NPM package or the file that you normally `require` when you are going to leverage a certain module.

log.js

```
module.exports = function (str) {
  return console.log(str);
}
```

In Node, you would simply write

node.js

```
var mymodule = require('./main')
mymodule();
```

For the browser, you want to export it as a global called `mymodule`. You therefore run `browserbuild` pointing to the working directory and supplying the name of the global variable to export and the main file:

```
browserbuild --main main --global mymodule main.js log.js > out.js.
```

What you're telling the `browserbuild` command is: compile the files `main.js` and `log.js` together, with the main module being `main` exposed as the global `mymodule`.

In addition, notice that at the end of the command I used > `compiled.js`. This ensures that the output that the command generates goes into the `compiled.js` file.

When you need to implement the library in the browser, all you do is include the `<script>` tag pointing to the `compiled.js` script:

```
<script src='compiled.js'>
```

The output of this generated script looks as follows:

compiled.js

```
(function(){var global = this;function debug(){return debug};function require(p,
 parent){ var path = require.resolve(p) , mod = require.modules[path]; if (!mod)
 throw new Error('failed to require "' + p + '" from ' + parent); if (!mod.exports)
 { mod.exports = {}; mod.call(mod.exports, mod, mod.exports, require.relative(path),
 global); } return mod.exports;}require.modules = {};require.resolve =
 function(path){ var orig = path , reg = path + '.js' , index = path + '/index.js';
 return require.modules[reg] && reg || require.modules[index] && index ||
 orig;};require.register = function(path, fn){ require.modules[path] = fn;};require.
 relative = function(parent) { return function(p){ if ('debug' == p) return debug;
 if ('.' != p.charAt(0)) return require(p); var path = parent.split('/') , segs =
 p.split('/'); path.pop(); for (var i = 0; i < segs.length; i++) { var seg =
 segs[i]; if ('..' == seg) path.pop(); else if ('.' != seg) path.push(seg); } return
 require(path.join('/'), parent); };};require.register("main.js", function(module,
 exports, require, global){

var log = require('./log');

module.exports = function () {
  log('Executed my module');
}

});require.register("log.js", function(module, exports, require, global){
module.exports = function (str) {
  return console.log(str);
}

});mymodule = require('main');
})();
```

The first section of the script is the implementation of the `require` function that the rest of the script uses. It's compiled into one line of code so that the impact of the compilation process on the length of the file is minimized.

The other interesting piece is that the `require.register` function exposes a `global` parameter. This is so that you don't have to rely on detecting whether a `window` is available to expose a certain global. You can write your scripts relying on Node.JS's `global` object, and in the browser it will point to the `window`.

Finally, the last section of the code is what exposes the *global* (in this case `mymodule`) and explains why we need to tell `broswerbuild` which module is the `main` one:

```
mymodule = require('main');
```

Another interesting feature of the browserbuild compilation process is the `if node` block, which allows you to use JavaScript comments to tell the compiler that a certain section of code should be stripped when compiling the module for the browser:

nodeonly.js

```
// if node
process.exit(1);
// end

console.log('browser and node');
```

In this case, the block gets removed from the browser version. If you execute

```
$ browserbuild --main nodeonly nodeonly.js
```

You'll notice the `process.exit` line will be gone:

```
// …
require.register("nodeonly.js", function(module, exports, require, global){
console.log('browser and node');
});nodeonly = require('nodeonly');
})();
```

To learn more about the different available options, you can execute `browserbuild --help` or refer to the project page located at http://github.com/learnboost/browserbuild.

SUMMARY

As it's been highlighted throughout the book, Node.JS has done a remarkable job at making writing JavaScript on the server-side a very pleasant activity.

At the core of its innovation lies the module system, something for which the browser environment has no de-facto equivalent.

This chapter started exploring the basic `runtime` methods of making code that can execute both on the server and the browser. By performing `typeof` checks, one can accomplish the feature detection of the module system, and provide an alternative exposure mechanism for the browser, such as globals.

But wrapping code manually in self-invoking functions, and executing `typeof` checks for every file of your library can definitely counteract the beautiful simplicity of the `require` system in Node, and that's the problem `browserbuild` allows you to solve. You are now empowered to write modules for Node.JS that can be compiled and executed in the browser with minimal friction.

The main advantage of this method is that your library gets eventually exposed as a global in the browser environment, just like jQuery or IO, which means you're not imposing a specific module system API for the end-user to leverage your code in a browser.

CHAPTER

16

TESTING

SO FAR, EVERY time you have written a Node program, you have verified it worked as expected by running it and observing that its behavior matched your expectations. This method of testing is often insufficient to ensure that programs work correctly and don't introduce new bugs as time goes by.

Automated testing is the process by which a series of programs are executed to verify that the intended function is in place. The first approach to automated testing in this chapter consists of creating one small node program per test and leveraging the native `assert` module.

Next, you optimize the process of writing assertions by leveraging a project called expect.js. You then explore how to organize testing by leveraging Mocha, a test framework.

Finally, for codebases that are meant to be run in browser and server environments, you will see how to take your existing tests and also run them on the browser.

SIMPLE TESTING

To get started, you'll need to identify a test subject. In other words, you'll decide what script or functionality you want to write tests for.

THE TEST SUBJECT

The test subject for this chapter is the application you wrote in Chapter 9 for searching tweets.

Here, you write a program which asserts that upon submitting a search keyword, a list of tweets is returned after the program looks for some indicative pieces of HTML. In this case, a list of tweets is composed of one or more `<li>` elements. Asserting the presence of the search keyword and the `<li>` string as part of the HTTP response should be sufficient for establishing that the application worked.

To start, navigate to the code examples and ensure that the application is running. Then point your browser to `http://localhost:3000`.

THE TEST STRATEGY

The most basic form of testing is writing a new node program whose exit code is 0 if the test passes or 1 if the test doesn't succeed.

If an uncaught exception is thrown, Node automatically exits with a failure error code for you, which fits this model nicely. In addition, you get a stack trace to understand where the error comes from. Therefore, when you write your tests, your goal is to assert that certain conditions are met or throw an exception otherwise. To this end, Node has a core module called `assert` that—like the name implies —ensures that a condition passes; otherwise, it raises an `AssertionError` as an exception.

As an example, write a test program that succeeds if the current timestamp is an even number or fails with a stack trace if it's an odd number:

```
/**
 * Module dependencies.
 */

var assert = require('assert');

/**
 * Assert condition
 */

var now = Date.now();
console.log(now);
assert.ok(now % 2 == 0);
```

You leverage `assert.ok` to guarantee that the value supplied is *truthy* (that is, it evaluates to `true` even if it's not `true`). If the number is divisible by 2 with no remainder, it means the number is even.

Now run the program a few times and look at the timestamps:

```
∞ simple-testing node assert-example.js
1325520251830
∞ simple-testing node assert-example.js
1325520252742
∞ simple-testing node assert-example.js
1325520253637

node.js:134
        throw e; // process.nextTick error, or 'error' event on first tick
        ^
AssertionError: true == false
    at Object.<anonymous> (assert-example.js:14:8)
    at Module._compile (module.js:411:26)
    at Object..js (module.js:417:10)
    at Module.load (module.js:343:31)
    at Function._load (module.js:302:12)
    at Array.<anonymous> (module.js:430:10)
    at EventEmitter._tickCallback (node.js:126:26)
```

In the first two cases, it's an even number, so the test exits cleanly. In the third execution, the timestamp is an odd number, and you therefore get a stack trace.

THE TEST PROGRAM

Now leverage `superagent` to make a GET request with the search term `bieber` and then analyze the response:

```
/**
 * Module dependencies.
 */

var request = require('superagent')
  , assert = require('assert')

/**
 * Tests /search?q=<tweet>
 */

request.get('http://localhost:3000')
  .data({ q: 'bieber' })
  .exec(function (res) {
```

```
    // assert correct status code
    assert.ok(200 == res.status);

    // assert presence of search keyword
    assert.ok(~res.text.toLowerCase().indexOf('bieber'));

    // assert list items
    assert.ok(~res.text.indexOf('<li>'));
  });
```

Notice that if the request produces an error, you throw it so that it becomes an uncaught exception and makes the program fail.

Remember you need to obtain `superagent` before you can run the tests:

```
npm install superagent@0.4.1
```

EXPECT.JS

In the preceding examples, you leverage `assert.ok` and a basic JavaScript expression.

When you're reading through tests, you might find it hard to understand what exactly is being tested for. For example, to assert that a string contains another, the easiest way to test it is to check for `indexOf` and apply the ~ operator, like you did previously.

Here, expect.js offers a single function called `expect` that turns

```
assert.ok(~res.text.indexOf('<li>'));
```

into

```
expect(res.text).to.contain('<li>'));
```

The expressiveness of expectations in something reminiscent of natural language makes writing and understanding tests a simpler task.

Expect.js is available through NPM as `expect.js` and its documentation can be found at https://github.com/learnboost/expect.js.

Next up you'll learn some of the basics of the expect.js API.

API OVERVIEW

The `expect` function is obtained by requiring the expect.js module:

```
var expect = require('expect.js')
```

Expect.js is completely interoperable with any module that already works with `assert`. Just like any of the functions exposed in the `assert` module, when an expectation is not met, an `AssertionError` is thrown.

Some of the most useful methods exposed by expect.js as of 0.1.2 are the following:

- `ok`: Asserts that the value is *truthy* or not

```
expect(1).to.be.ok();
expect(true).to.be.ok();
expect({}).to.be.ok();
expect(0).to.not.be.ok();
```

- `be` / `equal`: Asserts === equality

```
expect(1).to.be(1);
expect(NaN).not.to.equal(NaN);
expect(1).not.to.be(true);
expect('1').to.not.be(1);
```

- `eql`: Asserts loose equality that works with objects

```
expect({ a: 'b' }).to.eql({ a: 'b' });
expect(1).to.eql('1');
```

- `a`/`an`: Asserts `typeof` with support for `array` type and `instanceof`

```
// typeof with optional array
expect(5).to.be.a('number');
expect([]).to.be.an('array'); // works
expect([]).to.be.an('object'); // works too, since it uses typeof`
// constructors
expect(5).to.be.a(Number);
expect([]).to.be.an(Array);
expect(tobi).to.be.a(Ferret);
expect(person).to.be.a(Mammal);
```

- `match`: Asserts `String` regular expression match

```
expect(program.version).to.match(/[0-9]+\.[0-9]+\.[0-9]+/);
```

- `contain`: Asserts `indexOf` for an array or string

```
expect([1, 2]).to.contain(1);
expect('hello world').to.contain('world');
```

- `length`: Asserts array `.length`

```
expect([]).to.have.length(0);
expect([1,2,3]).to.have.length(3);
```

- `empty`: Asserts that an array is empty or not

```
expect([]).to.be.empty();
expect([1,2,3]).to.not.be.empty();
```

- `property`: Asserts presence of an own property (and value optionally)

```
expect(window).to.have.property('expect');expect(window).to.have.
  property('expect', expect)
expect({a: 'b'}).to.have.property('a');
```

- **key/keys:** Asserts the presence of a key; supports the `only` modifier

```js
js expect({ a: 'b' }).to.have.key('a');
expect({ a: 'b', c: 'd' }).to.only.have.keys('a', 'c');
expect({ a: 'b', c: 'd' }).to.only.have.keys(['a', 'c']);
expect({ a: 'b', c: 'd' }).to.not.only.have.key('a');
```

- **throwException:** Asserts that the `Function` throws or not when called

```js
expect(fn).to.throwException();
expect(fn2).to.not.throwException();
```

- **within:** Asserts a number within a range

```js
expect(1).to.be.within(0, Infinity);
```

- **greaterThan/above:** Asserts >

```js
expect(3).to.be.above(0); expect(5).to.be.greaterThan(3);
```

- **lessThan/below:** Asserts <

```js
expect(0).to.be.below(3); expect(1).to.be.lessThan(3);
```

Now that you've improved your assertion style, you can also refactor the tests organization with a framework called Mocha.

MOCHA

Mocha is a test framework that simplifies the process of writing tests that run in succession, running them and producing output that's helpful for the developer to observe.

Instead of having to write each test in a separate file, which could result in dozens of files that are unordered in the filesystem, you can use Mocha to structure your tests like this:

test.js

```js
describe('a topic', function () {

  it('should test something', function () {

  });

  describe('another topic', function () {

    it('should test something else', function () {

    });

  });

});
```

In the same spirit as expect.js, in test.js, the process of describing and organizing tests is natural.

All you need to do to run the tests is to leverage the `mocha` command. To get the `mocha` command, make sure to run `npm install -g mocha`. Then use

```
mocha test.js
```

Mocha can leverage multiple *reporters* to display the tests passing and running:

```
mocha test.js

  ..

  2 tests complete (0ms)
```

An alternative reporter, for example, is a `list`:

```
mocha -R list test.js

  a topic should test something: 0ms
  a topic another topic should test something else: 0ms

  2 tests complete (1ms)
```

As you see later, Mocha also has an HTML reporter, which enables you to take your tests to the browser.

TESTING ASYNCHRONOUS CODE

By default, Mocha executes one test after another immediately. Many times, however, you want to delay the execution of the next test after some async event occurs.

Consider the following test:

```
it('should not throw', function () {
  setTimeout(function () {
    throw new Error('An error!');
  }, 100);
});
```

This test *always* passes. The reason is that the timer is set, and there's nothing left to do, Mocha continues with the next one. Because no exceptions are raised *immediately* after setting the timeout, the test passes.

For tests in which exceptions could be raised in the future (that is, as a result of asynchronous behavior), you want to tell Mocha that you will notify it when you consider the test complete.

For that, you simply define an argument as part of the callback. In other words, as you saw in Chapter 2, you set the *arity* of the function (or the `function#length`) to 1:

```
it('should not throw', function (done) {
  setTimeout(function () {
    assert.ok(1 == 1);
  }, 100);
});
```

The test now behaves similarly to middleware. Mocha waits until the `done` function is called. If the function is not called within 2 seconds (by default), a timeout exception is raised to inform you on which test it's stuck. You can tweak this timeout by supplying the `-t` option to the `mocha` command. You also can customize it per test as follows:

```
it('will fail', function () {
  this.timeout(100);
  setTimeout(function () {
    // the test will timeout before this occurs
  }, 1000);
});
```

To make the test work, you invoke `done` after the assertions are done:

```
it('should not throw', function (done) {
  setTimeout(function () {
    assert.ok(1 == 1);
    done();
  }, 100);
});
```

Thus, you could rewrite the Bieber Twitter client in Mocha like this:

```
it('should find bieber tweets', function (done) {
  request.get('http://localhost:3000')
    .data({ q: 'bieber' })
    .exec(function (res) {

      // assert correct status code
      assert.ok(200 == res.status);

      // assert presence of search keyword
      assert.ok(~res.text.toLowerCase().indexOf('bieber'));

      // assert list items
      assert.ok(~res.text.indexOf('<li>'));

      done();
    });
});
```

Sometimes, a test can pass only when *more than one* asynchronous task run in parallel completes.

For this approach, you can use the typical trick of keeping a counter:

```
it('should complete three requests', function (done) {
  var total = 3;
  request.get('http://localhost:3000/1', function (res) {
    if (200 != res.status) throw new Error('Request error');--total || done();
  });
  request.get('http://localhost:3000/2', function (res) {
    if (200 != res.status) throw new Error('Request error');--total || done();
  });
  request.get('http://localhost:3000/3', function (res) {
    if (200 != res.status) throw new Error('Request error');;
    --total || done();
  });
});
```

Note that Mocha is smart enough to recognize that a certain uncaught exception belongs to a specific test. Because Mocha executes only one test at a time at any time, it knows to link any uncaught exceptions that are captured through `process.on('uncaughtException')` handler to the appropriate test.

BDD STYLE

The style described in the preceding section is called behavior-driven development (BDD).

In the following example, you test the behavior of Jade when supplied a template that contains a paragraph. You use it in combination with expect.js

First, you install Jade, Mocha, and expect.js:

```
$ npm install expect.js jade mocha
```

bdd.js

```
var expect = require('expect.js')
  , jade = require('jade');

describe('jade.render', function () {
  it('should render a paragraph', function () {
    expect(jade.render('p A paragraph')).to.be('<p>A paragraph</p>');
  });
});
```

Because you installed Mocha *locally*, you can execute it by finding it in `./node_modules/bin`:

```
$ ./node_modules/.bin/mocha bdd.js
```

TDD STYLE

The next style is called test-driven development (TDD). It's similar to BDD, but the organization is set around *suites* and *tests*.

Each suite can have *setup* and *teardown* functions associated with them. These functions are executed prior to each test in the suite, and they avoid code repetition while maximizing testing isolation.

For example, say you want to test the native Node `net` client. At the beginning of each test of the suite, you might want to initialize a client because each test in the suite leverages one, and at the end, you want to close the connection.

```
suite('net', function () {

  suite('Stream', function () {

    var client;

    suiteSetup(function () {
      client = net.connect(3000, 'localhost');
    });

    test('connect event', function (done) {
      client.on('connect', done);
    });

    test('receiving data', function (done) {
      client.write('');
      client.once('data', done);
    });

    suiteTeardown(function () {
      client.end();
    });

  });

});
```

EXPORTS STYLE

The exports style leverages the node module system to expose tests.

Each key exported constitutes the equivalent of a suite, and nested suites can appear as subobjects:

```
exports.Array = {
 '#indexOf()': {
   'should return -1 when the value is not present': function () {},
   'should return the correct index when the value is present': function () { }
 }
};
```

TAKING MOCHA TO THE BROWSER

Mocha is a project that was written for Node, but it can be compiled to be run in the browser.

The strategy for running tests in the browser (HTML) is straightforward:

1. Load the Mocha CSS and JS runtime.
2. Tell Mocha what test style you want to use (TDD, BDD, or exports).
3. Load your tests.
4. Run Mocha.

The expect.js project also runs in all modern and old browsers, which makes it the perfect companion for Mocha.

Setting up the project

You start by creating a `test/` folder that will contain the Mocha browser runtime files (mocha.css and mocha.js).

You can obtain both files by either copying them from the `node_modules/mocha` directory or downloading them directly from the git repository. For more information on how to download these files, refer to http://mochajs.com.

You also should load jQuery, expect.js, and your tests and then call `mocha.setup` to load the particular test style.

The `test/index.html` therefore looks like this:

test/index.html

```
<!doctype html>
<html>
  <head>
    <title>my tests</title>
    <link href="/mocha.css" rel="stylesheet" media="screen" />
    <script src="/jquery.js"></script>
    <script src="/mocha.js"></script>
```

test/index.html   (continued)

```
  <script src="/expect.js"></script>
  <script>mocha.setup('bdd');</script>
  <script src="/my-test.js"></script>
  <script>window.onload = function () { mocha.run(); };</script>
</head>
<body>
  <div id="mocha"></div>
</body>
</html>
```

As you can see, Mocha runs the `my-test` file, which you populate with a few simple array tests in BDD style:

my-test.js

```
describe('my tests', function () {
  it('should not throw', function () {
    expect(1 + 1).to.be(2);
  });
});
```

Serving up the directory

The easiest way to serve an entire directory as a website is to leverage a utility called `serve(1)`. A simple command-line program, `serve` runs `connect` static provider middleware for the directory you point it to:

```
$ serve .
```

You then simply point your browser to `http://localhost:3000`.

SUMMARY

You started off learning the easiest way to test a program, which is running a simple test script and expecting it to run successfully.

In order to verify that certain conditions are met within that test script, you used the core Node.JS module `assert`.

With that foundation in place, you set out to make stylistic and organization improvements to your tests with expect.js and Mocha, respectively. Expect allows you to express your tests very clearly, while Mocha gives you the ability to organize them around suites and empowers you to run tests in the browser environment. It also makes testing asynchronous code, as you saw, very elegant.

INDEX